SUSSEX PLACE-NAMES

their origins and meanings

Judith Glo----

G000016986

COUNTRYSIDE BOOKS
NEWBURY, BERKSHIRE

First published 1997
© Judith Glover 1997

All rights reserved. No reproduction
permitted without the prior permission
of the publisher:

COUNTRYSIDE BOOKS
3 Catherine Road
Newbury, Berkshire

ISBN 1 85306 484 X

*In loving memory of my father,
John Glover, who enjoyed many
happy days in Sussex*

Cover photo of Steyning supplied by Roger Holman.
Map by Trevor Yorke

Produced through MRM Associates Ltd., Reading
Printed by J. W. Arrowsmith Ltd., Bristol

Introduction

The *Anglo-Saxon Chronicle* calls it Suðsexe.
The name originally applied to the South Saxons
or *Sūðseaxe* (the *seax* was their distinctive
long-bladed knife) who invaded this part of
Roman Britain in AD 477. In time it came to be
used as the name of their territory, recorded in
AD 897 as Suðseaxnaland – the land of the South Saxons.

Place names are a bit like cryptic crossword clues. They contain all the information we need to decipher them – but until we can interpret them correctly they remain simply names on maps and roadsigns, hiding the answer to their origins within themselves.

Take Gatwick, for instance – a name most travellers through airports are familiar with. Break it down into its two component parts – gat and wick – and we find 'goat farm', telling us that somewhere beneath the tarmac of its busy runways Gatwick hides a humble little settlement many centuries old.

Its neighbour Crawley has grown out of all recognition since it became one of the New Towns of the post-war period, boosted by industry, commerce and the influx of commuters to residential estates. How many of them, I wonder, ever stop to enquire why such a fast-expanding place should have a name suggesting just the opposite? And what would they make of the fact that its first residents knew it as a crow-infested clearing or 'crawe ley'?

The place names of Sussex are a vital facet of the county's history (and by county I mean both East and West administrative areas). Whatever has happened here is reflected to a greater or lesser extent by what they can tell us. The very name 'Sussex' is in itself an incredible memorial to a race of people from the European mainland (in fact from the old Saxony region of Germany) who invaded and colonised the area long before their distant compatriots tried to do so again in two world wars.

Before the South Saxons arrived here the county had no separate identity as such. Its native British Celts were subjects of the Roman Empire, many of them employed on large estates like those at Fishbourne and Bignor. Within a few decades of the Saxon invasion in AD 477, those who had escaped the butchery had either fled westward or, starved into submission, had surrendered themselves to a lifetime of slavery. Their ancient Celtic language, their customs and

beliefs died with them, and only a shadow lingered on in the names they'd given to some of their hills and rivers.

Everywhere in the place names of Sussex, in towns and villages, hamlets and farms, woods and streams, it's the pugnacious Saxons who have left their mark. Their earliest settlements, established between AD 480 and 550, were densest along the coastal strip and open river valleys where they lived as tribal communities. We know this because they've left us clues in the names of those settlements – what etymologists, scholars who study the derivation and significance of words, call 'ingas' names – Goring, Worthing, Lancing, Angmering, to name but four of the 45 in Sussex.

A little later, as their new kingdom established itself and warriors exchanged their swords for ploughshares, the South Saxons moved further inland, carving out clearings or 'leys' in the forests, building new 'hams' or settlements and 'tons' or farmsteads. Their swine pastures were in the dense oakwoods north of the Downs, their flocks

4

grazed in watermeadows bordered by streams, their 'eys' or islands were surrounded by marshland flooded by the sea at each high tide. And the descriptions they gave to these places still exist to form the bedrock of the place names of the county.

Then in 1066, the Norman French arrived. After 500 years of peaceful evolution, and conversion to Christianity by St Wilfred of Northumbria in the 7th century, the South Saxons were no longer a war-loving race; indeed, they were no longer a separate kingdom. They were English. Although William the Conqueror was the new master, he was also a clever diplomat: instead of repeating history, he had no intention of destroying what could be turned to political and economic advantage.

Twenty years after the Battle of Hastings he ordered a major comprehensive survey of his new possessions. His officials visited every county, making what they could of the names the Saxon English had given their homes and land, and recording them in an often mangled

Normanised form in what would become known as the Domesday Book. Saxon manors found themselves with new lords with alien-sounding surnames that were added as a sort of feudal brand-mark, producing names like Hurstpierpoint, Hamsey, Herstmonceux and Horsted Keynes.

But though Sussex was now administered by Norman barons and divided into sub-divisions called Rapes, life for the lower orders went on in much the same fashion as it had before the Conquest. Parish registers, rentals, surveys and court records dating from the 13th to the 16th centuries provide us with the names of families that are now part of the general landscape, affixed to barns and crosses and village greens, woods and mills and hatch-gates.

The reigns of the Tudors, Stuarts and early Georgians saw Sussex becoming an important industrial centre, its ancient Wealden oak-woods felled to feed the flames of countless foundries producing iron to make the Navy's cannon, and leaving a legacy not just of hammer ponds and denuded woodlands, but of names like Cinder Hill and Furnace Green.

More recently still, the coming of the railway has stimulated the growth of coastal resorts and turned quiet country hamlets into thriving towns such as Burgess Hill, Hassocks and Haywards Heath. And still the change goes on. The place names of the new millenium will be reflecting the forward progression of Sussex just as they have been doing for the past 2,000 or so years.

Much of the information in this book formed the core of my earlier work on the same subject, first published in 1975. But all the entries have been reworked and expanded to include material on these more recent developments, as well as a completely fresh insight into the county's earlier history. In this I have been helped by the planning departments of East and West Sussex county councils, by the record offices of Chichester and Lewes, and by the local studies sections of public libraries – to all of whom I express my gratitude.

Judith Glover

GLOSSARY
of the most common elements in Sussex place-names

āc oak-tree
æsc ash-tree
bǣr swine pasture
bēce, bōc beech-tree
beorg mound, barrow
brōc marshy ground
brycg bridge
burh stonghold
burna stream, bourne
ceaster fortified camp
clif cliff, steep place
cnoll knoll, hillock
cumb valley, combe
denn woodland pasture
denu valley, dean
dūn hill, down
ēa river
ēg island
ersc stubble-field
falod fold
feld open land
ford ford
glind fenced enclosure
grāf grove
hæcc hatch-gate
hǣð heathland
hæg hedged enclosure
healh corner of land
hām settlement
hāmstede homestead
hamm watermeadow

holt thicket
horna horn, spit of land
hrycg ridge
hyll hill
hyrst wooded hill, wood
ingas people of, tribe
lacu watercourse
land land
lēah woodland clearing
lind lime-tree, linden
(ge)mǣre boundary
mere pool
mersc marsh
mōr wasteland, moor
ōfer bank, riverbank
ōra shore, border, bank
pytt pit, hollow
rīed cleared, ridded; clearing
scaga copse, shaw
sele, (ge)selle building
stede place
stīg path
strǣt Roman road, street
tēag enclosure, tye
tūn farmstead, manor
wīc farm
wielle spring
wisc bog meadow
worð enclosure, enclosed settlement
wudu wood
yfre hill brow

Words connecting place-name forms

alias otherwise known as

juxta next to, near

Note
Place-names set in SMALL CAPITALS in the A-Z entries are cross-referenced elsewhere.

· · A · ·

Abbot's Wood. Once land belonging to Battle Abbey, the present name first appears in 1540. Before then the place had been called Lynershe, 'stubble-field by the linden, or lime-tree', a name derived from *lind ersc* and found as Lindhersse in 1337 and Lynershe Wood in 1535.

Abingworth. Recorded as Abinge-worth in 1327, this was an area of enclosed land (*worð*) belonging to the Æbbingas, or Æbba's people, a tribe originating from Abinger in Surrey. They seem to have been a fairly important group, with several other settlements across the country – a hill (*dūn*) at Abingdon in Berk-shire, a corner of land (*healh*) at Abinghall in Gloucestershire, and a farmstead (*tūn*) at Abington in Cam-bridgeshire.

Adder Wells. One of those names smoothed away by Sussex speech. Once it was 'the spring by the apple-tree', recorded as Apeltre well in 1285 and Apterwell in 1470. But by 1825 it had been turned into Arters Wells, pronounced more or less 'adders'.

Adsdean. The early forms Addesden (1194) and Addesdene (1315) suggest a derivation of *Æddes dene*, describ-ing a dean or small valley belong-ing to an early settler called Æddi. The old name survives in that of Ads-dean House, near Westbourne.

Adur, River. The river was first given this name in Michael Dray-ton's *Polyolbion*, a topographical description of England published in 1622. Drayton mistakenly believed the Roman harbour of Portus Adurni (Portsmouth) had been situ-ated at the mouth of the Adur, and named the river accordingly. In ear-lier times it had been identified by the settlements along its course, thus we find it recorded as aqua de Brem-bre in 1249, from BRAMBER on its west bank; aqua de Schorham in 1263, from SHOREHAM at its mouth; aquam de Pende in 1301, from PEN, also at its mouth; and aqua de Cneppe around the year 1270, from KNEPP near its source.

Adversane. Originally a corner of land, or *hyrne*, attached to the now lost place of Hadfold, the name appears in 1279 as Hede-foldeshurne, then as Hadfoldsherne in 1711, and just under a century later as Hadfordshern. All that remains of Hadfold itself is nearby **Hadfold Farm**, taking its name from a fold or livestock enclosure belong-ing to an early settler called Hadda. It's noted as Haddesfolde and Hade-fold towards the end of the 13th cen-tury.

Agmerhurst. This was a hurst, or wooded hill, owned by an early set-tler named Angemǣr, whose main tribal settlement was at ANGMERING.

We find Agmerhurst recorded as Aghemeresherst in 1340 and Agmansherst in 1546, attaining its modern form by 1720.

Albourne. The tributary of the river Adur flowing through Albourne was once overhung with alder-trees, lending it the description of *alor burna*, 'the alder stream'. The name appears in its present form as early as 1401, developing from Aleburn noted in 1177.

Alciston. Traditionally pronounced Arlston, this Downland village originated as the *tūn* or farmstead of a South Saxon called Ælfsige. In the Domesday Book of 1086 it's recorded as Alsistone and subsequently appears as Alcistona in 1327. The manor and lands of Alciston formerly belonged to Battle Abbey, whose monks were sent to a monastery here for rest and retreat: **Court House Farm** incorporates part of the old 14th century buildings.

Aldingbourne. Documented as Aldingburne as early as AD 683, then as Ealdingburnan around two centuries later, the place name describes the bourne or stream now called Aldingbourne Rife, once the property of an early settler, Ealda – a personal name also found associated with ELLANORE. Aldingbourne itself is one of the oldest sites of Christianity in Sussex. Its Norman church of St Mary stands on the foundations of a monastery built here in the 7th century AD soon after St Wilfred's conversion of the South Saxon tribes.

Aldrington. Roman buildings were commonly utilised by the incoming Saxons for the construction of their new settlements. This is what seems to have happened at Aldrington, where the remains of a Roman posting station (unearthed here in 1818) were incorporated into the *tūn* or farmstead of a group calling itself the Ealdheringas – Ealdhere's people. In 1086 the Domesday Book records the place as Eldretune, and it appears as Aldringeton in 1200.

Aldsworth. The name is listed as Alderswerde in 1271, then leaps four centuries to appear as Aldesworth in 1660. It denotes the enclosure or *worð* of someone called Eald, whose personal name is a shortened form of both Ealda (found in connection with ALDINGBOURNE) and Ealdhere (ALDRINGTON).

Aldwick. Site of a farm considered old even as early as 1235, when it's referred to simply as Aldewyc – 'the old farm' – the place gave its name to the Aldwick Hundred, which was an area of land sufficient to provide a living for 100 families. Originally there were 67 such Hundreds in Sussex. Before 1428 this particular area was known as the Pagham Hundred, the meeting place being based at neighbouring Pagham, but after that date Aldwick became the more important settlement.

Alfriston. This was originally the farmstead or *tūn* of a Saxon of some note, Ælfric, his property being recorded as Alvricestone in the Domesday Book. The estate was awarded to Ælfric as a fief (land granted in return for military service) by King Alfred the Great – in fact there's a local tradition that it was at the Star Inn here that Alfred burned the famous cakes. The church of St Andrew stands on the site of an early monastic church in which was interred the body of St Lewinna, a Sussex girl martyred towards the end of the 7th century, making Alfriston an important centre of pilgrimage until her remains were stolen and taken to Flanders in 1058. The village's further claim to fame is its 14th century **Clergy House**, which was the first building ever to be acquired by the National Trust.

Allington. Although there's no hard evidence to connect Allington with Ælla, first king of the South Saxons, it's an interesting conjecture that either he or one of his family owned the *tūn* or farmstead here to the north-west of Lewes. Still a farm, it appears as Alintune in the Domesday Book and Alyngton around 1155. In 1328 it's mentioned as Esteralyngton – 'more easterly' – to avoid confusion with **Allington House** at nearby Chailey which was probably part of the same estate.

Almodington. A place name virtually unchanged since it first appeared in records of 1166 as Almodintona, denoting the farmstead of an early settler called Ealhmōd.

Amberley. The most popularly held theory among etymologists is that the name means 'the clearing by the river', from an ancient British word *amber* (river) which may have been given locally to the Arun, plus the Saxon ending *lēah* or clearing. The place is recorded as Amberle as early as AD 957. About the year 680 land in this area was granted by King Cædwalla to St Wilfred, who erected a church on the site of the present church of St Michael – this later building, together with a manor house, was begun by Bishop Luffa of Chichester around 1100. The manor house subsequently was used as the foundation of **Amberley Castle**, built late in the 14th century to guard the upper reaches of the Arun. Amberley stands in a delightful location on a low ridge overlooking the **Amberley Wild Brooks**, some 30 square miles of river marshes notable for fishing and boating – their description Wild comes originally from Weald.

Ambersham, North and **South.** Æmbresham in AD 963, this was the *hām* or settlement of a South Saxon named Æmbre. The place lay within the county of Hampshire up until 1832, when border changes brought it into Sussex.

Amberstone. Interestingly, the hamlet was originally called Amberford, marking the ford of Eamba. We find it mentioned as Ambeford in 1212. Then at some point during the next two centuries the place became identified by a prominent boundary stone here on the Hailsham-Hellingly parish border, appearing in 1470 as Ombefordstone. By 1588 the 'ford' had been dropped altogether, and the place name appears in its modern form. The South Saxon Eamba gave his name to several sites in this area. His ford crossed a tributary of Hurst Haven flowing across open land or *feld* which he owned – the now lost place of Ambefeld is recorded in 1180 – and his property extended to a clearing three miles away at HAMLYE BRIDGE.

Amblehurst. Æmela's hurst or wooded hill, this was Hamelehurst in 1195 and Amelhurst in 1340.

Ancton. Developing from the original Saxon *Annecan tūn* meaning Anneca's farmstead, the name appears as Ancketon in 1288.

Anderida. See PEVENSEY.

Angmering. This is another of those places where a Roman site was used as the foundation of a Saxon settlement. In the case of Angmering, the rebuilding goes back even further, because the Roman villa unearthed here in the 19th century was subsequently found to have been close to an Iron Age ditch, which gives the place a history of something like 2,500 years of continuous occupation. The Saxon tribe who have marked it with their identity were the Angemæringas, or people of a leader called Angemær, the name appearing as æt Angemæringum around AD 880, developing to Angmarrying in 1438. They also owned land at AGMERHURST. The neighbouring coastal resort of **Angmering-on-Sea** is a fairly recent development which has adopted the name of the old inland village.

Annington. A group known as the Anningas, or Anna's people, chose to settle themselves on a *dūn* or hill here on the South Downs, the place being recorded as æt Anningadun in AD 956, then as Aningatune just over a century later. At some point in its history Annington was also identified in Latin-written documents as Vetere Ponte, or 'the old bridge', appearing as Annyngdon *alias* Vetere Ponte in 1428. In fact we find a reference in 1296 to a 'villata de Veteri Ponte' by the old bridge across the Adur at nearby Bramber (a villata being a small country dwelling, maybe a farmhouse) so this seems to be how the alternative name originated.

Anscombe Wood. It's thought this name, recorded no earlier than 1688, derives ultimately from *Ānes cumb*. A combe can be either a deep little wooded valley, or – as seems more appropriate to this particular location in the Wivelsfield area – a hollow in a hillside. The personal name Ān tells us something about the individual who made his solitary home here, because the South Saxons used it as a nickname meaning 'the lonely one'.

Ansty. To reach Ansty in days gone by one would have needed to climb a fairly steep and narrow path to reach its hill-top site. The name means 'one-path', referring to a single-file way – *ān stīg* originally. It appears as Anstigh in 1313 and as Annstie in 1603.

Antye. This name contains the Sussex dialect word 'tye', a common or piece of open land, and is derived from the Saxon *tēag* which meant virtually the opposite, an enclosure. The recorded forms for Antye – Hentye in 1379 and Hantye in 1622 – suggest it was originally 'at the high enclosure' or *hēan tēage*, a supposition borne out by the upland situation of Antye Farm which is all that remains of the little early settlement here in the Wivelsfield area.

Appledram. See APULDRAM.

Applesham. Recorded in the Domesday Book of 1086 as Aplesham, this was the *hām* or settlement of a South Saxon rather appealingly called Appel. The name seems to be a diminutive of the personal name Appa, which we find in connection with AWBROOK. Applesham Farm here on the Downs above the river Adur is all that remains to identify the original site.

Apsley. Apsley Farm, just north of Thakeham, stands in what was long ago a clearing in a little wood of aspen-trees, which the Saxons called *æspe*. Its name is first recorded in 1073, as Absleia, appearing more recognisably some 200 years later as Apselegh.

Apuldram. Alternatively spelled Appledram, it's surely one of Sussex's most attractive place names, and with an equally attractive origin. There was a *hamm* or water-meadow here on the banks of the Chichester Canal enclosing some of the apple-trees that still grow so prolifically in the rich loam soil of this area. Early settlers would have known the spot as *apuldor hamm*, 'the apple-tree meadow'. It's Apeldreham in 1121, Appeldoreham in 1248, and Appuldram in 1440.

Ardingly. The Saxon word *lēah*, used to denote a cleared area of woodland, has given us -ley or -ly, one of our most common place-name endings. The clearing here at Ardingly was settled by a tribe known as the Eardingas, or Earda's people, and they probably chose the site because it made a strong defensive position above the narrow valley formed by one of the headwaters of the Ouse.

In 1107 the name appears as Erdingelega. By 1521 it had become Ardinglie. The village is nowadays famous for its public school, **Ardingly College**, which was opened here in 1870.

Argos Hill. Recorded as Argarshill in 1547, the place originally formed part of the family property of a Rotherfield landowner, Gilbert Orgar, who was living at the end of the 13th century. The name first appears in its modern form in 1724.

Arlington. Opinion is divided on the origin of this place name. It may describe the *tūn* or farmstead of a South Saxon called Eorla, or alternatively the farmstead of a nobleman or *eorl* (a word that actually meant 'warrior' and has given us our modern 'earl'). Whichever the correct interpretation, the Domesday Book tells us the place was Erlington in 1086. Interestingly, its Saxon church of St Pancras stands on the site of an earlier cemetery dating to the Roman occupation.

Arun, River. The river acquired its present name in the 13th century from the town of ARUNDEL which had developed on its west bank. But as late as 1263 we find it being referred to by its earlier name, Tarente, thought to be derived from an old British word *trisanton*, meaning 'trespasser' – even now the river can still cause extensive flooding of its valley. The name lives on in Tarrant Street in Arundel.

Arundel. Traditionally, the town was named after Hirondelle – 'the swallow' – horse of the legendary giant Bevis of Southampton who was warder of the gatehouse of Arundel Castle in Norman times, and a swallow is depicted on the town's coat-of-arms. More prosaically however, the name is from the hoarhound, a plant of the nettle family once growing in such profusion in the river valley here that the place was described as *hārhūne dell*, 'hoarhound dale'. It appears as Harundelle in the Domesday Book, and Arrundell a couple of centuries later. Arundel was used by the Romans as a station when they constructed their coastal road from Chichester to Pevensey. Later it was to become the property of Alfred the Great, who's believed to have built a stronghold here to defend the valley against sea raiders, and it remained a royal town until the reign of Harold Godwinson, last king of Saxon England. After the Norman Conquest Arundel was awarded to Roger de Montgomerie, who began the building of the castle soon after 1070 on the site of the earlier stronghold. It was through the descendants of Queen Adeliza, widow of Henry I, that the castle eventually passed into the ownership of the Dukes of Norfolk, premier peers of England, whose home it still remains.

Ash, Ashen, Ash Plats. See ASHLANDS.

Ashburnham. From a quiet rural settlement on the banks of a river overhung with ash-trees, Ashburnham was to develop into a major centre of the Sussex iron industry. Once it was *æsc burna hām*, 'the ashbourne settlement', recorded as Esseburneham in 1211 and Ashburnhame in 1320. By the late 16th century the river Ashbourne was

being dammed into huge ponds from which water was channelled to power the great drop-hammers used to make cannon for the Navy. The forge still exists – it was the last in Sussex to close, in 1802.

Ashdown Forest. The name is a lingering memory of the medieval landscape of Sussex, when this area was so thickly wooded with ash-trees that it was called 'the Ashen Down' or Ashendon. We find it listed as such in records of 1234. Once part of the great forest covering much of southern England, the *Sylva Anderida* of the Romans and the *Andredesweald* (Weald) of the Saxons, the Ashdown Forest was granted by Edward III in 1372 to his son John of Gaunt, Duke of Lancaster, and given the name Lancaster Great Park. It was to remain a royal hunting ground for more than 300 years. Ashdown is now a forest in name only, having been denuded over the centuries to feed the forges of the Sussex iron industry.

Ashfold. Several places in the county share this name, each of them derived from the same source – a livestock enclosure shaded by ash-trees. The oldest site is Ashfold at Slaugham, recorded as Asshefold in 1305. Ashfolds, Rusper, is Asshfoldes in 1428; and Ashfold, Lower Beeding, appears as Ashfolds Heath in 1609.

Ashgate. Site of one of the many gates or entrances into the Ashdown Forest, this one was clearly distinguished by a particular tree and is Assegate in 1279. The Saxon word *geat* still represents 'gate' in Sussex dialect.

Ashington. There are two possible interpretations. Ashington may have been the *tūn* or farmstead of a tribal group calling itself the Æscingas, or Æsc's people. On the other hand it just as easily could have been the farmstead of a group known as 'the dwellers by the ash-tree'. Whichever theory is correct, the place is recorded as Essingetona in 1073, and Asshyngton in 1397. The area round here is still quite heavily wooded.

Ashlands. A self-explanatory name, appearing as Asshelond in 1532. The widespread abundance of ash-trees throughout Sussex is obvious from a number of other place names, beside those given elsewhere in this book. **Ash Chalk Pits** and **Shaw** at Jevington was once the home of Jordan and Thomas de Asche listed in 1285, and is recorded as both the Ashe and Ash land during the time of Elizabeth I. **Ashen Wood**, Brightling, is named as such in 1636; while **Ashes Wood**, Battle, is Le Assh in 1419. **Ash Plats Wood**, Forest Row, appears as 'woodland called le Asplott' in 1598, Asplott meaning a plot of ground with ash-trees. The name may be compared with **Platt's Farm** at Burwash, which is Plott in 1493 and Plotts three centuries later, in 1823.

Ashleigh. This would originally have been a *lēah* or clearing in an ash wood. In 1271 it's Essele, appearing more recognisably in 1381 as Esshely. **Ashreed Wood** at Laughton had a similar beginning, though here the land was cleared of ash-trees in the sense of being ridded of them – we find it referred to as le Archreede in the time of Charles I. **Ash Reeds Copse**, Fernhurst, shar-ing the same meaning, is Essheredes in 1547.

Ashling, East and **West.** One of the many groups of Saxons colonising Sussex in the period known as the Dark Ages, after the Romans departed, chose this particular spot to put down their roots. They were the Æscelingas, the people of Æscel, and they've left their name here as their memorial – Estlinges in 1185, Ashlyng a century later. Eventually the settlement was to divide into two small hamlets, described around 1325 as Estasshelyng and Westasshlyng.

Ash Reeds Copse, Ashreed Wood. See ASHLEIGH.

Ashton Green. It began life as a *tūn* or farmstead identified by the proximity of a particular ash-tree and is Hastone in 1150, Asston in 1288.

Ashurst. An unspoilt village beside the Adur, with lovely views southward to the Downs, Ashurst shares its description of 'ash-tree hill' with the **Ashurst Woods** at Forest Row, Mayfield and West Hoathly, and **Ashurst Farm** at Plumpton. The village itself is the oldest of these sites, dating at least to the 13th century when it's recorded as Asshehurst. In its churchyard is the grave of Margaret Fairless Dowson (1869-1901) who as 'Michael Fairless', author of *The Roadmender*, a story of Sussex folk, wrote of the Adur valley here and the 'lean grey downs, keeping watch and ward between the country and the sea'.

Atherington. Listed as such in 1271, this was the Saxon *Æþelhering tūn*, the farmstead of Æþelhere. It grew to be a manor of some importance, being granted after the Norman Conquest to the Abbey of Seez in Normandy – the restored 13th century chapel of **Bailiffscourt** here is all that now remains of a grange inhabited by monks of that abbey. Atherington, in fact, is referred to in 1540 as Addrington *alias* Baliscourte. Sadly, coastal erosion in this area has caused such havoc that the chapel and mansion are the only buildings of any note still standing between Middleton and Littlehampton.

Atlingworth Barn. The place name ending -worth usually points to an early enclosure of some kind, whether it be land or even a stockaded village. This 'worth' belonged to a South Saxon tribal group, the Æþelingas, Æþel's people, and it's documented as Athelingeworthe in 1091, Adelyngworth in 1279.

Austford. There's some speculation about this name. The first evidence we have of it is rather late as place names go, 1483, when it appears as Alkysford. Etymologists believe it contains the Saxon personal name Ealh, and that the ford was a crossing over a tributary of the river Brede at this point. Interestingly, the same personal name crops up in connection with a stream at HAWKS-BOURNE some distance away.

Awbrook. The word 'brook' is still used in Sussex dialect to describe low-lying ground near a river, such as a marsh or watermeadow. The marshy land here was the property of an early settler called Appa. We find the name developing from Apebroke about the year 1270 to Awbrook in 1636.

· · B · ·

Babsham. Considering Babsham is one of the oldest surviving Saxon places in Sussex, nothing at all is known about its founder other than that he was called Bæbbi. He was just one of the many individual South Saxons who staked a claim to land here, leaving us only their names by which to remember them. Bæbbi's *hām* or settlement appears in a document of AD 680 as Bebbes ham. By 1473 it had become Babbesham, of which the modern form is a contraction.

Badland Shaw. See BATHURST.

Bailiffscourt. See ATHERINGTON.

Bainden. The place appears as Bayndenn in 1296. That -denn ending tells us it was originally a wood-

15

land pasture – commonly a swine pasture where the pigs fed on acorns or beechmast. The owner here was a Saxon settler called Bǣga, a personal name we come across again in connection with a valley at BAYCOMBE, a watermeadow at BAYHAM and an enclosure at BYWORTH.

Baker's Common. This was land once owned by William le Bakere who was living in the Framfield area in 1327. **Baker's Wood** derives its name in similar fashion from the Salehurst family of Walter atte Bakhouse – 'of the bakehouse' – recorded in the parish in 1309.

Balcombe. Sometimes place names throw up old and long forgotten mysteries. Balcombe is such a one. Why the South Saxons knew it as 'the evil valley' – *bealu cumb* – we shall never know. We can only guess that something very unpleasant cast a shadow dark enough to live on in the name of the little settlement which was to develop here on a ridge between two valleys. It's documented as Belecumbe in 1279. **Balcombe Forest** – together with the other Sussex 'forests' of Ashdown, Worth, Holmbush, Tilgate, Peasepottage and St Leonard's – is a last remnant of the immense Saxon *Andredesweald* that once covered the northern half of the county.

Baldslow. Lying at the north-west of a prehistoric track known as The Ridge, Baldslow stands on ground high enough to be the site of a beacon in days gone by. It's marked on Speed's map of Sussex (1610) as Balteslow Beacon. Much earlier this high land had been the property of a Saxon settler called Beald, and from

Bealdes hlǣw or Beald's hill, its name developed via Baldeslei recorded in 1086 in the Domesday Book, to the more recognisable Baldeslowe of 1296.

Balls Green. It gets its name from Rychard Balle, a native of Pulborough, who owned land hereabouts in the time of Elizabeth I.

Balmer. This was 'the mere by the stronghold' – *burh mere*. In the Domesday Book it's Bergemere, in 1279 Burwemere. By 1541 the name had been whittled down to Bormer – which is how it's still pronounced. The original mere, or pool, is nothing but a grassy pit, though traces of the ancient stronghold still remain high on Balmer Down, where Roman treasure has been found.

Balsdean. The Saxon personal name Beald – it meant 'the bold one' – has been noted already in connection with BALDSLOW. Here at Balsdean the same Beald – or it may have been another, equally as bold, who knows – had a dean or small valley, recorded about the year 1100 as Baldesdene.

Bantony. Recorded in the 17th century as Banton's land, this takes its name from Gilbert de Bamton, who is listed in documents of 1288. The surname spelling may be a clerical error, because we find another member of the same family, possibly Gilbert's daughter, referred to in 1327 as Katerina de Banton.

Banwell. Here just to the north of the Selsey peninsula in an area of lush fields and watercourses, a spring once welled up near a plot of ground where beans were grown. Its location earned it the description 'bean spring' (the Saxon word *wielle*, which has given us our 'well', meant a spring) and it's recorded in 1332 as Benewell. Banwell Farm is all that remains nowadays to keep the name alive.

Barcombe. Barcombe and its neighbour **Barcombe Cross** stand on the slopes of the Downs where waving fields of barley add their own particular beauty to the landscape. Barley has always been grown here. In fact Barcombe began its existence as a barley field or *bere camp* – the word 'bere' being a reminder that the Saxons used the grain for making ale as well as for food. Recorded as Berecomp in 1233 and Bercombe a short while later, the place was the 'middelborgh' of the Barcombe Hundred, the other divisions being Newick, the 'northborgh', and Hamsey, the 'southborgh'. A borgh was a tithing (a district containing ten households) of a Hundred, which as its name suggests was an area supporting 100 families.

Bardown. Early in its history Bardown was the site of a Roman furnace or bloomery, producing iron of a kind that could be forged into light tools and small weapons. Some time later the hillslope here was ploughed up for arable use and barley grown, hence the name 'barley down' or hill. It appears as Berdowne in 1410, Bardowne two centuries afterwards.

Barehurst. The vowel sounds of a place name are often a good clue to its original meaning. Barehurst looks as though it could have been

'barley hill', but *bere* (the Saxon word for barley) would have produced a name sounding more like Barhurst. The vowel sound points us more towards an original *bǽr*, a woodland pasture for swine, which fits the 'wooded hill' meaning of -hurst much better. The name is listed in the 13th century as Berehurst.

Barfold. Somewhere beneath the fields of Barfold Farm here at West Lavington there may still be evidence of the ancient stronghold or earthwork which early settlers converted for use as a fold for their livestock. Though there's no visual trace of any remains now, the spot was known as 'the fold by the stronghold' – *burh falod*. We find it called Burifold in 1300. Interestingly, it's documented in 1823 as Barvell, which tells us how the name was being pronounced in Regency days.

Bargham. See BARPHAM, UPPER and LOWER.

Barham. Once a barley meadow or *bere hamm*, Barham was the 12th century birthplace of Robert de Berham, who adopted the name of the village as his own. Robert was son of Reginald FitzUrse, one of the four knights responsible for the murder in 1170 of St Thomas à Becket in Canterbury Cathedral. Hundreds of years later Robert's own descendants, the Barham family, were to be among the greatest ironmasters of Sussex when production of iron made the county a major industrial centre between the 16th and early 19th centuries.

Barkfold. This is 'Beadeca's fold',

marking the spot where an early settler called Beadeca chose to keep his livestock. The place is recorded as Badekefold in 1327, Barkfolde in 1498.

Barkhale Wood. The wood stands on the slopes of Bignor Hill, site of a Neolithic causewayed camp, but its name contains no clue at all to that fact. Instead it appears in records of 1420 as Berkehale, derived from *beorc healh*, referring to a corner of land where birch-trees were growing.

Barkham. The early spelling Berchamme (1332) tells us this was once *beorc hamm* or birch-tree meadow. By 1611, the time of James I, it had become Barkeham.

Barklye. Berklegh in 1332 and Barkelegh in 1438, the name denotes a *lēah* or clearing in a wood of birch-trees. The ending -ly, -lie and -lye is very often pronounced 'lie' in Sussex place names.

Barlavington. A group of South Saxons called the Lāfingas, or Lāfa's people, had a farmstead hereabouts where they cultivated their barley crops. In their time it would have been identified as *bere Lāfinga tūn*. The Domesday Book of 1086 records it as Berleventone. How the name later developed is demonstrated in a document of 1616, where it's carefully noted down as Barlavington *alias* Berlavington *alias* Berlaton – this last form probably giving us the pronunciation of the day. Lāfa's people had their main settlement a short distance away at EAST LAVINGTON.

Barline. This is Bereglynde in 1279,

suggesting the origin of the name to be *bær glind* – 'glind' being a fenced enclosure and 'bær' a woodland pasture for swine. So this was a place where a swine pasture was fenced round. The name reappears as Berklinde in 1327, and by 1450 had become Barlynde.

Barnesden. See BARNSGATE.

Barnfold. See BARNHAM.

Barnham. During the Middle Ages Barnham was a fishing village on a tidal creek of the Arun. Much earlier in its history it had been the *hām* or settlement of a South Saxon called Beorna, and appears as Berneham in the Domesday Book. The same or another Beorna (his name meant 'the heroic one') owned an area of open land or *feld* at **Barnfold**, recorded as Bernefeld in 1279; and in the same year **Barnsfold**, originally a fold where he kept his livestock, is listed as Bernefolde.

Barnhorne, Upper and **Lower.** Originally one settlement, it lies amid the marshes of Hooe Level on a horn-shaped piece of land that elevates it above the low-lying area around. This horn was settled at an early date by a South Saxon named Byrna – we find it referred to as 'on byrna hornan' in a document of AD 772. By 1434 the place name had developed to Bernehorn, and is Barnehorne a century later.

Barnsfold. See BARNHAM.

Barnsgate. Recorded as Barnesgate in the time of Elizabeth I, this was one of the many gates leading into the Ashdown Forest, and was obviously identified by its proximity to some barn. Neighbouring **Barnesden** indicates the site of an old *denn* or woodland pasture in the same vicinity.

Barn's Green. The name is thought to have associations with the family of Thomas atte Berne – 'at the barn' – registered in the area in 1327.

Barnsnape. This is Brandeslep in 1255 and Bransnape in 1607. To find its derivation we need to look at its site. There's a steepish hillslope where Barnsnape Farm now stands, suggesting the original name was *brant slæp* or steep slippery place. Local pronunciation would account for the change from Bran- to Barn-.

Barpham, Upper and **Lower.** Until the 16th century the hamlet was known only as **Bargham**. We come across the first mention of any alternative name in a document of 1582, which refers to the place as Bargham *alias* Barffham. In fact the two names are interchangeable, though the Ordnance Survey map prefers Barpham. Bargham derives from the Saxon *beorg hām*, 'mound settlement' – the hamlet stands on the site of a Romano-British settlement built close to a burial mound. How or why it came to be known by the alias Barpham is a mystery, unless the dialect speech of Tudor Sussex influenced the change.

Barrowhill. A straightforward name, it refers to a hill with a barrow or burial mound on it, and is recorded as Berwehull in 1261.

Barton. See BERWICK.

Batchelor's Bump. A somewhat whimsical name, it comes from John Bachelor, a landowner living in the Guestling area during the time of the Tudors. It's been suggested the 'Bump' referred to a prominent hillock on his property.

Batchmere. The pool (mere) belonging to an early settler called Bæcci, this is listed as Baxchesmere in 1296 and Batchmore in 1627. Bæcci's pool probably drained into a tidal creek of Chichester Canal not far from Birdham.

Bathurst (Farm). First recorded in 1121, as Badeherste, the farm name preserves the memory of a South Saxon called Bada who owned a hurst or wooded hill here in the Warbleton area. We subsequently find the place documented at the beginning of the 14th century as Badhurst, and then Bathurst. The same Saxon personal name also occurs in connection with **Badland Shaw** not far away at Ewhurst. Here 'Bada's land' is first noted around the year 1220 as Badeland. By 1535 it had become Badlands, and the affix 'Shaw' – meaning a small wood or copse – was attached later on.

Bathurst Wood. It isn't recorded as such until 1724, so though this name may look the same as BATHURST FARM in the entry above, the two actually have slightly different derivations. Its appearance in a document of 1248 as Bodeherste suggests the Saxon personal name was Boda, making it originally *Bodan hyrst* or Boda's wooded hill. Subsequent records give the name as Bodherst (1432) and Botehurst (1457). We know the hill had a gate leading on

19

to it at one time, because we find a Bodherstgate here in 1248 and a Botherstgate 50 years later. Incidentally, Boda crops up again in connection with BUDDINGTON and BODIAM.

Batsford. Farms such as this one near Warbleton are often the last custodians of part of the history of Sussex, because they're all that's left to preserve the names of long-lost settlements and long-dead individuals. Batsford was once 'the ford of Bætel' – a personal name found nowhere else in the county. By the year 1100 Bætel's ford had become Betelesford, then Batelesford (1279) and subsequently Batesford (1319). His ford must have been a crossing place on a tributary of the Cuckmere in this vicinity.

Battenhurst. Another farm name with Saxon roots, this was originally 'Bēta's stubble-field' or *Bētan ersc*, recorded as Betenershe in the year 1200 and Bethenerse two centuries later.

Battle. This is surely one of the most famous places in British history. The town and its abbey church of St Martin's stand on the site of Senlac Moor, scene in 1066 of the so-called Battle of Hastings when William the Conqueror and his invading Normans defeated King Harold's Saxon English. The site is referred to in a Norman-French document written the same year as La Batailge – 'the battle place' – a description which lived on. Because Hastings was the nearest town of any importance at the time, it was used as a landmark to identify the location of the conflict. William's vow to build an abbey in thanksgiving for his victory

was fulfilled in 1094 when St Martin's was consecrated – traditionally its high altar marks the spot where King Harold died – and the small town which grew round it was known simply as Battle. The spelling is Bataille in 1251. The name of Senlac (from *sand lacu*, sandy watercourse) is preserved in that of the main street skirting the abbey precincts, Upper and Lower Lake. The stream, still flowing, probably looked sandy because of its reddish chalybeate water, but there was an old belief that it was coloured by the blood of those killed in the battle. St Martin's abbey was dissolved by Henry VIII. Part of the remains are now incorporated in a school for girls, but the grounds and other buildings are open to visitors.

Batworthpark. In 1306 this is Bedeworth *juxta* Arundel, 'juxta' meaning 'next to'. In 1436 we find it as Badworth. The site was once the *worð* or enclosure of an early settler called Bæda. Nowadays the name only survives in that of Batworthpark House, described in *The Castles and Mansions of Western Sussex* (1879) as 'one of the more ancient appendages of Arundel Castle'.

Baycombe. Research suggests that the personal name here is Bǣga (also found in connection with BAINDEN, BAYHAM and BYWORTH) and that this was Bǣga's combe or valley. The place is documented as Baycumbe in 1274.

Bayham Abbey. Founded between 1208 and 1211 by Sir Robert de Turneham, a distinguished crusader who raised several monastic foundations on his return from the Holy

Land, the abbey united two small houses of Premonstratensian monks, one from Brockley in Deptford (London), the other from Otteham near Polegate. It was originally known as Bels Lieux, or 'beautiful place', and gave its name to nearby BELLS YEW GREEN. After Henry VIII's dissolution of the monasteries the name gradually fell into disuse, and was in time replaced by that of the village of Bayham, just over the county border in Kent. Bayham itself has a Saxon origin, being the *hamm* or watermeadow of Bǣga – a personal name we also find at BAINDEN, BAYCOMBE and BYWORTH.

Beachy Head. Towering almost 600 ft above the sea, Beachy Head is one of Britain's most spectacular vantage points and marks the eastern termination of the South Downs. On a clear day one can see right the way from Dungeness to the Isle of Wight – and no doubt this glorious view accounts for its name. In the Norman-French spoken here after the Conquest it was 'beautiful headland' or *beu chef*. In 1264 we find it still spelled this way, but by 1546 it had been reduced to Bechy. And then long after everyone had forgotten the name meant 'headland' anyway, another Head was added for good measure.

Beacon Down. Since time out of mind, beacons, or signal fires, have been lit on hill-tops as a warning of danger. The one on Beacon Down, north of Waldron, was evidently prepared for use against the threat of the Spanish, because it's 'Beaken doune' on a map of 1584, just four years before the Spanish Armada was defeated. A much earlier one

was sited at **Beacon Hill**, Bishopstone. Here we find a reference to 'la Bekne' in 1374, halfway through the Hundred Years' War between England and France.

Bear Wood. It's been suggested the place has some connection with a Robert le Beer, known to have been living here in the Hartfield area in 1296. His surname seems to be from the old Saxon word *bær*, denoting woodland pasture where swine were kept, an interpretation which fits this particular location.

Becket's Barn. The building here is all that remains of an archbishop's palace belonging to the See of Canterbury, at which St Thomas à Becket is known to have stayed on official visitations. The church at nearby Pagham, dedicated to St Thomas, was probably built within a few decades of his murder in 1170.

Beckhall, Beckington. See BECKLEY.

Beckley. Once a Saxon royal possession, Beckley is mentioned in the Will of Alfred the Great as his lands at 'Beccanleah', bequeathed to his kinsman Osferthe. Some 20 years earlier, around AD 880, the place is called Beccanlea. There's no doubt it was originally *Beccan lēah*, the woodland clearing of a settler called Becca. Maybe this was the same Becca who had his farmstead at **Beckington Farm** not far away at Heathfield, listed about 1250 as Bekinton (from *Beccing tūn*). Another of the name owned a hedged enclosure or *hæg* away across the county at **Beckhall Farm**, Sutton – Beckehagh in 1327.

Beckworth. Recorded as le Backworth in 1631 during the reign of Charles I, etymologists think this may be ultimately derived from *Baccan worð*, meaning the enclosure of Bacca, a Saxon personal name found at PAXHILL.

Bedales. See BEDLAM WOOD.

Beddingham. Standing in downland country at the edge of the wide river valley of the Ouse, Beddingham began as a watermeadow (*hamm*) owned by a small Saxon tribe called the Bēadingas, or Bēada's people. It's referred to in a document dating roughly to the year AD 880 as Beadingahamme. Two centuries later the Domesday Book records it more recognisably as Bedingeham. The Bēadingas had their main settlement on the bank of the river Adur at BEEDING.

Bedham. This is Budeham in 1261 and Bedeham in 1563. It was originally the *hām* or settlement of a South Saxon called Buda – a personal name we also find connected with a farmstead at BUDDINGTON (Easebourne).

Bedlam Wood. Bedlam is the old name for a lunatic asylum. It came from the priory of St Mary of Bethlehem in London, a 15th century hospital which by the 17th century had become a notorious madhouse – the original Bedlam (the word is a corrupted abbreviation of Bethlehem). All this, however, is by the by because Bedlam Wood, at Mayfield, has a rather less dramatic history. It's recorded in 1352 as Beldamelond. Beldame, or beldam, is an obsolete term for a grandmother or

ancestress, so this may well have been land inherited from the maternal side of the family. Alternatively, it may share the same origin as **Beldameland Farm** at Wisborough Green, which we find variously listed as Bedellond (1369), Beldam lands (1623) and Bedhamland (1795). The 1369 form leads us to wonder whether the land here may have belonged to a beadle, a parish officer empowered to punish petty offenders. The title goes back to medieval days, when it's *bedel*, and gave rise to the surname le Budel which we find in connection with **Bedales** at Lindfield – a Thomas le Budel is recorded locally in 1301 and the place itself is given as Bedels in 1591.

Beechland. A simple, self-explanatory name, in 1441 it appears as Bechlond.

Beeding, Upper and **Lower.** The -ing ending is Saxon, from *ingas*, meaning 'people of', and is the clue that this was once a tribal settlement, home of the Bēadingas who took their name from their leader, Bēada. About AD 880 the place is mentioned as æt Beadingum, then later appears as Bedinges (1073) and Beding (1327). Upper and Lower Beeding are quite a few miles apart, Upper being further down beside the river Adur and therefore, geographically, lower than Lower Beeding. Upper Beeding was the tribe's original settlement (upper being used here in the sense of high or main, as in High Street) while Lower (lesser) Beeding, being on higher ground, was used for pasturing livestock. Bēada's people also owned pasture land at BEDDINGHAM.

Beeding Bridge. It's associated with Simon de Ponte de Beddinge, recorded in 1279, whose impressive surname informs us that he dwelt 'by the bridge of Beeding', crossing the Adur near Upper Beeding. **Beeding's Farm** and **Beedings**, both at Pulborough, take their name from William Bidyng, a native of Beeding, living early in the 14th century.

Beggars Bush. The spelling has hardly changed since the time of Elizabeth I, when it was Beggers-bush. **Beggars Copse** at Kirdford is similarly recorded as Begers Bush in 1740. It's tempting to imagine some poor wretch seeking refuge from the weather in the shelter of these bushes, but a prosaic interpretation is that the name probably has more to do with berries than beggars, and is derived from the Saxon word for a berry, *bēger*.

Beldameland. See BEDLAM WOOD.

Bellhurst. There are three places of this name in Sussex. Bellhurst at Etchingham was originally *Bellan hyrst*, being the wooded hill of a Saxon man rather prettily called Bella. It's Beleherst about 1260 and Belhurst some 20 years later. Bellhurst at Beckley shares the same history, appearing in the Domesday Book (1086) as Bellest; while Bellhurst at Wartling is Belherst early in the 14th century.

Bellreed Wood. The first evidence we have of the name comes in 1438, when it's mentioned as Balrede. Etymologists have suggested it may be derived from the Saxon *beolone rīed* – 'henbane rid' – referring to land cleared of henbane. This is a poiso-nous plant of the deadly nightshade family found growing wild in waste places and around the sites of ruins. Nowadays it's cultivated for medicinal use, particularly in the south and east of England.

Bells Yew Green. This attractive little village near the Kentish border derives its name from nearby BAYHAM ABBEY, which was known as Bels Lieux (medieval French for 'beautiful place') for a time after its foundation. Bells Yew is a rather charming corruption of that old name. It's variously recorded during the 17th century as Belsyoe, Bellisewe and Belsewes.

Bemzells Wood. The wood, together with Bemzells Farm here at Herstmonceux, marks the site of an ancient timber-framed building somewhere in the vicinity. What its use was we don't know, but it must have been a fairly sturdy construction because the name comes from *bēam sele*, describing a 'beam hall'. It's documented as Bembselle in 1296, Bemsell in 1360.

Benefold Copse. See BENNYFOLD.

Benfield. Benfield Farm at Hangleton occupies an area of open land where beans were once cultivated – probably the broad or 'common' bean, grown in Europe since prehistoric times. Its name, from *bēan feld*, appears as Benefeld in 1296.

Bennyfold. A good many of the county's minor names would be lost entirely but for the farms that still mark them on the map, preserving the location of long-vanished places. Bennyfold Farm at Petworth is a typical example. It stands on the site of a fold where an early settler called Bynna kept his livestock, and is Bunyfold in 1296, Benefolde in 1553. **Benefold Copse** at Lurgashall shares an almost identical origin, except the Saxon personal name here is Benna. From *Benning falod*, 'Benna's fold', the name had developed to Benyngfold by 1380.

Bentley. Bentley Farm at Framfield, and **Great Bentley Farm**, Cuckfield, are both recorded in the early part of the 14th century as Benetlegh. They're in places where the land had been cleared of *beonet* or 'bent grass' – describing long coarse grass such as rushes. Interestingly, this word has survived in Sussex dialect as 'bennets', used of long grass that bends with the wind.

Bepton. The Domesday Book (1086) records Bepton as Babintone, which is close to the older original name, *Bæbbing tūn* – the farmstead of a Saxon woman called Bæbbe. From Bebbinton (1240) it gradually became shortened in everyday speech until by 1527 we find the place referred to as both Bebyngton and Bebton. As a sidelight on history, Bæbbe was the name of Æthelfrith of Northumbria's queen, from whom Bamburgh (Northumberland) gets its derivation.

Bernhurst. The spelling has remained unchanged since 1288 when it referred to a barn by a hurst, or wooded hill. Our modern word barn comes originally from the Saxon *bere ærn* or 'barley house', a building where grain was stored.

Berryfield, Berryland. See BERRY LANE.

Berry Lane. A pretty name which belies its origin. Once it was 'the stronghold' or *burh*. We find it mentioned as le Bery in 1482, Berylane in 1495. No doubt the lane led up to the old earthwork on the hill at nearby Bersted. **Berry Farm**, Ardingly – documented as the Berry about the year 1600 – was earlier the home of William atte Bery (1327) whose surname meant 'by the stronghold'. There's no trace of any earthwork in this immediate vicinity, so the reference must be to Burstow Hill close by. **Berryfield** at Tangmere is Buryfeld in 1497. It has practically the same origin as the two **Berryland Farms** in the county, at Hurstpierpoint and Kirdford, their names referring to land near some vanished earthwork. Incidentally, *burh* later came to mean a fortified town and developed to our modern 'borough'.

Bersted. For almost 1,000 years there were two Bersteds here, North and South, straddling either side of the hill. Then in 1785 the village of South Bersted was purchased for redevelopment by Sir Richard Hotham, creator of the neighbouring coastal resort of BOGNOR REGIS, and it's since become virtually a suburb of Bognor. North Bersted appears to be the older of the two settlements. The first documented reference we have dates back to AD 680 when it's mentioned as both Beorgan stede and north beorgan stede – the *stede* or place of Beorga, an early Saxon settler. By the end of the 14th century the name had developed via Suthbergested (1272) and Northberghested (1327) to Bursted – which is how it's still pronounced.

Berwick. Recorded in the Domesday Book as Berewice, this was a Saxon *bere wīc*, or barley farm. A similar sort of farm, a *bere tūn*, occupied the site of **Barton Farm** at Pagham. Probably the only distinction between them was that a *bere wīc* was not protected within an enclosure like a *bere tūn*. Barton Farm is noted as Bertone broke in 1483, the 'brook' being marshy land in this coastal area.

Berwick St John. See COMPTON.

Bestbeech Hill. A descriptive name, it's first mentioned in 1780 as Best Beech Hill, maybe referring to some particularly handsome specimen of tree.

Betley. Bettelye in 1332, it was originally *Bettan lēah*, a clearing in woodland owned by a Saxon called Betta. He's one of the numerous early settlers of whom we find only a solitary instance in the place names of Sussex.

Bevendean. Here we meet a South Saxon of rather more consequence than many of his contemporaries. His name was Beofa, and besides tribal territory he owned land in his own right, including the valley at Bevendean, on the South Downs. Beofa's valley – *Beofan dene* – is Bevedene in the Domesday Book (1086) and Bevenden in 1230. He likewise owned a horn-shaped stretch of land protruding into marshes on the bank of Longford Stream at **Bevern Bridge**. Originally this would have been *Beofan horna*. Centuries on, when a bridge had been built across the stream, we find the place documented about 1100 as pontem de

Beuehorne, and later still, bridge of Bevehorne (1350) and Bevorne Bridge (1583). Beofa's tribal territory was at **Bevingford** where his people, the Beofingas, had their main enclosure. From *Beofinga worð* the name developed to Bebbyngewerth in 1296 and Bebyngworth in 1535. Then some time after the 16th century the ending was altered from -worth to -ford, a change no doubt influenced by Bevingford's closeness to a crossing over a tributary of the river Ouse.

Bevern Bridge, Bevingford. See BEVENDEAN.

Bevis's Thumb. This is the name fancifully given to a large Neolithic long barrow on Telegraph Hill at Compton. The legendary giant Bevis is closely associated with ARUNDEL. Folk tales describe him crossing from the Isle of Wight to Southampton in a single stride and living on a diet of a whole ox a week washed down with two hogsheads (roughly 490 litres) of beer.

Bewbush. After the Conquest of 1066 Norman-French names occasionally started appearing on the county map. BEACHY HEAD is one example. Bewbush is another. There must have been some attractive species of shrub growing hereabouts which particularly appealed to the eye, because the French origin of the name, *beau buisson*, meant 'beautiful thicket'. It's recorded as Beaubusson in 1317 and Beaubussh just under a century later.

Bexhill. The history of this popular seaside town reaches a long way back. It has its roots in Neolithic times, when a defensive earthwork was built on the hill where the parish church of St Peter's now stands. Low-lying marshland stretched beyond it to the sea. When the South Saxons arrived they found the old earthwork overgrown with the evergreen shrub called box, and after clearing the site, referred to it as *byxe lēah* – box-tree clearing. The name developed from Bixlea recorded in AD 772 to Bexelei in the Domesday Book. By 1406 it was Byxyll. Until the last decades of the 19th century the place was no more than a small village clustered about its hill, less than a mile from the sea. The modern resort developed after 1885, when Lord de la Warr, whose land included the old marshy area, began building on this coastal strip. Bexhill's famous **de la Warr Pavilion** commemorates his achievement.

Bexley Hill. See BOXAL BRIDGE.

Bible Bottom. Once known as The Devil's Book, this is a rectangular-shaped earthwork resembling an open book, lying on the side of Cliffe Hill. In times gone by when folk were more naively superstitious, they regarded many such ancient remains as the work of the Devil. Here the name has undergone a change for the better, so to speak.

Bibleham. See BIVELHAM.

Bigenor. See BOGNOR REGIS.

Biggen Holt. A name that hasn't changed much from its Saxon origin, *Bidan holt*. In fact it's recorded as such in AD 834, referring to a thicket of trees owned by someone called Bida.

Bigknowle. The earliest spelling appears in a document of 1296 as Bybeknolle, suggesting this was once the knoll or hillock of a settler named Bibba. By 1528 it had become Buknoll, reappearing as Bignold in 1703.

Bignor. Lying on the northern slopes of the Downs, this pretty village is the site of one of the most famous Roman villas in Britain, built towards the end of the 2nd century AD close to Stane Street. The ruins were uncovered in 1811, proving to be those of the administrative centre of an estate of about 2,000 acres. The villa itself covers about 4½ acres and contains some fine mosaic floors, including one depicting Venus and the Gladiator. Alas, the name of this estate didn't survive the Saxon invasion. Instead it was given the identity of its new owner, Bica, and the description 'hill brow', referring no doubt to Bignor Hill. So Bica's brow – *Bican yfre* – is the origin of the place name. It appears in the Domesday Book as Bigenevre. Two centuries later in 1284 it's Bygenore. Incidentally, Bica's name crops up again at PIGSTROOD.

Billingham. Byllingham in 1401, the place came into existence as the *hām* or settlement of the Billingas, a tribe taking its identity from its warrior leader Billa, nicknamed 'the dagger' (from their word *bil*). They also owned land at BILLINGSHURST.

Billingshurst. The site was a hurst, or wooded hill, on the territory of the Billingas, whose tribal settlement was at BILLINGHAM. From *Billingas hyrst* the name had developed to Bellingesherst by 1203, and

Billyngeshurst 50 years later. Billingshurst lies beside the Roman Stane Street running from Chichester to London, so maybe it's not too extraordinary that we find the name of the tribe's leader, Billa, connected with London's Billingsgate. Fancifully, Billingsgate is supposed to be called after a Roman surveyor, Belinus. Research suggests, however, that facts override the fancy, and that a branch of the Billingas migrated to London and settled near the site of the gate.

Bilsham. A map of 1732 shows the spelling to be Bilsom, which is how this name is still pronounced by Sussex natives. Earlier it appears as Bullesham (1236) and Bulsham *alias* Bilsham (1580). The earliest recorded form, in the Domesday Book, shows the name as Bilesham, so the origin seems to be *Bӯles hām* – Bӯli's settlement.

Binderton. In Saxon times women enjoyed a much higher status in society than they would later on in the Middle Ages. They were regarded as perfectly competent to manage property and enter into contracts dealing with the ownership of land. Here at Binderton we have one of the county's few surviving place-name examples of a Saxon lady of property. She was called Beornðryð and was mistress of a *tūn* or farmstead on this site. The Domesday Book documents it as Bertredtone. Just over a century later it was Bendrinton, and by the reign of Edward I (1279) it had become Bynderton.

Bineham. Somewhere in the vicinity, on a tributary of Longford Stream, there was once a water-meadow that held a trough or manger for the owner's livestock. From the descriptive 'manger meadow' or *binn hamm*, the place name developed via Bynhamme, found in 1332, to Bynham in Chagelegh (Chailey) recorded just 30 years after. The old word *binn* in due course produced the surname Bynne, Byne or Byn ('dweller by the manger') which occurs in connection with **Bines Green**, Ashurst, **South Binns**, Heathfield, and **Bines Farm** and **Gate**, West Grinstead. This last place appears as la Byne in Westgrynsted in 1454.

Bines Farm, Gate, Green. See BINE-HAM.

Bingletts Wood. Without the addition of the diminutive ending -let, this would be called Bingley Wood today. It's recorded as Bynglye in 1614. Earlier it was Byngelegh (1327), from *bing lēah* – 'hollow clearing' – describing a cleared patch of woodland containing a natural hollow. It lies near Heathfield in an area of well-wooded country.

Binsted. Like BENFIELD, this was land where beans were once cultivated. The name has the straightforward meaning of 'bean place', from *bēan stede*, and is Benestede in the Domesday Book, Biensted in 1332.

Birchen. The earliest recorded spelling – Birchenden (1262) – tells us that here was originally a *denn* or woodland pasture amongst birch-trees. By the time of the Civil War we know the name had been shortened in everyday use, because we find it documented as Byrchden *alias* Byrchenden in 1646. **Birchen Bridge**

near Nuthurst was either a bridge built of birch wood, or more likely, one near some distinguishing group of birch-trees. It's Birchenbridge in 1650. **Birchen Wood**, Brightling, means simply what it says, and appears as Berchenwode in 1336.

Birchetts Green. Recorded as la Birchette in 1309, the place was the home of a medieval landowner, William de la Byrchette, listed in the area in 1296. **Birchet's Wood** at Cuckfield shares a similar source, being originally the property of Ralph ate Birchet (1327). Both surnames describe someone whose dwelling was 'by the birch-trees'.

Birchgrove. Despite the apparently obvious derivation, the name actually has nothing at all to do with birch-trees. Its present form is quite modern and appears to be a corruption of Bunch Grove, recorded for the place in 1839. This in turn developed from Buntes Grove, found in 1564. Much earlier the Domesday Book lists it as Bontegrave, and around the year 1150 it's Buntes-graua. The origin is almost certainly *Buntes gräf*, referring to a grove of trees owned by a settler called Bunt.

Birdham. A picturesque village beside a tidal creek, Birdham has long attracted artists to its vicinity, as well as yachtsmen who come sailing here in Chichester Harbour. Its history as a Saxon settlement is first recorded in AD 683, when the name appears as Bridham. This suggests it was a spot noted for numerous flocks of birds, maybe a nesting colony, giving rise to the description *bridd hām*, or 'bird settlement'. We can see from a document of 1492 which refers to the name as both Byrdham and Bridham that by then it was being pronounced as it is today. Transference of the letter *r* in names isn't unusual and reflects the changes in everyday speech over the centuries.

Birling Gap. This cleft in the South Downs between Beachy Head and the mouth of the Cuckmere was originally home to a minor Saxon tribe known as the Bǣrelingas – Bǣrel's people. It must have made a strong defensive position above the sea, as well as being an excellent look-out point. The old tribal name had developed to Berlinges by 1210, and was Barlyng in 1363. In 1587 we first find it called Birling Gappe. During the 18th century the Gap was protected by a gate in a vain attempt to stop smugglers coming ashore and using the steep steps here to off-load their contraband.

Bishopstone. For almost 1,000 years Bishopstone belonged to the See of Canterbury. The connection began early in the 8th century AD, when the parish church of St Andrew was built, and lasted right until the 17th century when the place is recorded as Bushopston. With such an ecclesiastical history it's hardly surprising this was originally the farmstead of a bishop – though 'manor' is probably a more fitting description. The name developed from the old Saxon *biscopes tūn*, and is Biscopestone in the Norman Domesday Book.

Bittlesham. The first documented mention occurs comparatively late, in 1541, when the place is called Betilsham. Etymologists think it originally could have been *Bēteles* *hām* – settlement of a Saxon called Bētel. This interpretation is lent credence by the fact that the same personal name has been discovered in connection with a now lost place not far away, recorded about the year 1120 as Betlesparrioc. There's no doubt this was *Bēteles pearroc*, Bētel's paddock. Although we know the place was at Buckfold, unfortunately the exact location can't be identified.

Bivelham. Bivelham Farm, near Mayfield, preserves the name of a small settlement here beside the Rother. In 1288 it's recorded as Byvelehamme. Thirty years later it's Byvelham. The name derives from Saxon times, when it was *Bifelan hamm*, Bifela's watermeadow, so this is clearly a very old site. Interestingly, the farm is also known as Bibleham, pronounced 'Bibbelham' – an example of the way *v* changes to *b* in traditional Sussex dialect speech. Just a short distance along the river **Bivelham Forge Farm** and **Bridge** mark the location of an old foundry.

Blackboys. Blakeboyes in 1437, the village actually gets its name from Richard Blakeboy, whose home it was in 1398. Local tradition is rather more inventive, however, and credits the name to the so-called 'black boys' – charcoal handlers at the nearby iron foundries – who used the 14th century inn here to slake their thirst at the end of the day.

Blackbrook. Quite a few places in the county share this name. To understand its origin, it helps us to remember that in Sussex 'brook' doesn't necessarily mean a stream.

The word refers more generally to marshy ground. So here we have a description of black water-logged land found in connection with **Blackbrook Farm**, Petworth (called Blakebrok in 1330), **Blackbrook Farm**, Westmeston, **Blackbrooks**, Brightling, **Black Brooks**, Westfield, and **Blackbrooks Bridge** – of which there are two in fact, one at Chailey, the other at Sedlescombe.

Black Down. Owned by the National Trust, Black Down marks the highest point in Sussex, standing 919 ft above sea level, and commands some splendid views of the surrounding countryside. It was a favourite haunt of the poet Alfred Lord Tennyson, who used to walk here along the track now known as **Tennyson's Lane** from his home, Aldworth House, just across the Surrey border. Black Down is recorded in 1610 as Blackdoune Beacon. The name is obviously descriptive. Perhaps the summit had been blackened by fire at some time.

Blackfold Barn. See BLACKHAM.

Blackford. Blakeford in 1272, the name probably describes the mud-discoloured waters of a tributary of Hurst Haven which was forded near the spot where Blackford Farm now stands. The old bridge here is recorded as Blakford brige in 1517.

Blackham. This seems to have got its name from *blæc hamm* or 'black watermeadow', from dark marshy ground in the vicinity. It's documented as Blacheham around 1095, and Blakeham just under a century later. Similarly, **Blackfold Barn** at Balcombe stands on what was once

29

'black open land' or *blæc feld* – Blakefeld in 1308. And the same derivation, indicating dark-coloured soil, is shared by **Blackland Copse**, Henfield (Blakelond 1296), **Blackland Wood**, Forest Row (Blackland Croft 1625), **Blacklands**, Slinfold (Blakelond 1338), and **Black Lane**, Itchingfield – described as Blake lond in Hechingfeld in 1318.

Blackhurst. Dark undergrowth or tree cover probably gave this place its description of black hurst or wood. We find it referred to as Blackehurste in 1390. **Blakehurst Farm** at Warningcamp has the same origin, being la Blakehurst in 1263.

Blackland, Black Lane. See BLACKHAM.

Blackstock Bridge. Somewhere in the area there was once a stretch of open land identified by some prominent blackened stock or tree stump. It's mentioned as Blakestokfeld in the time of Edward II. The -field ending was dropped from the name after a bridge had been built here spanning a tributary of Wallers Haven. Another black (maybe burnt) tree stump marked the site which **Blackstock Farm** at Hellingly now occupies. This appears as Blakestocke in 1272.

Blackstone. The earliest record of the name (1262) gives the spelling as Blexinton, which suggests to scholars that it was originally *Blæcsiging tūn*, denoting the farmstead of a Saxon warrior called Blæcsige. His name has a somewhat formidable interpretation: it meant 'black victory'. By 1373 the place spelling had become Blaxton, and on Speed's

map of Sussex (1610) it's Blackson.

Blackwell Wood. Water from a spring welling up at this spot couldn't have been too palatable, nor very salubrious for that matter. The unpleasant discoloration earned it its name, recorded in 1296 as Blakewelle. Another 'black well' or spring rose in the vicinity of **Blackwell Farm**, East Grinstead – in 1593 spelt exactly as it is today.

Blatchington, East and **West.** Although the two places lie a fair distance apart, they share a common beginning. Each came into existence as the *tūn* or farmstead of a Saxon warrior-farmer bearing the sinisterly evocative nickname 'the black one' – Blæcca. From *Blæccing tūn*, both names had developed to Blechyngton by the first half of the 13th century. The 'East' and 'West' prefixes were added quite some time afterwards, succeeding an earlier form of identity that distinguished one place from the other by their locations. Thus we find West Blatchington referred to as Blechington *juxta* Shorham (near Shoreham) in 1340, and East Blatchington as Blachington *juxta* Sefford (near Seaford) just under 40 years later.

Bleatham. The name is pronounced 'Bleat-ham' and its spelling has remained unchanged since Saxon times. The first settlers surely must have found the spot a bleak and cheerless place to live, since they called it 'the miserable settlement'. Their word *blēat* is still used in Sussex to describe a biting cold wind – which may give us some clue why Bleatham was so miserable. Unusually, the parish has the alternative name **Egdean** which scholars consider to be derived from *Ecgan dene* – Ecga's valley. It's recorded as Egedene in 1279. Who knows, maybe Ecga was one of the hardy Saxons who chose to stay on here when others had abandoned the site.

Bletchingley. Blecchingelegh in 1279, this was a *lēah* or cleared area of woodland in the tribal territory of the Blæccingas, or Blæcca's people. Their leader – 'the black one' – may have been the same individual who had two farmsteads of his own, at EAST and WEST BLATCHINGTON. As with most Sussex place names that end in -ly or -ley, the final syllable of this name is emphasised as 'lie'.

Boarshead. Recorded as Boreshead in the time of Mary I (1556) the name is suggested to have come from some particular stone shaped like the head of a boar. However, it's possible the origin stems back to the practice of animal sacrifice when, in pagan worship, the head of a slaughtered animal was set up on a pole. There are examples in neighbouring counties of this ritual being preserved in place names, including Broxhead, Hampshire (a badger) and Eversheds, Surrey (a wild boar).

Boarzell. Before they became extinct in this country, wild boar had been hunted for centuries as beasts of the chase. Boarzell was once 'boars hill', and so obviously a place where these animals were to be found. From *bāres hyll*, the name developed via Baresselle (1123) and Borselle (1296) to Boorsill, recorded in 1724. The old Sussex dialect pronunciation of *s* as *z* has clearly affected the modern spelling.

Bodiam. The early spellings, Bodeham in 1086 and Bodihamme in 1259, seem to indicate this was originally *Bodan hamm*, the watermeadow of a Saxon called Boda (a personal name we also find in connection with BATHURST WOOD and BUDDINGTON). Until recently Bodiam was generally pronounced 'Bodjum'. It's a pleasant Wealden village, its big attraction being the moated castle standing on a mound between the Rother and the Kent Ditch – the latter a dividing line between the counties of Kent and Sussex. In the Domesday Book (1086) Osbert de Bodeham is recorded as living here in a timbered hall as thane, holding the land in return for military service. From his family the manor passed in 1250 to the de Wardeux family, and just over a century later it descended through marriage to Sir Edward Dalyngrigge, a knight of East Grinstead. The Rother was at that period navigable as far as Bodiam Bridge, and in 1385 Sir Edward was granted special licence by Richard II to build Bodiam Castle as an inland defence guarding the river valley. It was dismantled during the Civil War by Sir William Waller, then subsequently purchased by Lord Curzon in 1917, and left to the National Trust at his death in 1926.

Bodle Street Green. This is Bodylstret in 1539 and Bodell Strete half a century later. The name was acquired from the Bothel family, property owners recorded in the area between 1318 and 1346.

Bognor Regis. For a thoroughly modern, popular family seaside resort, Bognor has the distinction of being one of the oldest recorded Saxon sites in the county. It appears in a document of AD 680 as Bucgan ora – Bucge's shore – referring to a strip of shelving beach used as a landing place. Its owner, Bucge, is one of the few Saxon women we find commemorated in Sussex's place names. Her landing place was to grow into a medieval fishing hamlet, recorded as Buggenore in 1275, Bogenor in 1405. And we know that it had two inland swine pastures, one at **Little Bognor** (Bogenore in 1248), the other at **Bigenor Farm** (Bogenore in 1279). Its prosperity as a coastal resort began soon after 1785. In that year a wealthy London hat-maker, Sir Richard Hotham, bought 1,600 acres of land in the area which he developed with the intention of creating a rival 'watering place' to Brighton. He renamed his new town Hothampton, but this went out of fashion soon after Sir Richard's death in 1790. Bognor was granted the royal affix Regis (a Latin word meaning 'of the king') following the convalescence of George V at nearby Aldwick in 1928.

Bolebroke. The gatehouse of Bolebroke Castle, built between 1475 and 1500, is believed to be the oldest brick building in Sussex. It originally belonged to the Dalyngrigge family, one of whom built the castle at BODIAM. Bolebroke seems to have come into existence as a strip of marshy land where a bull was kept, hence the description 'bull marsh' (the word 'brook' more generally refers to water-logged ground in Sussex). Its name appears as Bolebrok in 1249, and as Bolbrocke *alias* Boolebrocke in 1588.

Bolney. The various spellings of the name – Bolleneye in 1279, Bolneye in 1325 – point to a Saxon origin of *Bollan ēg*, or Bolla's island. The derivation suggests the site was once an island of firm ground surrounded by marsh here beside a tributary of the Adur.

Bolnore. The only historical record of this name dates from the Tudor period, just after Elizabeth I's succession, when we find it given as Bulnore. Etymologists think it may have developed from *Bulan ora* – Bula's bank, or edge – a reference to the steep hillside here.

Boltro Road. At some time there was a 'bull trough' in the vicinity, used as a means of identifying this location. It's described as Booltrowe in 1606 and Bulltrowe two years later, the spelling indicating that 'trough' was earlier pronounced the same way as 'plough'. As a point of interest, the word came from Saxon *trog*, which has also given us 'trug' – the shallow wooden basket traditionally made by Sussex craftsmen.

Bonswick. Although this has a Saxon look about it, Bonswick is actually a surname, acquired from the local family of Bonnicke, or Bonwycke, documented here in 1575. **Bonwicks Place** at Ifield shares a similar history, being recorded as Bonewekes in 1567 and taking its name from the family of Walter Bonwyk of Roffey (1296).

Bopeep. This is surely one of the prettiest names in Sussex, conjuring a picture of Little Bopeep and her sheep. But alas, its history isn't quite as idyllic. Recorded as Bo-Peep in

Alciston in the Turnpike Act of 1792, it's believed the name is a sardonic reference to the turnpike keeper, peeping through his small window on the watch for travellers along what is now the main A27 road. The earliest reference to bo-peep as the act of looking out is found in 1364, when one Alice Causton had to 'play bo-pepe thorowe a pillory' for selling short measures of ale. A variation is the children's game of playing peep-bo between their fingers.

Borde Hill. The name – spelled Boorde Hill in 1606 – came from the family of Borde, or Boorde, of neighbouring Cuckfield, who appear frequently in parish records from 1497 onwards. In 1893 Borde Hill House was purchased by Colonel Stephenson Clarke, who began a unique collection of plants and trees here. His son, Sir Ralph Clarke, set up **Borde Hill Garden** as a registered charity in 1965, opening these beautiful grounds to the visiting public.

Boreham Bridge. The site was once a watermeadow occupying an area of raised land alongside a tributary of Wallers Haven. The name in fact means 'elevated meadow', from *bor hamm*. Boreham Bridge is recorded as Borhambregge in 1418. **Boreham Street**, close by, could well be the original site, appearing as Borham in 1262.

Boringwheel Mill. The earliest mention dates from 1658, the time of Oliver Cromwell, when we come across a reference to Boreing wheele pond. During the period of the Sussex iron industry the place was the site of a mill where cannon and similar ordnance were bored.

Bosham. A picturesque village on a small peninsula between two tidal creeks, Bosham is steeped in the early history of Sussex. We can trace its name (pronounced 'Bozzum') as far back as AD 750, when it's referred to as Bosanhamm – the watermeadow of Bōsa. The neighbouring Hundred of Bosmere in Hampshire contains this same personal name, suggesting Bōsa was a fairly important settler. Before his time, the Romans had had a camp here, and it's thought Vespasian – commander of the 2nd Legion in Britain and later Emperor of Rome – owned a villa in the vicinity. King Canute certainly had a palace at Bosham. Tradition claims it was here that he ordered the waves to retreat. The manor later passed into the possession of Earl Godwine of Wessex, and through him to his son Harold, last king of Saxon England. In fact it was from the watermeadow now known as Quay Meadow that Harold embarked for France in 1064 on his fateful visit to William of Normandy. The Bayeux Tapestry shows him on his way to Mass at Bosham church before the voyage, and it's possible his body was brought back here for burial beneath the chancel arch after his death at the Battle of Hastings two years later. **Bosham Hoe**, on a little inlet at the tip of the peninsula, gets its affix from *hōh*, meaning a spur of land.

Boship. Boship Farm, at Hellingly, is on the site of an early type of co-operative, a *gebūrscipe* – the Saxon word literally meant 'association of peasants'. In 1442 the name is recorded as Boureship. By 1565 this had become Bowershipp. And in 1823 the spelling is Boarship.

Bosney. Here we have the same personal name – maybe even the same Saxon individual – encountered at BOSHAM. Bosney was once Bōsa's hedged enclosure, or *hæg* – a word that has given us our modern 'hay', a hedge or fence, and also 'hayward', someone who saw to the maintenance of enclosures and kept cattle from breaking through. From Saxon *Bōsan hæg* the place name had developed to Bosinhey by the mid 12th century, and was Boseney in 1296.

Bostal Hill. Bostal is a common Sussex dialect word for the steep paths running up the slopes of the Downs. Its derivation is either *beorg stigel*, 'mound stile', referring to a barrier at the foot of the track, or else *borg steall*, 'security place', applied originally to a hill-top refuge and perhaps later transferred to the track leading up to it. Bostal Hill, near Alciston on the South Downs, is described as Borstalle in 1327, and the Borstall ten years later. Similarly, **Bostal Road**, Poynings, appears as Borstalle in 1296.

Botley Wood. This is Bottelegh in 1296 and Botleghe in 1546. It contains the Saxon personal name Botta, together with *lēah*, a cleared area of woodland, giving us an original meaning of Botta's clearing.

Botolphs. The hamlet takes its name from its parish church, dedicated to St Botolph who died about AD 680 and was one of the most popular saints of medieval England. It's recorded as de Sancto Botulpho in 1288, Botoulf in 1395, and Botulphes in 1453. The present church is Norman, built on the foundations of a Saxon church which is believed to have been known as St Peter's-by-the-Bridge – a bridge once spanned the Adur close by, erected as part of the Roman trade route carrying Cornish tin to the port of Pevensey.

Bow Hill. Some scholars consider the 1194 spelling, Bochella, to be a clerical error for Boghella, which makes more sense if we accept the origin of this name to be *boga hyll*, a reference to its shape – 'bow hill'. It's certainly recorded as Bowehill in 1540. The group of barrows on the hill traditionally contain the remains of Saxons killed in a battle fought here in AD 895 between Danish marauders and the men of Chichester.

Bowley. The -ley ending tells us this was once a Saxon *lēah*, a clearing in woodland. The first part of the name (recorded as Bouely in 1296) is a personal name, perhaps Bofa. Bowley Farm here at North Mundham is all that remains of his little site.

Boxal Bridge. This has associations with the family of Boxall who figure prominently in the registers of Kirdford from 1586 onwards. They took their surname from the now lost place of Boxholte – 'box-tree thicket' – which lay within Kirdford parish. **Boxalland Farm** here, and another of the same name at Lurgashall, and **Boxall's Moor**, Linchmere, were probably likewise connected with this family at some time, as was **Bexley Hill** at Fernhurst, which is recorded as Boxall Hill in 1736. All these places lie within a few miles of each other.

Boxgrove. The site of an ancient grove of box-trees which gave Boxgrove its name, this unassuming village at the foot of the Downs is known to archaeologists the world over because of a bone uncovered in a gravel pit here in 1993. It proved to be the oldest human remains ever found in Europe, dating back an incredible half a million years, and was christened Boxgrove Man after its discovery place. The village's other claim to distinction is the priory, founded in the 12th century by Robert de Haye as a cell of the Benedictine Abbey of Lessay in Normandy. After the dissolution of the monasteries in 1537, much of the building – including its magnificent nave – was saved from destruction by Lord de la Warr, lord of the manor, and incorporated in the present church of SS Mary and Blaise.

Bracklesham. This little place, which has given its name to Bracklesham Bay, west of Selsey Bill, is one of the county's older Saxon sites. Its recorded history goes back to AD 714, when it's documented as Braclæshamstede, the homestead of a settler called Braccol. Just over two centuries later, in AD 945, the name is more recognisable as Brakelesham.

Bradford's Bridge. At first glance the derivation seems obvious. But there was never a Mr Bradford to give his name to the place. The spelling is Bretford in 1327, telling us it was originally 'the bright ford', describing the shining clear water flowing past this spot. By the time of Elizabeth I the spelling had altered, and we find it referred to as Bradford brook.

Brailsham. Brailsham Farm near Waldron stands on the site of a *hām* or settlement that belonged to a Saxon, Brægel. From the original *Brægeles hām*, the name had developed to Breilesham by 1230 and Brailesham some 20 or so years later.

Bramber. The name is from the Saxon *brēmer*, meaning 'thicket of broom'. It's mentioned as Bremre in AD 956, and Brembre in the Domesday Book. The rape, or county division of Bramber was given by William the Conqueror to William de Braose, who built Bramber Castle on the site of a Saxon stronghold guarding the lower reaches of the Adur. The river has narrowed a good deal since then, but it originally flowed past the foot of the castle mound. In fact traces of the old landing stage have been uncovered close to the Norman church. Bramber is home to the **National Butterfly Museum**, which is attached to St Mary's, a 15th century timber-framed house built for the monks who were Wardens of the Bridge here.

Brambletye. 'Tye' is used in Sussex dialect speech to mean a common or large open field. It comes from Saxon *tēag*, signifying an enclosure. So Brambletye was once enclosed land where brambles grew in profusion. It's recorded as Brembeltie in 1091, Brambeltye in 1282.

Branshill. Branshill Farm near Battle stands on a site originally known as Brembelshulle – 'brambles hill'. It's documented as such around 1240. The modern name seems to be a contraction of this.

Brantridge. This is 'the steep ridge',

aptly describing its situation on a promontory of the forest ridge. The Saxon word for 'steep' was *brant*, thus we find the name appearing as Branteregg in 1292.

Breach. Recorded as la Breche in 1261, the place gets its name from the Saxon *bræc*, used of land newly breached, or broken up for cultivation. **Breechlands** near Hurstpierpoint has a similar origin. In 1327 it was the home of Robert ate Breche.

Breadsall. Somewhere in the vicinity of Breadsall Farm, near Battle, once stood a building constructed of planks or boards – perhaps clad with the type of weather-boarding still commonly seen on properties in the south-east. That old *bred geselle* – 'board building' – identified the site, variously listed as Bregesele (1189), Bruggeshull (1359) and Bridgesell (1724).

Brede. The original little settlement on a spur of land overlooking the broad valley known as Brede Level, through which flows the river Brede. It was this valley that gave the place its descriptive name of 'breadth, broadness' (originally *brædu*) which had become Brada by 1166 and Brede half a century later. **Brede Place**, an imposing Tudor mansion, is mentioned in 1546 as the 'hall of Foorde', taking the name of some nearby river crossing. A Robert atte Forde is registered here in 1296.

Breechlands. See BREACH.

Bremere Rife. Like so many other words in the Sussex dialect, 'rife' has a Saxon origin and usually signifies a ditch across open land. Bremere is from *brōm mōr*, 'broom moor', describing wasteland covered in broom-bushes. It's Brumore in 1166, Bremore in 1397.

Brickhurst Wood. This began as 'breach hurst', a wooded hill by land newly breached or broken up for cultivation. We find it mentioned as Brecherst around the year 1230. **Brickhurst Farm**, Laughton, has an entirely different derivation, though. Recorded in 1543 as Bryggers after the family who owned it, the modern spelling shows the common corruption of final -ers to -hurst. The same surname in its more recognisable form of Bridger (meaning bridge-keeper) occurs in connection with **Bridgers Mill**, Haywards Heath, where the Bridger family are recorded in the local parish registers of the mid 17th century.

Bricklehurst. See BRIGHTLING.

Bridgers Mill. See BRICKHURST.

Bridgwick Pit. The medieval spellings Bretteswick and Brecteswicke suggest a Saxon origin of *Beorhtes wīc* – Beorht's farm. 'Pit' is a late affix, referring to a dip or hollow hereabouts on the South Downs.

Brightford. The name explains itself, being a description of the crystal clear water of the stream which was forded at this point before entering the sea between Worthing and Lancing. It's mentioned as Bretford in 1191. Interestingly, the Domesday Book (1086) gives the name as Bredford, a spelling persisting in BRADFORD'S BRIDGE, which shares the same origin.

Brightling. An ancient village set among the wooded hills of the Weald, Brightling began its existence as home of a minor Saxon tribe known as the Beorhtelingas – Beorhtela's people. In 1016 it's mentioned as æt Byrhtlingan, then changes from Brichelinges (1248) to Brightlinge (1535). Beorhtela himself had land just a few miles north, at Ticehurst, where **Bricklehurst Manor** stands on the site of his hurst or wooded hill. From *Beorhtelan hyrst* the name developed via Breytleherst to Brikelherst. **Brightling Park** was the home of a notable local eccentric, 'Mad Jack' Fuller, ironmaster and one-time MP for Lewes, who died in 1834. He was responsible for building several prominent landmarks in the area, including the obelisk on Brightling Down and the 'Sugar Loaf' folly at Dallington. He's buried in Brightling churchyard beneath a 60 ft pyramid.

Brighton. Until Brighton was developed as one of the principal watering-places of Regency England, it was known as Brightelmstone, a name that had persisted in one form or another for something like 1,000 years, having entered history as *Beorhthelmes tūn*, the farmstead of a warrior-farmer called Beorhthelm – 'bright helmet'. The Domesday Book spells the name Bristelmestune, and by 1493 this had become Brightelmeston. 'Brighton' as an abbreviated version only came into popular use early last century. The original little Saxon farmstead grew into a small fishing village, valued by the Normans at a rent of 4,000 herrings a year. It remained a cluster of fishermen's cottages centred round **The Lanes** until the early 1750s, when a Dr Richard Russell of Lewes published a book on the healing properties of its seawater. This attracted visitors to come and 'take the waters' and made Brighton into a fashionable spa. The town owes most of its prosperity and development, though, to the Prince Regent, who moved here in 1784 to his 'respectable farmhouse' – now **Brighton Pavilion**.

Brinfast. Somewhere beneath the fields of Brinfast Farm, North Mundham, lies the site of an early stronghold known in Saxon times as *Brȳnes fæsten*, or Brȳni's fastness. The first record we have of the place is from the year AD 683 when it's Brunefasten. By 1340 this had been modified slightly to Brunefast. Brȳni also owned the stream dividing neighbouring Bersted from Felpham, mentioned around the year AD 895 as Brynesfleot. We find his name connected with another Saxon stronghold across the county near Pulborough, at **Brinsbury Farm**. Here the site was a *burh*, a fortified place little different from a fastness (which, as the name suggests, was 'held fast'). *Brȳnes burh* became Brunnesburi (1195) and a century later, Brunesbury.

Brinkhurst Furze. See BRINKSOLE.

Brinksole. This was the *syle* or mire of a settler named Brynca – most probably a wallowing-place for his livestock. The spelling appears as Brinckeshole and Brunkesole during the 13th century. Brynca also seems to have been owner of a hurst, or wooded hill, a short distance away at **Brinkhurst Furze**, recorded as Brinkehurst in 1296.

Brinsbury. See BRINFAST.

Brittenden. See BRYCKDEN.

Broadbourne. This is Broad Bourne in 1835, referring to a tributary of the river Adur. The old local name, a humorous variation, is Broadbones.

Broadbridge. Self-descriptive, it's Bradebrigge in 1192, indicating a bridge just to the north of Bosham. The same origin is shared by the various **Broadbridge Farms** at Horsham, Slinfold and Washington, all of which are first found recorded late in the 13th century. **Broadbridge Heath**, near Warnham, appears as Bradbruggesheth in 1441, describing heathland by a bridge crossing the Arun just here.

Broadhurst. Recorded as Bredehurst in the time of Henry III, the name describes a hurst, or wooded hill, overlooking the broad valley of the eastern Rother.

Broad Oak. Presumably the tree was 'broad' in the sense of having a large trunk or spread of branches. Before 1567, when the place is mentioned as Broadoke, it was known as Motts after the Mott family living in the area during the 16th century. Quite possibly a member of the same family gave his name to **Motts Mill** near Groombridge.

Broad Rife. 'Rife' or 'rhythe', a dialect word for a ditch running across open land, is derived from the Saxon *rið*, a rill or small stream. When Selsey was an actual island, the 'broad rill' here emptied directly into the sea. In 1327 the spelling was Braderithe.

Broadwater. This was the name once given to a wide tongue of sea stretching inland between Worthing and Lancing. In a document of AD 946 it's referred to as æt bradan wætere – 'at the broad water'. The Domesday Book records it as Bradewatre, by which time the name had been transferred to the little settlement later to develop as Broadwater village. It's now been virtually engulfed by the growth of Worthing.

Brockfield. See BROCKHURST.

Brockhurst. 'Brock' is our traditional country name for a badger, and comes directly from *brocc*, which is what the Saxons called the animal. Here at Brockhurst was a wooded hill where badgers had burrowed to make a sett. In 1337 the place is described as Brokhurst in Walda, meaning 'in the weald or forest'. Earlier, the Domesday Book spelled the name Biochest. Sharing the same origin is **Brockhurst Farm** at Lurgashall, home in 1279 of Richard de Brokehurst; and **Brockshill Farm**, Hartfield, which is Brokeshull – 'badger's hill' – in 1288. **Brockfield**, near Wadhurst, similarly may have been a place associated with these animals, or it may have been 'brook field'. It appears as Brokefield in 1600.

Brook. The Saxon word *brōc* from which we get 'brook' had the literal meaning of 'water breaking forth'. It's a meaning that has persisted in Sussex, where a brook isn't so much a small stream as an area of marshy, water-logged ground. Besides describing a particular site, the word also gave rise to the surname variously recorded as del Brok, atte

Brouk, ate Broke, etc – 'dweller by marshy ground' – which we find connected with the numerous Brook, Brookhouse and Brookland place names in the county.

Brooksmarle. See BROXMEAD.

Broomden. The spelling is Brunynden in 1272. This suggests a Saxon derivation, *Brūning denn*, referring to the woodland pasture of someone called Brūn – a fairly common nickname meaning 'the brownhaired / skinned one' which in time was to produce the surname Brown.

Broomfield. It's a description of open land covered with broombushes. Broomfield near Withyham is recorded as Bromfeld in 1296. The same spelling but a slightly later date (1452) is shared by Broomfield, Hadlow Down. **Broomlye Farm**, Newick, was the home in 1340 of Edmund de Bromleghe, whose name tells us he was 'dwelling by the broom clearing'. A broom-covered watermeadow lay on the site of **Broomham** at Catsfield – Bromhamme in 1340. And we find a similar origin for Broomham, Guestling (Bromham 1220), Broomham, Heathfield (Bromhame 1296) and Broomham, Laughton (Bromham 1287). Incidentally, the original household brooms, or besoms, were made of broom twigs, hence their name.

Broomhill. In 1648, the time of the Civil War, this name is documented as Promehill *alias* Bromehill. Medieval records give it as Prunhill and Prumhelle, while the earliest, dating from the late 12th century, is Promhelle. It's obviously 'plum-tree hill' or *prume hyll* – but what is especially remarkable is that it's a rare example of the use of a South Saxon dialect word in a place name. The usual word was *plume*, from which we get 'plum'. The South Saxons used *prume*, from which possibly comes 'prune'.

Brown Bread Street. This seems to be a fanciful type of field name, referring to the appearance or quality of the soil. Similar names elsewhere include Beans and Bacon, and Spicecake.

Broxmead. Like BROCKHURST, Broxmead was once associated with badgers. Somewhere round here the animals had a burrow, or sett – the Saxon word was *smēagel*, giving the place the description 'brock's burrow'. The name changes from Broksmegl (1296) to Broxmele (1332) before becoming Brocksmede in 1556. **Brooksmarle**, near Burwash, shares exactly the same origin, but the spelling has developed differently. Early in the 13th century it's Broxmegle. Then by 1265 it's become Broxmedle, and two centuries later we find it referred to as Brokemayll *alias* Brokemayles.

Broyle, East and West. Interestingly, this name preserves a common medieval term for enclosed park or woodland stocked with deer and other beasts of the chase. During the reign of Henry III it was a royal hunting ground, documented as Brullius Regis, or the king's broyle. Later in the 13th century it's mentioned as boscus de Bruyll, referring to woodland here. **Broyle Place** at Ringmer obviously gets its name from the same source. Originally a bishop's palace belonging to the See of Canterbury, it's called Bruil in 1229 and le Broyl by Ryngemere in 1307.

Bryckden. Recorded in 1487 as land belonging to John Brekeden, the place is called Brickenden in 1611. Probably the same medieval landowner is also responsible for nearby **Brittenden**, since confusion between *k* and *t* isn't unusual in the development of place names.

Buckfold. See BUCKHAM.

Buckham. The earliest recorded form of this name spells it Bochamme, which tells us it was once a *hamm* or watermeadow identified by some particular beech-tree. Almost two centuries later, in 1489, we find the spelling altered to Bukham. **Buckfold Farm** at Petworth must be on the site of a fold overshadowed by beeches. It's Bocfolde in 1273. And **Buckholt**, near Dallington, is recorded in 1275 as the home of Peter atte Buckholt – 'dweller by the beech thicket'. This is also the origin of **Buckholt Farm**, Bexhill (variously listed as Bocholte, Bogholte and Bukholte) as well as **Buckwell Farm**, Ashburnham – Bukholte in 1296. In this instance the name seems to have been altered by colloquial speech to something like 'Buckell'.

Buckholt. See BUCKHAM.

Bucks Green. It owes its name to Richard Buck who was living here in the Rudgwick area before 1725, the date his Will was published.

Bucksteep. 'Steep place overgrown

with beeches', the name appears as Bocstepe around 1120 and Bukstepe in 1351. Bucksteep lies in fairly hilly, wooded countryside.

Buckwell. See BUCKHAM.

Buckwish. Bokewysshe in 1327, Buckwish Farm at Henfield takes its name from a beech-shaded watermeadow drained by one of the tributary streams of the Adur. The Saxon *wisc* used of marshy meadowland has survived in Sussex dialect speech as 'wish', with the same meaning.

Buddington (Easebourne). This was the *tūn* or farmstead of an early settler called Buda – a personal name we also find associated with BEDHAM. The Domesday Book of 1086 lists it as Botintone. In 1265 it's Budington, which is much closer to the original *Buding tūn*.

Buddington (Wiston). Although they may look identical, this Buddington has a slightly different history to the previous entry. It began as a Saxon tribal farmstead belonging to the Bodingas, or Boda's people, and took its identity from them as *Bodinga tūn*. It's recorded as Bodingetona in 1073, and Bodington in 1578. But by this later date local pronunciation had already affected the name's spelling, because we find the place listed as Buddingeton in 1483. The personal name Boda also crops up at BATHURST and BODIAM.

Budham Wood. The wood lies on a bend of the Rother in meadowland described early on as 'pratum de Budeham' – Budham meadow. Some scholars believe the name is manorial since the place once bordered land belonging to Radulphus de Bodeham, a native of nearby Bedham, whom we find recorded in 1296. Alternatively, it may share the same derivation as Bedham itself and be Buda's watermeadow or *hamm*.

Bugsell, Bugsill Lane. See BUXSHALLS.

Bulverhythe. Lying in a sheltered coastal valley between the higher areas of Hastings and Bexhill, Bulverhythe was the main harbour of the citizens of Hastings until around the end of the 15th century. The origin of its name, *burhwara hȳð*, literally translates as 'burghers' landing place'. By 1229 this had become Burewarehethe. In 1430 it's Bolverhethe. And in 1672 we find it as Bulverhyde.

Buncton. The name preserves the identity of a minor South Saxon tribe, the Buningas, or Buna's people, who had their *tūn* or farmstead on this site. The Domesday Book notes the place as Bongetune, while records of the 13th century refer to it as Bungeton. The modern name has developed from Bonketon, a form first recorded in 1323.

Burchetts. This medieval word, once used to describe a clump of birch-trees, is noted as Byrchettes in 1580. Similarly, **Burchetts Wood** at Herstmonceux appears as Burchettes in the same period. The corresponding surname atte Byrchette, or Burchett, meaning 'dweller by the birch clump', can be found in connection with the **Burchett's Farms** at Keymer and Wisborough Green.

Burfield. Originally *burh feld* – 'open land near a stronghold' – this is documented as Burgfeud in 1273. The actual stronghold is thought to have been Bosham close by.

Burgess Hill. Burgess Hill is a comparatively modern development that has grown considerably since the opening of the London-Brighton railway line in 1841. It owes its name to the family of John Burgeys, registered in the Clayton area between 1296 and 1332, and appears as Burges Hill during the period of Elizabeth I. The family surname originally denoted a *bourgeois*, the inhabitant of a borough.

Burgham. See BURPHAM.

Buriton. Like BARCOMBE across the county, this small village stands on the slopes of the Downs, where barley has been cultivated since well before the Saxons arrived. It came into existence as a *bere tūn* or barley farm, being mentioned as Bertone in 1380. The usual modern form of this type of place name is Barton, but here the name shows the obvious influence of neighbouring Buriton just over the Hampshire border.

Burleigh Arches. Long before it became a manor belonging to the See of Canterbury, this was a Saxon site, first recorded in the year AD 765 as Burhlea – 'stronghold clearing' – referring to a cleared area of woodland either close to or containing some sort of fortified structure. The Domesday Book spells the name Berchelie. Medieval records give it as Burghele, Burle and Berlegh. By 1543 it's Burlyarch, taking the affix 'arch' or 'arches' from a scribal contraction used by clerks for *archiepis-copi* – 'of the archbishop'.

Burpham. In Saxon times invasions by marauding Danes were an ever present threat, particularly along the rivers. It was to guard against such incursions that Alfred the Great built a stronghold here at Burpham, along with another on the opposite bank of the Arun at Arundel. Within a couple of decades a small settlement had developed. In AD 920 it's referred to as Burhham, 'the settlement beside the stronghold'. For centuries the name was spelled Burgham, then in 1558 we find it as Burfeham, and in 1631 as Burgham *alias* Burfam – a pronunciation that has lasted ever since. **Burgham** near Etchingham has retained the older spelling. Here too there was a stronghold settlement – it protected a Saxon ford across the river Limden.

Bursteye. Pronounced 'Burst-eye', it hardly seems the most attractive name. But its modern form is a contraction and doesn't do justice to its original meaning of 'birchen path', describing a path shaded by birch-trees here in the vicinity of Bursteye Farm at Ardingly. In 1287 the name's mentioned as Byrchenestye. By the time of James I (1614) we find it already being shortened, appearing as Birchenstie *alias* Birstie.

Burstow Hill. It gets its name from John de Burgstowe, originally a native of Burstow in Surrey, who settled in this area about the middle of the 13th century.

Burton. As a rule, the place name Burton signifies a farmstead by an early stronghold, but in this instance we find a somewhat different derivation. Originally *Bodecan tūn*, it was the farmstead of a Saxon settler, Bodeca. The Domesday Book gives the name as Botechitone. Medieval records refer to it as Boudeketon, Bodgeton and Bouketon. By 1582 these forms had been contracted to give us Bodyton *alias* Burton.

Burwash. Somewhere along the ridge between the Rother and the Dudwell on which this lovely village developed, there once stood some kind of *burh* or fortified place. A particular field close by identified the site as *burh ersc* – literally 'stronghold stubble-field' – a description that in time produced the forms Burhercse (1170) and Burgasshe (1378). Later on the name appears as Burgherssh *alias* Burwassh, and in 1603 it's Burwash *alias* Burrysh – this last spelling showing the pronunciation, which has persisted in the old Sussex rhyme 'To love and to cherish, from Battle to Berrish'. Just south of the village stands **Bateman's**, home of the writer Rudyard Kipling from 1902 until his death in 1936. He used the house and surrounding downland landscape in some of his best-loved stories, including *Puck of Pook's Hill*, *Rewards and Fairies* and *Traffics and Discoveries*. Inside, Bateman's is almost exactly as Kipling left it, and is now a National Trust property open to the public.

Bury. The Arun seems to have been a well-guarded river, with Saxon strongholds at ARUNDEL, BURPHAM and here at Bury. There's no trace of any site now, so this particular *burh* was probably a small ditch-and-rampart earthwork near the riverside. In 1086 the Domesday Book records the name as Berie. By 1271 it's become Bury. And in 1711 the spelling is Berry – which is how the name is still pronounced. **Bury House** was the home of John Galsworthy, author of *The Forsyte Saga*. After his death in 1933 his ashes were scattered on the Sussex Downs. **Great** and **Little Bury**, East Lavington, was originally the family home of Richard atte Bury – 'dweller by the stronghold' – registered in the parish in 1296.

Buss's Green. It has associations with the family of William le Bussh, or le Bousse, registered in the Wadhurst area in 1327. Their surname is chiefly a Kentish one, derived from an old word meaning 'bushel-barrell'.

Butcher's Cross. The place takes its name from Edward Butcher of Mayfield parish, alive at the start of the reign of Henry VIII. Unless it referred to a crossroads here, the affix probably describes a boundary cross. The occupational surname of Bochier or Butcher is likewise found in connection with **Butcher's Cross**, Hartfield, **Butcher's Farms** at Bolney and Buxted, **Butchers Row**, West Grinstead, and **Butcher's Woods** at Wadhurst and Worth.

Buxshalls. A document of the year AD 765 records the site as bocgeselle – 'beech building'. It tells us nothing about the building as such or what it was used for, only that it stood near some particular beech-tree. That old reference had produced the name Bokesulle by the end of the 13th century, developing to Buxshells

recorded in 1621. A similar building by a beech gave rise to the name of **Bugsell Farm** at Salehurst. This appears as Bokeselle around 1260, then became Boghesell (1306) before leaping the centuries to reappear as Bugshill in 1893. At first glance it looks as though **Bugshill Lane** at Bepton shares the same origin. But this is Bokestile in 1261, probably 'beechwood slope'.

Buxted. The spellings Boxstede in 1278 and Buksted in 1306 suggest 'beech place', from *bōc stede*. The original village was situated inside **Buxted Park**. But in the 1830s Lord Liverpool, who owned the Park at that time, decided the villagers were interfering with his privacy and had Buxted re-sited in its present position outside his grounds.

Bylsborough. This owes its origin to a Saxon with the oddly modern name of Bill (maybe a warrior nickname, 'the dagger') who owned a grave-mound or barrow here. Traces of a round barrow have been found near Bylsborough Farm. Bill's barrow – *Billes beorg* – in time became Billesberg, recorded in 1262, which then developed to Bilsberry by 1686. The place's proximity to Woodmancote is referred to in a document of 1305 as Billesberegh *juxta* Wodemanecote.

Byworth. Etymologists interpret Begworth, Behgworth and Byworthe – all identifying Byworth in 1279 – as *Bǣgan worð*, Bǣga's enclosure. This is a Saxon personal name dotted elsewhere about the county at BAINDEN, BAYCOMBE and BAYHAM, and the now lost place of Begeherst.

··C··

Cadborough. See GATEBOROUGH.

Cade Street. Until around the middle of the 17th century this was known as Cat Street, a medieval name open to a number of interpretations. Some scholars think it may be a corruption of 'cart street' – in fact the place is recorded as Cartstrete in 1330, but more often than not the spelling is Cattestrete or Catstreete, with Kattestrete the oldest (1288). The street is a Roman road that ran close by. The cat could have been an animal, or a personal name (as at CATSFIELD) or perhaps the historical slang expression for a harlot. The change of name to Cade Street commemorates Jack Cade, leader of the Kentish rebellion of 1450, who was trying to flee to the coast when he was captured and killed in a garden here. A monument marks the spot where he's believed to have died.

Cakeham. It's Cacham in 1226, Cakham about 1400, and Cackham in 1823, telling us how the name is still pronounced. To begin with, it was *Caccan hām*, Cacca's settlement. Incidentally, **Cakeham Manor**, dating to the early 13th century, was once a palace of the Bishops of Chichester.

Calceto Priory. The site of this 12th century priory at Arundel was originally 'Pinna's settlement' (*Pinnan hām*) recorded as Pinham in 1151. But after the building of the priory – a house of Augustinian Canons, dedicated to St Bartholomew – that old name was abandoned. In its place we find Calceto de Arundel (1200), la Chauceye (1275) and Prior de Calceto (1332), forms incorporating the Norman-French word *caucié* (an embankment) applied to the causeway which the monks built to connect Arundel with the hill on the opposite side of the Arun valley.

Calcot. This was the 'cold cottage' mentioned as Calkott in 1612. Either Calcot Farm here at Steyning stands in a particularly draughty location, or its name has the same meaning as COLDHARBOUR, suggesting a wayside shelter for travellers.

Caldbec Hill. The Saxon word for cold was *cald*. The Norman-French for spring was *bec*. Together they give us 'cold beck', probably a reference to the spring that still rises on the hillside. Caldbec was the scene of the main fighting between Saxons and Normans in 1066 at the so-called Battle of Hastings. King Harold chose the hill to bar William's advance northwards, and might easily have won the conflict had not his soldiers on the left flank disobeyed orders to stand fast and instead charged down into the valley below Caldbec in pursuit of the Normans, who were feigning a retreat. This action opened a breach on the hill for the enemy to reach Harold's army from behind, with disastrous results.

Calem Wood. In the Middle Ages this was a watermeadow bordering one of the tributary streams of the Rother. Recorded as Carleham in 1320 and Carlham in 1460, it was the property of a man called Carle (a medieval personal name), maybe the same Carle who owned land not very far away at KEYSFORD BRIDGE.

Camber. Cameras and Camber go together, especially in the summer season when Camber Sands is such a popular spot for spending a day by the sea. In fact the association with cameras goes a lot further back than might be supposed. Camber actually owes its derivation to the Anglo-French word *cambre*, which in turn came from Latin *camera*, meaning a room or chamber. The name seems originally to have been used as a description of the confined space of the old medieval harbour, and developed from Portus Camera, noted in 1397, to Caumbre and then le Cambre. **Camber Castle** was one of a chain of fortifications built by Henry VIII during the French invasion threat of the late 1530s. It was constructed on a spit of land commanding one side of the Rother estuary, but the estuary has long since silted up, stranding the castle inland and allowing the development of Camber village.

Camp. The word is used here in its original meaning of field, derived from Latin *campus*, a plain. It appears as les Compes during Tudor times, and Compcrofte, Eastcompe

in 1639. **Camp Hill**, Maresfield, shares the same derivation and is Campysshill in 1564.

Cansiron. See CRANEDEAN.

Carcombe Wood. See CATSFIELD.

Carfax. Horsham is the only place in the country, besides Oxford, to have a Carfax. It's a dialect term describing the junction of four or more roads, probably derived from the Latin word *quadrifurcus*, literally 'four forks', which later became *carrefourgs*, or crossways, in Old French. Horsham Carfax is mentioned in 1548 as the 'street called Scarfax'.

Carthagena. The farmhouse, at Somerley, was built from the timbers of the *Carthagena*, one of the galleons of the Spanish Armada which grounded off Bracklesham Bay in 1588. The same fate befell many of her sister ships, wrecked along the coast after storms had blown the fleet off course, forcing it to struggle home to Spain via the north of Scotland.

Casteye Wood. See CATSFIELD.

Castlefields. This is Castelfeld in 1455. The 'castle' is actually the remains of an earthwork – the word comes from Latin *castellum*, a fortress. Similarly, **Castle Copse** at Lurgashall is mentioned as Castlefeild in 1683 and must lie near an old site.

Catsfield. Opinions are divided on the derivation of this particular place name. Some scholars interpret it as 'Catt's land', the *feld* or unenclosed land of a Saxon called Catt. Others suggest the origin is 'land frequented by feral cats'. The Domesday Book adds to the confusion by documenting the name in 1086 as Cedesfeld and Cedesfelle. Later records are closer to the Saxon original, giving it as Catesfeld, Cattesfelde and Catisfelde. The same argument applies to **Catsland** and **Catsfold**, two farms at Henfield. They may have been Catt's land (Catteslonde in 1279) and Catt's fold. Or just as feasibly they could have been places where feral cats were often seen roaming. This is certainly the interpretation of **Carcombe Wood**, Whatlington – Catecumbe about 1200 – a combe or valley where the animals were found. And also **Casteye Wood**, Balcombe, where there was a narrow track they used – the name is Cattestye in 1296, Casty in 1564.

Cavalry Quarters. Near Fernhurst, the place is believed to have acquired its unusual name from a troop of Royalist cavalry who concealed themselves here in 1643 while nearby Cowdray was occupied by Parliamentary forces.

Chailey. Somewhere on this high, breezy spot on the South Downs gorse-bushes once grew in profusion. The first Saxon settlement was in a place where the bushes had been cleared away, hence *ceacge lēah* or 'gorse clearing'. In 1087 the name appears as Cheagele. Two centuries later it's Chageleye. And by 1588 it's become Chayly. The village boasts a fine smock mill on its common, standing within sight of the renowned **Heritage Crafts School** for handicapped children.

Chalcraft Barn. See CHALDER.

Chalder. The name means 'calf bank' and must refer to a slope of land here in the vicinity of Chalder Farm, Sidlesham, where calves were pastured. From *cealf ōra*, we find it called Chalfor in 1275, Chaluore in 1380. After this there's a long gap until 1823, when a map of Sussex refers to the place as Chalders Farm. Not far away at Bersted is **Chalcraft Barn**, on the site of a 'calf croft' or field mentioned as Chaluecroft in 1271 – a spelling and date shared by **Chalcraft Copse** at Funtington.

Chalkham. Chalkham Farm on the Downs at South Malling came into existence as the *hām* or settlement of a small group of Saxons called the Scealcingas. We know nothing about them except that their name meant 'the warriors' – an apt enough description of first-generation settlers. The place name is noted in 1340 as Schalkyngeham. At some time this would have developed to Chalkingham, but there are no later records to tell us at what date the present abbreviated form first appeared.

Chalvington. This little downland village was originally *Cealfing tūn*, the farmstead of an early settler called Cealfa – 'the calf' – maybe describing a mild-mannered, simple individual. The Domesday Book gives the place name as both Caveltone and Calvintone. By the 14th century the spelling is Chalvyngton. Documents of the Tudor period tell us the name was already shortened in everyday speech, because in 1576 we find it referred to as Chalvington *alias* Chaunton – which is more or less how it's still pronounced.

Chancton, Upper and **Lower.** This is listed as Cengeltune in the Domesday Book of 1086, a spelling not too far removed from the original Saxon *sængel tūn*, which had the meaning of 'farmstead near a thicket of brushwood'. Around the year 1230 the name is Changelthone, becoming Changeton, then Chankton (1488).

Chanctonbury Hill. The name ending -bury is usually a reliable indication of an earthwork or other ancient defensive site. Chanctonbury was the *burh* or stronghold near CHANCTON, and it's recorded as hill of Changebury in 1351, Chanckberie hill in 1587. The stronghold is an Iron Age earthwork known as **the Ring,** containing a beech grove which is a notable landmark, planted in 1760. According to Sussex legend the Ring is haunted by the ghost of a Saxon warrior, killed at the Battle of Hastings, returning to search for the treasure he'd buried here. Another legend maintains Chanctonbury Hill was formed from a great clod of earth thrown from the Devil's shovel as he dug the DEVIL'S DYKE above Poynings.

Chapmans Town. It derives its name from the family of Virgilius Chepman, registered in the parish of Warbleton in 1295. His surname tells us he was a chapman, an itinerant trader – from which we get the term 'chap'.

Charleston (Westdean). 'Churl' is nowadays used as a derogatory reference to someone ill-bred and surly. But once it meant nothing worse than a country labourer. The original churls – the Saxon word was *ceorl* – were freemen of the lowest rank, and later villeins or feudal tenants. A group of them worked a farmstead here at Charleston. In 1086 the Domesday Book notes it as Cerletone. During the medieval period the name developed to Charlton, but then a rogue *s* crept in, probably influenced by neighbouring CHARLESTON at West Firle, and we find it recorded as Charlston in 1622. Incidentally, the grounds of **Charleston Manor** here are open to the public. Two other churls' farmsteads lay on the sites of **Charlton**, near Singleton, mentioned as Cherleton in 1271, and **Charlton Court**, Steyning – Cherleton *juxta* Stenyng in 1307. The number of Charltons scattered throughout the country shows how many of these freeholdings there were belonging to peasants released from their local lord's bondage.

Charleston (West Firle). Some scholars think this may have been a farmstead where charlock, or wild mustard, grew. Others favour a Saxon personal name, Ceorl-lāc, making the origin of the place name *Ceorl-lāces tūn*, a theory which seems supported by the Domesday Book entry, Cerlocestone. This later developed to Cherlakeston, Charlokeston and Charlaxton. By 1614 it appears as Challston *alias* Charleston. Further research suggests the place also may have been known at some time as East Firle, from its proximity to West Firle and to distinguish it from CHARLESTON near Westdean.

Charlton. See CHARLESTON.

Charlwood. The name refers to woodland once owned by churls, or feudal tenants. It's first noted in

47

1296, as Cherlewod. Three centuries or so later, in 1611, the name is spelled Charelwood.

Charman Dean. Charemanys in 1521, the place originally had links with the Charman family of Broadwater, registered in the district in 1557 and 1560. The affix is descriptive of a dean or small valley.

Chatfields. From Chatefeld, Chetfeld and Chettefeld, all recorded late in the 13th century, it's possible to deduce an origin of *Ceattan feld*, open land belonging to an early settler, Ceatta. Later natives of Chatfields seem to have carried the name to two other places in the county, because **Chatfield's Farm**, Cowfold, was the home of Richard Chatfield in 1610; and **Chatfield Shaw**, Chiddingly, has associations with the family of Thomas Chatfeld, listed in 1562.

Chelwood. See CHELWORTH.

Chelworth. The first documented records of this name are found comparatively late, in the mid 16th century, when it's given as Chelworthe Common and Chellworth Gate. Scholars suggest it must be manorial in origin, deriving from Chilworth in Surrey – which was Cēola's *worð* or enclosure. Chelworth and its neighbours, **Chelwood Common** and **Chelwood Gate**, obviously share the same source, with -worth changing to -wood as a way of distinguishing them.

Chestham Park. This is Chustham in 1305 and Chestham soon after. The site may have been known as 'the chest settlement', so called

because of the discovery nearby of a Roman coffin-burial – *ciest* meant a chest or box, and by inference, a coffin. Alternatively, the name may be derived from an abbreviated form of *cisten*, chestnut, in which case it can be interpreted as 'settlement by a chestnut-tree'. Research has also brought to light a medieval word *cheste*, meaning strife, which could point us to some old forgotten dispute here.

Chesworth. 'Worth' is a common element in English place names, deriving from the old *worð*, an enclosure of some kind – generally a farm. Here on the site of Chesworth Farm near Horsham, an early settler called Ceorr owned just such a place. It's recorded as Cherseworth in 1281 and Chusworth in 1418, before leaping a few centuries to reappear as Cheesworth in 1743.

Chichester. Sussex's cathedral city was a settlement of the Regni tribe before the Romans chose the site for their fortified town of Noviomagus, or 'New Market'. It was destroyed soon after AD 477 in the wake of an invasion led by the Saxon war-chief Ælla and his sons Cissa, Cymen and Wlencing. Cissa took the place as his own, building a stronghold among the ruins and naming it after himself – *Cissan ceastre*, Cissa's fort. Tradition also gives him credit for a second stronghold, at CISSBURY. In AD 895 Chichester is documented as Cisseceastre, becoming Cicestre in the Domesday Book, and then Chichestre in 1417. The city still retains stretches of its original Roman wall, together with many other outstanding features which include the 15th century Market

Cross and magnificent cathedral, begun about 1091 by Bishop Ralph the Norman.

Chiddingly. Like a number of other of the county's names, the -ly ending is emphasised as 'lie' and tells us the place was originally a cleared area of woodland. Here the *lēah* or clearing belonged to a Saxon tribal group called the Cittingas, Citta's people – their leader could have been the same Citta who owned his own land at CHITCOMBE and CHITHURST. Chiddingly is recorded as Cetelingei in the Domesday Book (1086), then changes from Chitingeleghe to Chittinglegh before it becomes Chittinly in the 17th century. Sussex dialect speech is probably responsible for the softening of *t* to *d*. The Cittingas had a second woodland clearing at **Chiddingly Wood**, West Hoathly. As early as AD 765 we find this documented as Citangaleahge. By 1621 it's referred to as both Chittinglie and Little Chittinglye, no doubt to avoid confusion with Chiddingly proper.

Chidham. During the 12th and 13th centuries the name is spelled Chedeham. By the time of the Tudors it's Chudham. Its Saxon origin, *ceode hām*, has the curious literal interpretation of 'bag settlement'. Research suggests this is a reference to one of the tidal creeks on which the village lies, a theory lent weight by the fact that Bosham Channel has a narrow opening which to early settlers may have resembled the shape of a tied bag or sack.

Chilgrove. Lying in a deep-cut valley on the South Downs, this attractive village has developed on the site of an ancient grove of trees. Its particular location served to identify the spot as 'the gulley grove' – *ceole grāf* – which had developed to Chelegrave by the year 1200. The name shows an interesting use of the Saxon word *ceole*. Its actual meaning was 'throat', but just as our modern word 'gorge' also means throat, so it could be used as a topographical description. Not far from Chilgrove the valley is closed by the ridge of Bow Hill where two concentric ramparts mark the site of an Iron Age fort called **Goosehill Camp**.

Chilley. In early times this was a little island of firm ground surrounded by the tidal marshes of Pevensey Haven. Identified as *Cillan ēg* – Cilla's island – after the settler who owned it, the name's variously spelled Chylley, Chelie and Chillye from the 13th century up to the time of Charles II. Maybe a native of this little place gave his name to **Chillies** near Buxted, which is recorded as Chyllegh in 1537, Chillis in 1750, and was known to belong to a John Chilley in Tudor days.

Chillies. See CHILLEY.

Chillinghurst. According to etymologists, here we have the same Saxon personal name found at CHILLEY. In this instance it's associated with a hurst, or wooded hill – Chelenhurst in 1288, Chillenershs 50 years later. The place lies in well-wooded countryside north of the Downs.

Chills Down. Noted as Childowne in 1585, the place gets its name from John le Child who was living locally in the West Dean area in 1309. His surname suggests a youth of gentle birth, as in the ballads *Childe Roland* and *Childe Harold*.

Chilsham. Documents of the period 1287-1327 refer to Chilsham as Chelewesham, which suggests to etymologists a Saxon origin, *Cēolwīges hamm* – the watermeadow of an early settler, Cēolwīg. The place lies beside Nunningham Stream. In 1522 it's mentioned as Chelsham Gate, and three centuries later a map of Sussex gives it as Chilsum, telling us how the name is pronounced locally.

Chilt, River. Recorded in 1357 as le Chilte, this is a back-formation from WEST CHILTINGTON, where the river rises from a spring-fed pond beside the church.

Chilthurst. It's nice to imagine this hurst, or wooded hill, was once upon a time a favourite spot where local children played. In fact the name is the only one in Sussex showing an original use of the Saxon word *cild*, child, and it appears as Childeherst, Childhurst and Chilthurst during the 13th century. Like its neighbour CHILSHAM, the hamlet lies on Nunningham Stream. In the Tudor period there was a bridge here, noted as Chylters brige in 1517, Chilteherst bregge in 1540.

Chiltington, East and West. These two separate place names may well be identical in origin, with East and West added at a late date to distinguish them. **West Chiltington** seems to be derived from an old British name, *celte*, meaning 'high' – the village stands in an elevated position above the Arun, near a hill that scholars think could once have been known as the Chilte. **East Chilting-** ton lies at the foot of the Downs, and therefore also near high ground. The name suggests, then, an origin of *Celtinga tūn* – 'farmstead of the Celtingas, or dwellers by the high place'. An alternative argument is that it contains a Saxon personal name, Cilta, and is 'farmstead of Cilta's people'. West Chiltington is recorded as Cillingtun in AD 969, Cilletone in the Domesday Book, and Chiltyngton *juxta* Thakham in 1342 (from its proximity to Thakeham). East Chiltington is Childentune in 1086, Chiltigton *juxta* Lewes in 1283.

Chilver Bridge. Long before any bridge was built here, there was a crossing-place over the Cuckmere called 'the gravel ford'. The word gravel actually comes from the old French *gravele*, which replaced in common use the original Saxon *cisil* or chesil found in this place name. In 1252 it's Chisilford. By 1686 a bridge had been built, mentioned as Chissleford bridge. Then during the following century the name was gradually shortened in everyday speech, appearing as Chilver bridge in 1796.

Chitcombe. See CHITHURST.

Chithurst. The 11th cenury church is built on a mound believed to have been the site of a pagan temple, probably belonging to the Iron Age tribe occupying the hill fort in nearby **Hammer Wood.** Long after they'd gone a Saxon called Citta laid claim to the place – maybe the same Citta whose tribal property was at CHIDDINGLY. Citta's wooded hill – *Cittan hyrst* – was entered in the Domesday Book of 1086 as Titesherste. In 13th century records it's more accurately rendered as Chytehurst and Chiteherst. The personal name Citta crops up again in connection with a combe, or small valley, at **Chitcombe**, which appears as Chitecumbe and Chytecumbe between 1220 and 1340.

Chittinghurst. Recorded in 1320 as Shotyngherst, the place is known to have been the home 25 years earlier of Matthew de Shottyngherst, but the name itself presents a mystery. Etymologists offer no suggestion, other than that it obviously contains as a final element -hurst, denoting a wooded hill. There's nothing to tell us whether the other element is a personal name or a topographical description, though the medieval word *shotten*, meaning 'shot out' may possibly give us a clue and account for the change of initial Sh- to Ch- as a matter of taste.

Chittlebirch. Early settlers have left their names appended to farms and settlements, valleys and hills all over the county. Here at Chittlebirch Farm, near Sedlescombe, we find one – Cetol – attached to a birch-tree. Why this particular tree should have been singled out, who knows – perhaps it was a boundary post or some kind of waymark. In time, Cetol's birch gave its name to the site, preserved for posterity as Chetelisbirch (1288) and Chiltebirche (1418).

Chuck Hatch. This is le Chukhach in 1467, Churk Hatche in 1611, and Chuckhatch gate, Chuckehatch greene in 1642. It's also referred to in 1559 as Chuckelandes, and identified one of the many hatch-gates leading into the Ashdown Forest.

'Chuck' has survived as a Sussex dialect word meaning a block of wood, so it's feasible chucks were either cut or stacked near this gate.

Church Acre. Obviously an area of cultivated land, perhaps tithe land, belonging to a church. We find mention of Church aker brigge here in 1590, crossing one of the streams in Pevensey Levels, and Church acre drove in 1840 – drove being the dialect term for an unfenced road leading through a farm to different fields. There are several **Church Farms**, **Church Houses**, **Churchlands** and **Church Woods** in the county, all once associated with, belonging to, or situated by, a church.

Church Norton. This seems to have been the north *tūn* or farmstead of the church of St Peter's, Selsey. Its chapel – dedicated to St Wilfred, converter of the heathen Saxons – was formerly the chancel of Selsey church.

Chyngton. The derivation of this farm name at Seaford is uncertain, but scholars think it probably reflects a Saxon tribal name, the Cintingas – Cinta's people – found connected with Chinthurst in Surrey and a lost Chintebrok in Kent. Chyngton is recorded as Chintinges in 1180, Chintynge in 1235. On a map of 1823 the spelling is the same as the pronunciation, Chinton.

Cinder Hill. This is 'le Synder' in 1590, and 'waste called the Synder' in 1622, unattractively referring to old iron-smelting works close by. The slag from furnaces used in the Sussex iron industry between the

16th and early 19th centuries has also left us with the names of **Cinder Hill**, Horsted Keynes, **Cinderhill Cottages**, Dallington, and **Cinderford Cottages**, Herstmonceux, recorded as Synderford in 1540.

Cissbury. The name is part fact, part fiction. For countless centuries this huge Neolithic hill-fort was known simply as Bury – 'the stronghold' – but in Tudor days a little romance was woven into its history, linking it to Cissa, son of the warrior chief of the South Saxons, whose own stronghold was at CHICHESTER. A survey of the Sussex coast done at the time of the Spanish Armada names Cissbury as Sieberie hille. On Speed's map of Sussex (1610) it's Sissabury. Not until 1724 do we find it spelled Cissbury. Constructed between 400 and 250 BC, it was the Iron Age capital of this area of the Downs. Its massive ramparts continued to be fortified until 50 BC when it became the centre of a farming community, then the ramparts were re-fortified towards the end of the Roman occupation to protect the inhabitants against Saxon raiders. The site is now maintained by the National Trust.

Clapham. Etymologists suggest the first element of this name is a rarely found word *clopp*, which meant a log or a tree-stump. Clapham lies in an area of ancient woodland and would certainly have been a *hām* or settlement where logs were plentiful. The Domesday Book spells the name Clopeham, and it appears as Clopham right up to the time of Charles I, when we find it referred to as Clopham *alias* Clapham. The site of **Clapham House** at Litlington

probably shares the same origin, being recorded as Clopham throughout the period 1224-1466.

Clappers. The stream just here was originally spanned by a primitive clapper bridge, simply a plank of wood raised on piles and laid across as a gangway. Records of the early 14th century show a John le Claper, or atte Clapere, living in the neighbourhood – in other words dwelling 'by the clapper'. These rough and ready bridges were obviously also to be found at **Clappers Bridge** (there are two such places in the county, one at Barcombe, the other at Isfield) and **Clappers Wood**, Heathfield, which has a stream flowing through it.

Clapwater. Noted as Clappwater early in the reign of Elizabeth I, it lies close to the site of a watermill described in 1206 as 'Clapmella' or Clap Mill. The name was probably applied in mimicry of the noise made by the mill paddles as they 'clapped' or slapped down on the surface of the water.

Claverham. This is Claveham, Clavreham and Clavesham in the Domesday Book (1086) and Clavreham throughout the medieval period. In Saxon times it had been a clover meadow or *clæfre hamm*, providing rich pasturage for livestock. **Clearhedge Wood** at Waldron lies on a ridge of land where clover grew. It's Clavregge in 1288, Claregge in 1429.

Clayton. A village noted for its famous windmills, 'Jack', a smock mill, and 'Jill', a post mill, standing together on Clayton Hill. Much of the parish lies on gault – a series of beds of clay and marl – so it's hardly surprising the name interprets as 'the clay farmstead' (from *clǣg tūn*) describing the site of the first small settlement here. In 1086 the Domesday Book refers to it as Claitune, and in 1121 it's Claetona, before becoming Clayton during the following century. Beds of clay have likewise resulted in several **Clayton** and **Clayland Farms** in Sussex, as well as **Old Clayton**, Sullington. Incidentally, that old word *clǣg* survives in dialect speech as 'claggy', used of sticky soil.

Clearhedge Wood. See CLAVERHAM.

Clemsfold. See CLIMPING.

Cliffe Hill. There are tumuli in the vicinity, and a Neolithic long barrow on Cliffe Hill itself, proving the area must have been inhabited from at least the late Stone Age. Its name obviously describes a high, steep-sided place, and appears as la Clyve in 1248, Clyf 50 years or so later. In 1345 it's noted as Clyve by Lewes, to distinguish this particular 'cliff' from another at **Clive Vale**, Hastings, recorded as Cleve in 1366, Clyffe lands in 1578 – 'Vale' refers to a depression in the Downs just here. **Cliff End** at Pett literally tells us where the line of coastal cliffs from Hastings finishes, and is Cliveshende about 1197, Clyvesende in 1262.

Climping. The village lies a mile inland from the sea, on the western side of the Arun estuary. Its original settlers were a Saxon tribe called the Climpingas, who took their identity from their leader, Climpe. His name tells us something of his appearance, because it was a nickname meaning 'the lumpy one' – probably describing a bulky, pot-bellied man. The Domesday Book records the place as Clepinges. In the 13th century it's Clympinges, losing its ending to become Climping around 1260. 'The lumpy one' had land of his own at **Clemsfold** near Slinfold, where we find Climpe's fold noted as Climpesfaude in 1285, Clymesfold *alias* Clempesfold in 1624. And the same nickname crops up again in connection with a hill ridge at a now lost place near Mayfield recorded in 1443 as Clymperegge.

Clive Vale. See CLIFFE HILL.

Coates. The name simply means 'cottages' – not the cosy roses-round-the-door kind of cottage beloved of artists, but the humble wattle-and-daub cot of the medieval peasant. There was probably a row of them here, forming the nucleus of the later, larger settlement recorded as Kotes about 1142, and Cotes up until the mid 15th century. **Cote**, near Durrington, is known to have been the home of William atte Cote (1296) – 'dweller at the cot'.

Cobden. The modern spelling has not changed since its first appearance in 1500. Before then it had been Coppeden (1256) and Copden (1479), indicating a Saxon origin, *Coppan dene* – Coppa's valley. The name is preserved by Cobden Farm, high on the Downs near Sullington.

Cob Brook, Cobham, Cob Lane. See COPFORD.

Cockhaise. See COCKING.

Cocking. One of the things that strikes visitors to this pretty little place is that the woodwork of the cottages is painted a uniform deep yellow, common to all villages managed by the Cowdray Estate. Until the 13th century its name is variously spelled Cochinges (1086), Cokinges or Cockinges, indicating it was originally the territory of a Saxon group known as the Coccingas, or Cocca's people. Scholars think the personal name (a nickname meaning 'the cock') is to be found at **Cokeham** – Cocca's *hām* or settlement – which the Domesday Book records as Cocheham, and is Coukham in 1357. They're undecided whether **Cockhaise Farm** at Lindfield was Cocca's brushwood or cock-bird's brushwood, though the latter interpretation seems marginally more likely. It's Cokehese in 1279, Cockeys in 1590, and Cokehayes in 1636.

Codmore Hill. The name appears as Codemere in 1288, suggesting its derivation is *Coddan mere* – Codda's pool. Given the location, the pool must have been at the foot of the hill, in the vicinity of Codmore Farm.

Coggins Mill. This is actually a corruption of Colkins Mill, mentioned as Colkynesmell in 1315 and Colkins mill in 1668. Interestingly it gives us an example of the personal name Colkyn which was once upon a time quite common in Sussex.

Coghurst. Although it has the appearance of being a -hurst place name, in fact this one began as Coghert's, through its connection with the family of a John Coghert registered in the Guestling area in 1327.

Coldharbour. Places called Coldharbour are found all over the country – in fact there were 307 of them at the last count. They mark the site of wayside shelters that literally harboured travellers in cold and inclement weather. The term began as a Saxon one, *herebeorg* (denoting a temporary army encampment) then developed to *cald hereberwe* in the Middle Ages. These roadside refuges have given their name to some 26 places in Sussex, including **Coldharbour** near Salehurst (Coleharbour 1823), **Coldharbour Farm**, Chiddingly (Coleharber 1698) and **Coldharbour Farm**, Worth (Cold harbor 1727).

Coldwaltham. In the days when vast forests of oak covered the rolling plain to the north of the Downs, a group of settlers made a home for themselves here in one of the forest clearings, felling more trees to accommodate their growing numbers. The place was known simply as 'the forest settlement' – *weald hām* – and it's one of the county's oldest recorded Saxon sites, documented in AD 683 as Uualdham and in AD 957 as Waltham. Curiously the Domesday Book makes no mention of it. In 1340 we find its name referred to as Cold Waltham, reflecting its bleak situation on what by now was open heathland. Less than a century later it's also called Est (East) Waltham, distinguishing it from West Waltham, now UPWALTHAM.

Coleham. See COLWORTH.

Coleman's Hatch. The name comes from the family of Edmund and Richard Coleman – maybe father and son – registered in the parish of Hartfield in 1279 and 1327. Their surname (more common in Kent) suggests they followed the occupation of charcoal-burner, found in connection with COLLIER'S GREEN. Coleman's Hatch is recorded as Colmanhacche in 1495 and Colmanshacche 40 years later – the 'hatch' being a wicket-gate opening on to woodland close by. **Colmanshatch Wood** at Newick probably shares a similar origin, appearing as Colemanshech in 1352.

Colgate. A hamlet attractively situated in the highest part of St Leonard's Forest, it once had connections with the family of Godelene de la Collegate, registered in the area in 1279. The gate here – one of many leading into the forest – must have been close to an early iron-smelting works, since the family name meant 'dweller at the (char)coal gate'. In fact there's a **Hammer Pond** two miles south whose waters were probably used to power the machinery.

Colhook Common. See COLWORTH.

Collier's Green. There are two in the county, one near Ewhurst, the other at Warbleton. The first gained its name from the family of Robert le Coliere, recorded around 1240; the second from John le Coleyere, recorded in 1288. Their surname tells us that both were charcoal-burners. Later, during the 16th and 17th centuries when the Sussex iron industry was at its height, the title of collier strictly applied to the foreman of a smelting works, while those working under him were known as 'burners' or 'black boys'.

Collington, Collumn Hill, Colner. See COLWORTH.

Coltstaple. We have a choice of different spellings for this name. Early in the 15th century it appears as Coltstapole and Collestaple. In 1650 it's Coulstaple. And on a map of 1823 it's shown as Coldstaple. No certain interpretation is possible, but etymologists think it could derive from *Colles stapol* – Coll's post – referring perhaps to a boundary mark on the land of an early settler, Coll, here in the neighbourhood of Coltstaple Farm at Horsham.

Colwood. In 1617 it's listed as Collwoode, Collwood streate and Colewood gate. Much earlier, in 1296, the place was the home of Christian de Kolewode, whose name describes him as dwelling 'by the (char)coal wood'. In fact there were extensive charcoal works here at one time, associated with the county's iron-smelting industry.

Colworth. We meet the Saxon personal name Cola in connection with no fewer than eight places in Sussex. Given their distribution it seems unlikely the same Cola was responsible for all of them; but then neither can we rule out the possibility that one particular individual was important enough to own land at several of these sites. The oldest on record is Colworth, near Oving, where Cola had an enclosure or *worð*. The place appears in a document of AD 988 at æt Coleworð, and is Coleworth in 1288. There was a similar kind of enclosure – maybe a farm – at Colworth near West Dean, which is Colwerthe in 1309. At Fletching, **Coleham Farm** stands on the site of Cola's *hamm* or water-meadow. In 1296 it was the home of Walter de Coleham, who adopted his name from the place. Interestingly, we find another Walter de Coleham in the parish of Sutton in 1288, living on the site of Cola's *hām* or settlement. It's now called **Collumn Hill** (the modern spelling of this name seems to be a fanciful corruption of dialectal Cole'm). A hook-shaped strip of land belonging to Cola explains the name of **Colhook Common** at North Chapel – Colhok in 1281, Colehoke roughly 30 years after. **Collington** near Bexhill, originally *Coling tūn* – Cola's farmstead – is referred to as Colington late in the 12th century. This derivation seems to be shared by **Collington Wood**, Ticehurst – it's Colinton in the time of Henry III. Finally, **Colner Farm** at Bosham preserves the site of *Colan mere*, Cola's pool. The name appears in a document of 1279 as Colem'e, scribal shorthand for Colemere.

Combe. The Saxon *cumb* has given us combe or coombe, a word defined as 'a deep little wooded valley, a hollow in a hillside'. Combe as a place name is dotted all over the map of Sussex – at **Combe** near Wadhurst (Cumbe around 1197), as well as **Combe Barn**, Westfield, **Combe Bottom**, Westdean, **Combe Hill** at Jevington and Ninfield, and **Combe Wood**, Mayfield. It's also the origin of the widespread medieval surname atte Cumbe or de Cumbe – 'dweller by, or in, the valley' – frequently found associated with such names. An alternative spelling has given us **Coombe** at West Firle (Cumbe around 1200) and **Coombe** near West Hoathly (Cumbe 1327), together with **Coombe Bottom**, Stopham, **Coombe Lane**, Burpham, and **Coombelands**, Pulborough. **Coombe Place Farm** at Offham is on the site of the Battle of Lewes, fought in 1264.

Comphurst. In the reign of Henry VIII the place is recorded as Compers and Comperscrosse. A little later in the Tudor period it's Comps Crosse. A survey made of the county in 1724 rather quaintly notes it as Compost, while a map of 1823 calls it Comphouse. The name originated with a medieval owner, John Comper, who was a member of the family of atte Compe – 'dweller by the field' – registered in Wartling early in the 14th century.

Compton. This is a place name fairly common throughout middle and southern England. It means 'valley farmstead', from the Saxon *cumb tūn* – a description that nicely fits the downland location of Compton. The Domesday Book lists the place as Contone, but 70 years or so earlier in 1015 it was more accurately recorded as Cumtun, becoming Cumpton by 1224. The village is also sometimes distinguished as **Compton St John**, because of its connection with a Norman-descended family of that name between the 12th and 14th centuries. **Compton Wood** likewise appears in the Domesday Book as Contone. In 1280 it's given as Cumpton in parochia de Westferle – 'in the parish of West Firle'. We also find it occasionally named as **Compton Berwick** or **Berwick St John**, from its proximity to BERWICK and its association with the Knights of St John of Jerusalem (the Knights Hospitallers) who at one time held land here.

Coneyburrow. See CONEYHURST.

Coneyhurst. In 1574, during the reign of Elizabeth I, the place is described as communen voc. Coneyhurst – common land called Coneyhurst. In fact until very recently the place remained a common, no doubt still supporting a sizeable population of the rabbits, or conies, which originally gave the place its name. Although hares have always been native to these islands, rabbits weren't introduced until the 12th century. They soon became valued both as a source of food and for their fur, widely used for trimming clothes and lining capes, but being prolific breeders they spread everywhere. We come across coney burrows (the old term for rabbit warrens) at several named sites in Sussex. **Coneyburrow Wood**, Waldron, is described as Coneyburyfeld in 1679. **Coneyburrow Shaw**, Mayfield, similarly appears as Conyberry field around 30 years earlier. In 1547 **Conyboro** at Barcombe is called Coney Burrow, and a short time after, **Coneycroft Wood**, Warnham, is Conyefelde.

Cooden. Although it doesn't look like it in its modern form, this is actually one of the Saxon tribal -ing names that appear with such frequency on the county map. As late as 1719 we find it referred to as Couding, while a century or so earlier it's Cowdinge downe. The place was originally settled by a group called the Cōdingas – Cōda's people. Somewhere nearby we know they had a *lēah* or clearing because part of Cooden is recorded as Codyngelegh in 1375. And a spot just here on the coast is mentioned very early on as Codanclife – Cōda's cliff or steep place. Nowadays Cooden is virtually part of the popular seaside resort of Bexhill.

Cooksbridge. Cooke's Bridge in 1590, the place lies on a tributary of the Ouse and takes its name from the family of Thomas Coke of Hamsey who are registered a short time earlier, in 1543. Their surname, in its later form, has given us **Cook's Cottages**, Nuthurst, **Cook's Farm**, Northiam, **Cook's House**, West Burton, and **Cook's Wood**, Bolney.

Coolhurst. Records go no further back than the Tudor period, when this name appears as Colehyrst and Coolehurste. It's probably to be taken as a straightforward description, though whether 'cool' means breezy or shady is a matter of choice.

Coombe. See COMBE.

Coombes. The name accurately reflects the topography, since there are quite a few combes or valleys in this area of the Adur between Steyning and Shoreham. In AD 956 Coombes itself is referred to as cumbhæma gemære – 'the boundary of the valley settlements'. In 1073 it's called Cumba, the Saxon word for valleys. And in 1086 the Domesday Book notes it as Cumbe. Not until the 13th century do we find the plural form Cumbes or Combes recorded.

Coombewick. This is Comenwyke in 1615, Comewick in 1823. Much earlier it had been the home of Roger de Cumbwyke, a native of Steyning recorded in 1296, and John de Cumbwyk, recorded in 1327 – their surname tells us they lived 'at the valley farm'.

Cooper's Green. The village green came into existence as a grassy area shared by the community for all kinds of different pursuits, from recreation to drying clothes and meting out justice in the stocks. Cooper's Green obviously developed round such a site, taking its name from the family of William le Coupere, natives of nearby Sheffield, registered here in 1327. Their occupational surname – cooper or cask-maker – is likewise associated with **Cooper's Corner**, Salehurst, **Cooper's Cross**, Herstmonceux, and **Cooper's Heath**, Iping.

Cootham. Documents of the Tudor period give a variety of different spellings – Cowdam *alias* Coodam *alias* Coteham (1556) and Codeham *alias* Coteham (1582). The name is still pronounced Coteham. In the Domesday Book it's Codeham, derived from *Cūdan hām*, the settlement of a Saxon called Cūda – maybe the same individual identified with a hill not very far away at CUDLOW BARN.

Copford. It came into existence as a shallow crossing-place on one of the tributaries of the Cuckmere river, and took the identity of an early settler called Cobba. 'Cobba's ford' became Cobbeford by the early 13th century, and Copeford sometime later. We encounter the same Saxon personal name at **Cobham** near Rotherfield – Cobeham in 1332, and originally Cobba's *hamm* or watermeadow. **Cob Brook**, at West Hoathly, lies on the site of a Cobbe-

melne (Cob Mill) mentioned in 1308, near **Cob Lane** leading to Ardingly. Both names share a descent from the same source.

Cophall. It's recorded in 1438 as Coppedhall, referring to a hall or manorhouse with a capped roof – that is, one with a high, steep pitch. The same description applies to **Copshall** at Guestling – Copped hawle in 1500 – and **Copyhall** near Chithurst – Coppet Hall in 1823.

Copsale. Together with neighbouring **Copsale** (formerly Cobsale) **Court**, the place appears as Cobsale in 1650, Copsale in 1795, and Cobshill in 1823. The second part of the name is almost certainly derived from *healh*, meaning a nook or corner of land. The first part could be a personal name, Cobb, or the dialect word 'cob' given as a nickname to a large, strong man.

Copshall. See COPHALL.

Copthorne. This is 'cropped or capped thorn' – a thorn-tree that had been pollarded by having its topmost branches pruned back to produce a close head of fresh shoots. The place is mentioned as Coppethorne in 1437.

Copwood. The spelling hasn't changed since the name was first recorded in 1694. It probably describes a small wood of 'capped' or pollarded trees.

Copyhall. See COPHALL.

Corsley. This name, and that of **Cousley Wood**, present a problem. We know they share an identical origin as the site of a Saxon *lēah* or cleared area of woodland. The difficulty lies with the first element, which etymologists believe to be either an unrecorded personal name, or something akin to an old British word meaning marshland. The latter seems more likely, since Corsley lies in an area well-watered by streams. It's first mentioned late in the 13th century as Coreslie and Corsle, then reappears as Coseley in 1758 and Corslea in 1813. Cousley Wood, not far away at Wadhurst, also lies in an area of streams. Here too we find the name recorded as Coreslie, before it gains the addition of 'wood' to become Corslewode in 1437 – probably to distinguish it from Corsley.

Cotchford. Somewhere on the site of Cotchford Farm at Hartfield there was once a 'queach enclosure'. Queach is a word seldom heard nowadays but still in the dictionary – it means a thicket, and first came into use at the start of the 14th century as *queche*. So this was a piece of enclosed land, a 'worth', surrounded by thickets. It's recorded as Quecheworth in documents dating 1274-1321. Then in 1535 the name alters its ending to appear as Cochefford, reflecting the proximity of a stream in the vicinity. In 1627 it's noted as Quotchford *alias* Cotchford *alias* Quetchworth, showing how the original name had survived over the centuries. Cotchford was the home of the children's author A.A.Milne, who made the farmhouse the setting for *The House at Pooh Corner* (1928).

Cote. See COATES.

Cottenden. This began as a *denn* or woodland pasture belonging to an early settler called Cotela, its name developing from *Coteling denn* to Cotelingdene (1180) and then Codelendenne (1332). The modern form is obviously a contraction.

Coultershaw. The old pronunciation of this name (-haw, not -shaw) tells us its origin is *hōh*, describing a spur of land owned here by a Saxon, Cuþhere. During the 13th century we find it spelled Cuteresho and Coutersho. By 1535 it's Cowtershall. And in 1610 a map of Sussex gives it as Cawdershaw. The place lies on a tributary of the Arun, hence its alternative identity, Coultershaw Bridge.

Courtup. The research of family names suggests Courtup may be the source of the surname Courthope, frequently found in Sussex. It's derived from *Curtan hop* – Curta's enclosed valley – and the site (now a farm) is noted as Curtehope in 1310, Courthope a century later.

Cousley Wood. See CORSLEY.

Covehurst Bay. Covehurst Wood, on the cliffs overlooking the Bay, is probably the original 'hurst by the cove', described as Coueherst or Coveherst early on in the 14th century. The Bay itself is fairly shallow and lies on a scenic stretch of coast between Hastings and Fairlight Cove.

Cowbeech. Like COPTHORNE, the name refers to a 'capped' or pollarded tree, in this case a beech, once used to identify a particular location. It's recorded in 1261 as Coppetebeche, then it gradually gets shortened – Coppebeche (1517) and

Cobbeach (1622) – until it finally appears as Cobeech in 1724.

Cowden. There are two places sharing this name. Both lie on the sites of medieval cow pastures. Cowden near Wartling is Kudenn in 1296, Coudenne 20 years later; while Cowden near Mayfield already had its modern spelling by 1333.

Cowdray Park. It's one of the jewels in Sussex's crown, with a romantically tragic history clinging to its magnificent ruins. The original name for the place came from a Saxon word *sængel*, meaning 'brushwood thicket', recorded as la Sengle in 1272 and Single Park as late as 1529. At some time during the 13th century Norman-French influence introduced an alternative name, *coudraie* or 'hazel hedge', noted as la Coudreye in 1279 and la Codray six years later. Cowdray Park is famous for its summer polo tournaments. More famous still (at least in Sussex legend) is the so-called Cowdray Curse attached to the Montagus who owned the now ruined house, a Tudor mansion gutted by fire in 1793. A week after this disaster Lord Montagu died in a boating accident and his branch of the family was extinguished – supposedly fulfilling a curse laid on the first owner by a monk of Battle Abbey at the time of the dissolution of the monasteries. Cowdray shares the origin of its name with **Cowdry Farm** at Birdham – la Coudree in 1288, Cowdree around a century and a half later.

Cowfold. A description needing no explanation, it's Cufaude in 1255, Coufold in 1336 and Cowfolde in 1589.

Coxbrook. The only early record of this name dates from 1279, when it's given as Cockisbrok. Etymologists read this as *Cocces brōc* – an area of marshy ground owned by an early settler called Cocc, a nickname that has many possibilities. On the other hand, it could have been marshy ground frequented by cock-birds.

Crabbet Park. See CRAB ROW.

Crab Row. No one seems to know how the crab, a wild bitter apple, came by its name, but it has been eaten by man since earliest times and may well have been the original fruit that tempted Adam and Eve. Crab Row near Eartham, noted simply as le Crabb in 1609, must have been a row of rural dwellings near a particular crab-apple tree. **Crab Farm**, Mayfield, is on land recorded in 1489 as Crabbefeld, or crab-tree field. And **Crabbet Park**, Worth – Crabbetts in 1504 – was earlier the home of John de Crabbewyke (1296) whose surname tells us he lived at a farm where crab-apples grew.

Crainham Wood. See CRANEDEAN.

Cralle Place. Cralle Place, near Warbleton, was built by Sir John Lade in 1724, but its name reminds us it stands on a much older site. Those living here in medieval days knew it as 'the crow clearing', so it was obviously a spot where such birds were seen in numbers. Interestingly, the name shares the same origin as CRAWLEY but has retained its spelling of 1288, and is pronounced 'Crawl'. In 1541 it's noted as Crawlebrigge, from its proximity to a tributary of the Cuckmere.

Cranedean. Cranes and herons may be birds of the same family, but their names have a slightly different history. Crane is from the Saxon *cran*, while heron has an Old French origin, *hairon*. Confusingly, etymologists refer to cranes as herons in names like Cranedean, which they interpret as 'heron down, or hill'. The place is mentioned as Cranedoune in 1609. **Crane Down**, Jevington, with the same meaning, appears as Cranedoun in 1535. **Crainham Wood** at Ewhurst, near the Rother, is on what was once a *hamm* or water meadow where herons were seen, recorded as Cranham at the start of the 13th century. **Cranesden** near Mayfield was similarly a *denn* or pasture associated with these birds, and is Cranysden in 1547. A stretch of marshy wasteland used by herons gave rise to the name of **Cranmer Barn** near Henfield – Cranmore in 1602. And scholars suggest **Cansiron** at Forest Row may be derived from *cranes hyrne*, 'heron's corner'. Between 1415 and 1520 the name appears as Canserne and Cannesherne (in 1579 there's a reference to Carneserne fordge, which possibly explains the -iron ending of the modern name). Finally, **Crimbourne Farm** near Kirdford lies near a 'heron stream' or bourne, and is recorded as Cranbourne as late as 1795.

Cranesden. See CRANEDEAN.

Crawley. Modern Crawley – an amalgamation of THREE BRIDGES, IFIELD and old Crawley village – is one of the original 'new towns' that came into existence as a result of the New Towns Act of 1946. It's now a large and still expanding industrial community whose development has been encouraged by the proximity of GATWICK AIRPORT – all a very far cry from the crow-infested clearing in Tilgate Forest from which the town has grown. Its name has Saxon roots – *crawe lēah*. We find it spelled Crauleia in 1203, then Crawele just under 50 years later, and Crawley in 1316. A few miles to the east, **Crawley Down** has borrowed its neighbour's identity, being Crauledune in 1272, Crawleydone in 1437.

Creed. This is a slightly unusual name. It's given as Cride in 1296 and Crede by the time of Henry VIII. Etymologists think its origin is a lost Saxon word *crȳde*, derived from another that meant weeds or plants, and they suggest Creed Farm here at Bosham must stand on the site of some kind of early garden, or at least a spot where plants were grown.

Creep Wood. One of the old meanings of 'creep' is a narrow passage or recess. That's the sense in which it's used here to describe the deep, narrow valley where Creep Wood lies. The name has hardly changed since 1208, when it's given as Crepe.

Crimbourne. See CRANEDEAN.

Crimsham. Crimsham Farm, near the coastal village of Pagham, has one of Sussex's oldest recorded Saxon place names. Despite the passage of some 13 centuries it has remained virtually unchanged since it first appeared in a document of AD 680 as Crymesham – the *hām* or settlement of Crȳmi. Crȳmi himself seems to have been the butt of personal jokes about his size, because his name tells us he was unkindly nicknamed 'the crumb'.

Cripp's Corner. It lies at the corner or junction of five roads, and gets its name from a John Cryps who was registered in the parish of Ewhurst in 1432. A later John Cripps, living in the reign of Henry VIII, gave his name to **Cripps's Corner** at Forest Row, while **Cripp's Farm**, Cuckfield, used to be the home of Nicholas Cripse, recorded here in 1648. Their surname in its various forms came from an old nickname meaning 'crisp or curly haired'.

Crockerhill. A crocker was a crockery-maker or potter, so we can guess that the hill here was the site of an early pottery. It appears as Crockerehull in 1220, Crokkereshelle in 1428. There was also a pottery – literally a 'crock place' – at **Crockstead** near Framfield, recorded as Crocstede in 1268 and Crocksted in the time of Elizabeth I.

Crockhurst. Scholars believe this place name – Crokehurst in 1535 – is partly derived from an old British word *cruc*, meaning 'hill'. The -hurst ending simply echoes this as an explanatory addition. Interestingly, we find a lost Crockhurst at Horsham (noted as Crochurst in 1254) referred to in a list of Saxon swine pastures as crochyrst. Since these pastures were generally on wooded hillslopes, there's good reason to suppose the original meaning of the name was indeed just 'hill'.

Crockstead. See CROCKERHILL.

Cross-in-Hand. The sign on the village pub depicts a hand holding aloft a quartered standard, reflecting the tradition that Cross-in-Hand got its name as a meeting place of Knights Crusaders journeying to Rye for embarkation to the Holy Land. The name appears in a Latin document of 1547 as *via cruce manus*, which half a century later is rendered into English as Crosse atte Hand, or Crosse in Hand. In the absence of any other explanation, it seems tradition for once could be right.

Crouch Ham. In 1609 the place is referred to as le Doune (the hill) called Croucham. This probably had the meaning of 'enclosure near the cross' – an interpretation given weight by the fact that we find a Simon atte Cruche living 'by the cross' just half a mile away in 1327. The Middle Ages were times of intense religious belief and crosses were a common feature of the landscape, whether as preaching crosses, wayside shrines or boundary markers. So it's not surprising that the surname atte Cruche, or de Cruce, from the medieval word *crouche*, cross, has given us a number of place names in Sussex, including **Crouch Farm**, Barlavington, **Crouch Hill**, Henfield, **Crouchhouse Farm**, Stedham, **Crouchland**, Kirdford, **Crouchlands Farm**, Cuckfield, and **Crouch's Farm**, Warbleton.

Crowborough. Crowborough used to be part of the parish of Rotherfield until 1880. Now, even though it's an expanding dormitory town for London commuters, it's still a village at heart, perched on its hill at the edge of the Ashdown Forest. At one time, long before the commuters, the hill was noted only for the number of crows it attracted, hence its name. In 1390 this is recorded as Crowbergh. In 1587 it appears as Crowbarrowe.

And Speed's map of Sussex (1610) gives it as Crowboro Hill. The creator of fiction's most famous detective, Sir Arthur Conan Doyle, lived here at **Windlesham** from 1907 until his death in 1930, writing many of his Sherlock Holmes stories. As requested, he was buried in the garden of the house, but his remains were exhumed after the Second World War and reburied at Minstead in Hampshire.

Crowham. Despite the apparent connection with crows, Crowham in fact has a much prettier origin. Here on the banks of the river Brede lay a watermeadow where saffron grew, and the Saxon description *croh hamm* – 'saffron meadow' – developed to Crohhame and Croham during the 13th century. In 1662 the name is interestingly recorded as Crougham *alias* Croffham, giving us the pronunciation of the time. Saffron, a species of crocus, is still widely used both as an orange-yellow dye and a flavouring for food.

Crowhurst. Crowhurst has two possible origins, neither of them to do with crows. The site is mentioned in a document of AD 772 as on Croghyrste. Scholars debate whether the first element here means 'mud' or 'tendril', but either way, the second element is certainly *hyrst*, a wooded hill. The name subsequently appears as Croherst in the Domesday Book (1086), Crauhurst in 1316, and Crowehurst in 1535. **Crowhurst** near Burwash does, however, mean what it looks like, a 'crow-infested hill', appearing as Crawehurstbrigge in 1279. And **Crowhurst Farm**, Mountfield, shares the same description – it's Crowherst in 1296.

Crowlink. The name is first recorded in the 13th century, as Crawelinke and Crowlinke, and means 'crow rise' – rising ground frequented by these birds, high on the downland cliffs overlooking the sea. It's the only spot apart from Birling Gap where descent to the shoreline is possible between Eastbourne and Cuckmere Haven. Interestingly, the Saxon word *hlinc* or 'link' is still used in Sussex to describe a wooded bank on the side of a hill.

Crumbles, The. It's the stretch of coast between Langney Point and Pevensey Bay, once the scene of a gruesome murder but nowadays better noted for its holiday caravan sites. The name is an old one, and has stayed almost unchanged since it first appeared late in the 13th century as la Crumble. Its meaning seems a little uncertain, but scholars suggest it's derived from the medieval word *crumbe* or *crombe*, crumb or fragment, used in this case to describe a small parcel of land.

Crypt. A name conjuring up all sorts of Gothic horrors, it's first mentioned as a family surname, variously spelled de la Gripe, ate Gripe and atte Cripe, recorded here in the parish of Cocking between 1265 and 1327. The name meant 'dweller by the drain', apparently a description of the small deep-cut valley in which Crypt Farm lies, which probably acted as a natural drain during heavy rainfall. The old word *grype* found in this name has survived in Sussex dialect as 'grip', used of a small ditch.

Cuckfield. The earliest records give it as Kukufeld and Cucufeld, obviously a reference to open land haunted by the cuckoo-bird. However, the Saxon word for the cuckoo was *gēac* (preserved in Sussex dialect as 'gowk') so the place name seems to have originated as an imitation of the bird's distinctive call. Not until the 13th century do we find it noted as Cukfeld, becoming Cookfield by 1422. The family of Harold Godwinson, last king of Saxon England, owned several manors in this area. After the Conquest, William de Warenne, who administered the Rape or county division of Lewes, used Cuckfield as a hunting lodge, and he and his wife Gundrada founded a church here on the site of the 13th century Holy Trinity church. Nowadays a favourite attraction is the donkey races held on summer bank holiday.

Cuckmere, River. One of the earliest meanings of the word 'quick' signified something alive, living (as in the expression 'the quick and the dead'). This is the sense in which we find it used of the Cuckmere – literally 'the living mere or pool' – to describe its fast-flowing water. From *cwicu mere* the name developed to Cokemere, Cookemere and Coukmere during the 14th century, subsequently appearing as The Cuckmer during the reign of Elizabeth I.

Cuckmere Haven. The haven, or harbour, of the CUCKMERE river, this secluded little bay is recorded as Cokemerehaven in 1352, and the Haven of Kockmare in 1582. There has never been any true harbour here, but the place was certainly a 'haven' for smugglers during the 18th and 19th centuries.

Cudlow Barn. For centuries, Cudlow itself was a parish on the edge of the sea near Climping. But changes to the coastal landscape gradually destroyed it and now it lies submerged beneath the waves, leaving Cudlow Barn to stand as a last surviving trace of the old name. Long before the sea claimed the land, there was a hill here belonging to a Saxon called Cūda – perhaps the same individual whose settlement was at COOTHAM. From *Cūdan hlǣw* – Cūda's hill – the name appears as Cudelawe, Codelawe and Codelowe during the 13th century. In Tudor times old Cudlow is mentioned as Cudlo Haven.

Cullinghurst. See CUTTINGLYE WOOD.

Cuttinglye Wood. Although the early spellings are a little confusing, this is almost certainly a Saxon tribal name, *Cufelinga lēah*, indicating a woodland clearing belonging to the people of Cufela. The oldest documented forms give the name as Couelingeley (1286) and Covelyngeleye (1344). Later on we find it spelled Coblingeleghe (1476) and Coddinglighe (1567). An Ordnance Survey map of 1896 shows it as Cut-and-lie Wood, which is more or less how the name is still pronounced. We come across the personal name Cufela again at **Cullinghurst**, near Hartfield. Here it's connected with a hurst or wooded hill, recorded as Covelynghurst in 1354, Colyngehurst in 1500.

·· D ··

Dadland Shaw. See DUDWELL.

Daleham. Dale is a word we associate more with the northern English landscape, but we find it occasionally used in its original Saxon form *dæl* in the southern counties – at ARUNDEL, for instance. Daleham, close to the river Ouse, lies on the site of what was once a *dæl hamm*, a dale (or valley) watermeadow recorded as Dalehamme in 1327 and rather curiously as Deal Haurum in 1691.

Dallingridge. In the days when the Ashdown Forest was part of the vast oakwood covering the entire length of the Weald, the ridge of land on which Dallingridge Farm lies, near Forest Row, must have made a convenient and well-protected site. It took the name of the Saxon tribe who owned it, the Dædelingas, or Dædel's people, and appears as Dadelingregge in 1271, then Dallyngerygg just over a quarter of a century later.

Dallington. Dalinton in the Domesday Book, and Dallington in 1265, this was originally *Dealling tūn*, the farmstead of Dealla, an early settler. The village's most prominent landmark is its 40 ft high **Sugar Loaf**, a conical folly built early in the 19th century by 'Mad Jack' Fuller, local squire and ironmaster, who lived at BRIGHTLING. **Dallington Forest** acquired its name from the village, and is noted in 1334 as 'wood called the chase of Dalynton'.

Danegate. The name more accurately should be Downgate. Once the site of a gate leading on to a down or hill nearby, we find it recorded as Dounegate in 1428, Dengate a century later, then Dungate in 1721. It looks as though the place name was altered to its present form during the 19th century to give it a pseudo-historical connection with neighbouring SAXONBURY, which itself is a fanciful Victorian corruption.

Danehill. The parish was formed in 1898 from parts of Fletching and Horsted Keynes. Originally it was a *denn* or woodland pasture, noted as Denne in 1279 before its description expanded to become Denhill in 1437. Late in the 18th century it's mentioned as Danehill *alias* Danhill. **Great and Little Danhill Farms** at Thakeham acquired their name from the family of la Dene – 'of the valley' – registered in the area in 1271.

Dankton Barn. Etymologists offer the theory that Dankton Barn must lie very close to a place recorded in the Domesday Book of 1086 as the manor of Denton, whose boundaries ran between Coombes and Sompting. The name Denton suggests 'valley farmstead', and Dankton Barn does indeed lie in a small valley, so maybe the two place names share a common origin.

Danny. This is Denye in 1296, Danye 50 years later, and Danny-Park by the time of Elizabeth I. Its site, in the valley of a tributary river, was once an island of firm ground surrounded by marsh, hence 'valley island' or *denu ēg*. Danny Park, once known as the Great Wood of Hurst, began with the enclosure of the 'wood of Daneghithe' or Danny haven, by Simon de Pierpoint early in the 13th century. The original manorhouse here, home of the de Pierpoint family who gave their name to nearby HURSTPIERPOINT, was destroyed by fire about 1350 as an act of vengeance after the last of that line had sadistically burned to death some of his serfs. The house was rebuilt by George Goring, later Earl of Norwich, between 1582 and 1593. **Danworth Farm**, a few miles to the north, lies on the site of a valley enclosure or 'worth' mentioned as Deneworth in 1332 and little Danworth land in 1617.

Danworth. See DANNY.

Darwell. The name is shared by a number of places in the Mountfield area – Darwell Wood, Darwell Beech, Darwell Hill, Darwell Reservoir and Darwell Hole, as well as Darwell Furnace Farm which stands on the site of the old iron furnace here. The name was originally 'deer fold', describing an enclosure specifically for containing deer. It's mentioned as Derefold in 1294, la Derefolde and Derefeld around 30 years later. Sussex dialect pronunciation

of *f* as *v* later corrupted it to Darvel, as illustrated by Darwell Hole – Derfould Hole and Darvoll Hole early in the 1600s, becoming Darvel Hole by 1724. **Durfold Farm**, Warnham, gives a further example of the way this name has changed – it's Derefolde in 1330, and then Durvell in 1823. Neighbouring **Durvall's Gill** has kept the 19th century spelling.

Daux, Great and **Little.** This is Dorks Farm in 1656, Dawks in 1795, and Dorks again in 1823, a good indication of the name's pronunciation. Much earlier, in 1296, it was the home of Richard atte Douwehok, suggesting that earlier still a hook of land here was owned by a Saxon woman called Duhchæ, giving us an origin of *Duhchwe hōc* for the name.

Deadman's Oak. The name must surely commemorate some old act of violence, perhaps a suicide by hanging. It's referred to as Deadmans Oake in 1703.

Dean, East and **West.** These two attractive downland villages lie only a few miles apart at either end of the valley of the river Lavant. They're distinguished from one another in 1150 as Estdena – 'east valley' – and West, while West Dean is further identified in 1337 as Westden by Sengelton (Singleton). The village may also be the site of a place called Edelingedene referred to in a charter of Æthelred the Unready (978-1016). It was somewhere near here that Danish invaders were repulsed by the men of Hampshire in the year 1001 – and West Dean lies only five miles from the county border. The name Edelingedene interprets as 'valley of the princes' from the

Saxon *æþelinga dene*, being presumably the property of a royal manor in the area.

Deanland. Denlond in 1339 tells us this is old pasture (*denn*) in wooded country. **Deanland Farm**, Warbleton, lies on similar land, recorded as Denland in 1566.

Dean's Green. It acquired its name from the family of Richard atte Dene – 'dweller in the valley' – registered in the parish of Barcombe in 1296. **Dean's Mill** near Lindfield has a different origin. Once part of the manorial property of the Dean of South Malling, it's mentioned as Deanes Mill in 1625.

Dedisham. The variety of spellings for this place name makes precise interpretation a little difficult. It first appears in 1257 as Doddesham. Thirty years later it's Daddisham. In 1408 we find it called Dadysham. And an itinerary of 1675 gives it as Detsum. Etymologists think the most likely derivation is the *hām* or settlement of Dæddi.

Deerswood. Saxons used their word *dēor* to mean wild animals in general, and only later did it come to be applied specifically to deer. The word was also used as a personal name (or rather a nickname) suggesting someone with the qualities of a wild animal. Here at Deerswood we find such an individual owning a *worð* or enclosure, recorded early in the medieval period as Deresworthe in Ifeud (Ifield). There are no later records to tell us at what date the not uncommon change from -worth to -wood took place.

Dell Quay. La Delle in 1280, Dell Key in 1671, the name signifies a hollow or depression – probably with reference to the eastern arm of the Chichester Channel on which Dell Quay lies, since a map of 1578 mentions the Channel as Dell flu – flux, or flow. The quay was Chichester's harbour in Roman times and continued to serve as the city's port until 1824, when a canal was cut from Birdham to link the harbour with the river Arun at Ford. It remains a popular area with yachtsmen.

Dencombe. Dencombe came into existence as *Denecan cumb*, the combe or valley of a settler called Deneca. The earliest spelling is Denechecumbe (1121), followed by Denekecumbe (1296) and then Denecombe (1304). It lies not far from Slaugham in the valley of the Ouse.

Denne. This has the simple straightforward meaning of 'woodland pasture', appearing as la Denne in 1328. **Denne Park** near Horsham shares the same origin. In 1283 it was the home of William atte Denne, whose name tells us he lived 'by the pasture'.

Denniker, The. Here we have one of those names worn down over the years by Sussex speech. During the reign of Charles I (1644) it's recorded as Deane acre – 'valley acre' – describing a parcel of land on this valley site.

Densworth. The ending -worth almost always signifies an enclosed place of some kind – an animal enclosure, farm, or even a small well-protected settlement. Densworth occupies just such a site, originally owned by someone with the oddly modern-sounding name of Dene. The spelling has hardly changed at all since 1261, when it's listed as Deneswrth (*sic*).

Denton. There can be no confusion about the derivation of this particular name because it's recorded as Denton – 'the valley farmstead' – in a document dating as far back as AD 801. **Denton Hill** above is noted in 1377 as 'montem de Denton voc. Denbourghdown' – the hill of Denton called Denbourghdown, showing a curious duplication of 'bourgh' and 'down' which both mean hill.

Denwood. This was once woodland bordering a *denn* or pasture, first mentioned as Denwood in 1682. **Den Wood** near Linch has a different origin. It lies at the top of a small valley or dean, which in 1332 was the home of Thomas atte Dene – 'dweller in the valley'.

Dern Wood. Around the year 1240 this location is referred to as a grange, or farm estate, called Derne. In 1513 the name is exactly the same, the Derne. The spelling is too constant for it to mean anything other than 'hidden away' (from *dierne*), a description that suits the place almost as well today.

Derridge. Derridge Farm, near Rotherfield, stands on a ridge of land in thickly wooded countryside. In medieval times it was a haunt of deer, hence its name, 'deer ridge', recorded as Doregg in 1458, Dorage a century after, and Durrage in 1823.

Devil's Dyke. The Dyke is actually

an earthwork dating back some 2,000 years, but local legend offers a more sinister explanation for this cleft in the Downs. Intending to punish the people of Sussex for their conversion to Christianity, the Devil began digging a trench from the sea to drown them all. But an old woman watching him from the darkness held up her candle, and mistaking its light for the rising sun the Devil fled, leaving his work unfinished. He is also associated in Sussex lore with the **Devil's Bog** in Ashdown Forest, the **Devil's Ditch** near Halnaker, the **Devil's Humps,** a group of barrows on Bow Hill, the **Devil's Jumps**, a similar group on Treyford Hill, and **Devil's Road** at Billingshurst.

Dial Green. This is one of those place names that's changed spelling, and therefore meaning, in the last 100 years or so. It's called Tile Green in 1801, probably referring to a kiln in the neighbourhood where house tiles were manufactured.

Dial Post. In 1702 this little hamlet near West Grinstead is noted as Dial Post Farme. In the absence of any other explanation, the most obvious is that the name refers to a post supporting a sundial – in those days often the means of telling the time.

Dicker, Upper and **Lower.** These two hamlets lie next to each other on old common land called the Dicker, site of a foundry dating from the time of Sussex's iron industry. It's been suggested they owe their name to the ten-rod 'dickers' of iron paid in lieu of tax or rent by some ironworks. The word originated as Latin *dicora*, meaning ten or tenth, which developed to medieval *dyker*. Since Dicker appears as Dyker or Dykere throughout the 13th century, the connection seems evident.

Diddlesfold. See DIDLING.

Didling. The early forms Dedlinges and Dudelinges tell us this was the territory of a Saxon tribal group known as the Dyddelingas, or Dyddel's people. Around the year 1260 the name was shortened a little to Didelinge, but it kept its final *e* into the Tudor period and beyond, appearing as Dedlinge in 1545. The same tribe may well have had more land a little to the north near Lurgashall, on the site of **Diddlesfold**. This was originally *Dyddeles falod* – Dyddel's fold – recorded as Dudelesfald about 1156, Dudelesfolde in 1312.

Dinglesden. The only possible clue to the origin of this particular name is a reference in a document of 1279 to an Adam de Tingelden, living locally in the parish of Peasmarsh. Without further material to work on it's difficult to give a derivation. The first element may be either *tÿnincel*, 'small farmstead', or *þengel*, 'prince', and the second element *denn*, 'woodland pasture' or *denu*, 'valley'.

Ditchling. A charming village with a long royal pedigree, Ditchling lies at the foot of Ditchling Beacon, at 813 ft one of the highest points on the South Downs. Its name is a memento of its early Saxon history, when this was the tribal territory of the Dicelingas, or Dicel's people. In his Will, Alfred the Great refers to it as Diccelingas; and two centuries later the Domesday Book lists it as Diceninges, Dicelinges and Digelinges. By the late Tudor period the name had become Dichlinge. The Neolithic earthwork in the vicinity was used by the Romans as a fortified camp approached by **the Nye**, a sunken trackway by which the village can still be reached. Later, Ditchling was to become the administrative centre of a large estate belonging to King Alfred – the royal palace is believed to have occupied a site close to St Margaret's church, parts of which date to this period. Opposite St Margaret's stands a 16th century gem, **Anne of Cleves' House**, given by Henry VIII to his fourth wife as part of their divorce settlement in 1540.

Doleham. Doleham Farm, on the banks of the river Brede near Westfield, lies on medieval meadowland once divided into strips or 'doles' – a word still used in Sussex to describe a division of communal land. Apart from being spelled Dowlham in 1795, its name has stayed unchanged since first recorded in 1199.

Donnington. See DUNCTON.

Downash. Like ASHDOWN, this originally described high ground distinguished by a prominent ash-tree, perhaps used as a landmark. It's recorded as Downassh in 1432, Downashe in 1508, and may well be identical with a place called La Dune by Heylesham (Hailsham) in 1298. If so, it shares its name with **Down Level** close by in the Pevensey marshes. **Downash** near Ticehurst has a slightly different origin. In 1266 we find the name as Downe Wyste, a form repeated in 1535 as

Downwyst. Interestingly, 'wist' is a dialect word referring to a measure of land, so here we probably had hill pasture divided up in a certain way.

Downbarn. This doesn't appear as Downbarn until 1734. Much earlier, in 1287, the place is recorded simply as the Downe, describing its elevated location.

Downford. In 1620 it's spelled Downeforde, in reference to an old ford crossing the Rother nearby at the foot of a slight hill.

Downley. The name originated as *dūn lēah*, a cleared area of woodland on a down or hill. In 1271 it's given as Dunlee, then in 1591 as Downeley in Singleton. **Downley Bottom** near Harting is similarly mentioned as Downeley in 1565. And early in the 14th century we find **Dunly Wood**, Waldron, variously listed as Dounle, le Dunleye and Dounlee.

Dragons Green. A fearsome dragon once lived in this part of St Leonard's Forest, causing such devastation that St Leonard himself was forced to get rid of it. After a terrible battle (or so the legend goes) the dragon was slain, and wherever St Leonard's blood had been spilled patches of lily-of-the-valley appeared. On a less fanciful note, there was an ordinary family of Dragons, natives of Roffey, living nearby in the parish of Cowfold in 1296, so this place name probably originated with them. Certainly, **Dragon's Farm** at Cowfold (called Dragons in 1682) owes its name to their ownership.

Drayton. This isn't an easy one to explain. The name itself derives from Saxon *dræg tūn*, which interprets literally as 'drag farmstead'. Scholars suggest it was a place of portage – a site close to a track along which timber was hauled. The earliest reference to the name comes around the year 1200 when it's recorded as Dreyton, Draiton and Drayton. In 1509 it's Dreeton, showing the pronunciation at that date.

Drungewick. See DURRINGTON.

Duckreed Wood. This pretty country name has almost as pretty an origin. It describes a rill, or small stream, haunted by ducks. Early in the 14th century the place was the home of Dion de Dugrith – 'dweller by the duck rill'. In the time of Henry VIII its name appears as Dugredde.

Duddleswell. Our modern word 'well' comes from Saxon *wielle*, a spring, a place where water wells from the ground. The spring on the hillslope just here belonged to somebody called Dudel, giving us 'Dudel's well', recorded as Doudeleswell in 1295, Duddellyswell a little under two centuries later.

Dudsland. This is a name hardly changed at all by the passage of time. In medieval days the site of Dudsland Farm at Hadlow Down was owned by someone of whom we know nothing more than his name – Dudd. In 1327 the place was noted as Dodeslonde, and by 1547 it had already begun appearing in its modern form.

Dudwell. Dudwell has a similar origin to DUDDLESWELL, except here the personal name is Dudda, producing the early forms Dudewelle and Dodewell. This could have been the same Dudda who owned land not far away at Northiam, where **Dadland Shaw** is recorded as Dudilande and Dodylonde in the 13th century. Dudwell itself shares its name with a tributary of the eastern Rother.

Dumpford. We don't know for certain, but it's possible there's been a watermill here beside the river since early medieval times – maybe even on the same site as the present mill. The place name is the clue, telling us there was a ford hereabouts near a spot where the river had been dammed to provide water power. The early spellings vary between Demetford, Demeford and Dempford, before appearing as Dumford in 1724.

Duncton. Some of our earliest Saxon settlers were obviously more notable than others. Quite a number were tribal leaders; but for the majority, their only testimonial is the isolated names of farms and woods. Dunneca, the Saxon responsible for the existence of Duncton, was probably of the notable variety. He was wealthy enough to own two farmsteads, one here and another just south of Chichester at **Donnington**, both sites being of sufficient importance to appear in the Domesday Book. It's interesting to compare the way these two identical place names developed. Duncton is Donechitone in 1086, Doneketon in 1261, and Downcton in 1641. Donnington is Dunketone in AD 966, Cloninctune in 1086, Doneketon in 1275, and Donghton *alias* Donnyngton in 1558.

Obviously, confusion between the two led to a necessary alteration of identity during the Tudor period.

Dunhurst. This is simply 'the hill wood' or down hurst, describing the small hill on which the place stands. It's called La Dunhurst in 1279.

Dunly Wood. See DOWNLEY.

Durfold. See DARWELL.

Durford. Durford lies on a tributary of the western Rother, at a spot where there was once a fording place used by deer and other animals. The 'deer ford' is first recorded in 1183 as Dereford, a spelling that changes to Durford in 1545. **Durhamford** near Sedlescombe shares much the same origin, except that here the ford crossed the river Brede from the bank of a *hamm* or watermeadow. In 1296 it's given as Deramford.

Durrington. This came into existence as the *tūn* or farmstead of a Saxon tribal leader called Dēora. The place is recorded as Derentune in the Domesday Book, but its first mention is possibly older than that because research suggests it may be identical with a Derantun granted by King Æthelstan to one of his thanes. In 1640 the village location is referred to as Derrington in Tarring. Dēora's people, the Dēoringas, owned a communal farm on the site of **Drungewick**. Originally *Dēoringa wīc*, the name developed to Derengewyk in 1288, and Duringewike 50 years after that. In 1724 it appears rather curiously spelled Drensweek.

$\cdot\cdot$ E $\cdot\cdot$

Early. See EARNLEY.

Earnley. Of all the areas of Sussex settled by the South Saxons, the Selsey peninsula is probably the oldest. Certainly, Earnley is no exception. This little coastal village with its 14th century church and flint-walled barns lies on the site of an ancient clearing that was once the haunt of ernes, or sea-eagles. In a document of AD 780 the name is given as Earneleagh, while a little later, in 930, it's Earneleia. The descriptive 'eagle clearing' may also be the origin of **Early Farm**, near Wadhurst. This appears as Arleygh in the 15th century, having been the home of Agnes de Arlegh in 1296.

Eartham. Eartham translates literally as 'earth settlement' – in other words, a settlement surrounded by ploughed land. It's spelled Urtham in 1279. Just over 100 years later we find it referred to as Ertham Bovedon, a form repeated in 1547 as Ertham *alias* Bowdown. Bovedon (or Bowdown) was the name given to the manor of Eartham, describing its position 'above on the down'.

Easebourne. The village, one of those managed by the Cowdray Estate, lies close to the western Rother and owes its name to a Saxon called Ēsa who owned a bourne – maybe a stretch of the Rother itself – near the site. The Domesday Book of 1086 reproduces the name as Ese-burne. In 1500 it's Esbourn – virtually how it's still pronounced. **Easebourne Priory**, a convent of Augustinian nuns founded about 1230 by John de Bohun, was dissolved by Henry VIII and now forms part of the church of St Margaret's. Inside the church is the tomb of the 1st Lord Montagu, who in 1591 entertained Elizabeth I at Cowdray House.

Eason's Green. Although it's called Easons in 1686, the name is more accurately given as Eston Grene in 1543. This was 'the east *tūn* or farm-stead' probably with reference to Little Horsted, a few miles to the west. It's first mentioned early in the 14th century as Estone and Esteton.

Eastbourne. One of the county's premier coastal attractions, East-bourne gets its name from the bourne, or stream, that still flows from a spring near St Mary's parish church to form a lake in Motcombe Gardens. The Domesday Book notes the place simply as Burne or Borne. By 1310 it had become Estbourne, to avoid confusion with another Bourne, now WESTBOURNE. There is evidence of a Roman settlement in the area, and the town was a royal manor of both Alfred the Great and Edward the Confessor. The original village settlement lay about a mile inland round St Mary's, but in 1834 it was inherited by William

Cavendish, 7th Duke of Devonshire, who subsequently designed and developed the elegant resort that is Eastbourne today. For sportsmen, one of the town's most popular venues is the county cricket ground, **The Saffrons**, preserving the name of Saffron Gardens, recorded in 1535, where this crocus-type plant was cultivated for use as a dye and a food flavouring.

Eastbrook. Spelled Eastbroke in 1571, this originally must have been an area of boggy ground lying to the east of Southwick parish.

Eastdean. Its name – dean or valley – perfectly fits the village location in a hollow in the Downs. Alfred the Great had a manor here mentioned as Dene. A little later, to avoid confusion with another significant valley settlement to the west (now EAST and WEST DEAN) the place was distinguished as 'east' and is mentioned as both Dene and Esdene in the Domesday Book. In 1322 its situation is further clarified as Estdene by Seford (Seaford).

East Dean. See DEAN, EAST and WEST.

Eastergate. This attractive name with its suggestion of springtime began simply as Gate. The Domesday Book records it as such in 1086, with reference to a particular gate leading on to common land here. Late in the 13th century it became 'the eastern gate' to distinguish it from another at WESTERGATE, and in this form appears as Estergate or Estregate from 1263 onwards.

East Grinstead. A bustling market town whose charter dates from 1221, East Grinstead came into existence as a green stede (place) of abundant verdant growth. Late in the 12th century we find it called Grenesteda, but already by 1271 it's distinguished as Estgrenested to avoid confusion with a similar 'green place' at WEST GRINSTEAD. It's also identified as lying '*juxta* Eaduluebregge (next to Edenbridge, Kent) in 1288. Among the town's architectural attractions are the restored timber-framed houses in the High Street, and **Sackville College**, a finely preserved Jacobean building, founded by Thomas Sackville, Earl of Dorset, as a hospice for the poor and disabled.

East Guldeford. It's called New Guldeford in 1511, Est (East) Guldeford a few years later, taking its name from Guildford in Surrey. In 1505 an entry in the Register of Bishop James notes that in that year 'the church of New Guldeford, within the marisco (marsh) commonly called Guldeford Innyng, now reclaimed from the sea and made dry land by Richard Guldeford, Kt., having been newly built at his expense' was consecrated as the parish church by the Bishop. The Guldeford family originated from Guildford. In 1480 Sir Richard had rented 1,500 acres of the Romney marshes from the Abbey of Robertsbridge for a payment of 12d a year. This was the beginning of East Guldeford – called New or East to distinguish it from Guildford proper.

East Hale Bottom. It preserves the name of one of the six tithings – manors rendering a tenth of their annual produce – of the Hundred of Eastbourne. We don't know exactly where the original 'east hall' stood, but it's recorded as æt Easthealle as early as AD 963, appearing in 1086 as Eshalle and in 1316 as Easthall. 'Bottom' describes the downland location.

East Hampnett. Like its neighbour WESTHAMPNETT, East Hampnett lies a little over 50 ft above sea level on ground rising up from the coast towards the Downs. Both places were originally Saxon farmsteads. The earliest record we have of East Hampnett is a charter of the year AD 680, when the area is referred to as terram heantunensem – 'at the land of the high farmstead'. The Domesday Book notes the place as Antone. By the end of the 13th century it had become Esthamton – 'East' to avoid confusion with its neighbour. The French diminutive ending -et was added to the name about the same period, and it appeared as Esthamton *alias* Esthamptonette in 1347.

Eastland. A description given to land lying east of a particular parish, it's resulted in the names of **Eastland Coppice**, Wilmingon (Ruffe Eastland coppice 1653), **Eastlands Farm**, Cowfold (Esteland 1646), **Eastlands**, Whatlington (Estlond c.1200), **Eastland Shaw**, Brede (Estlond 1410) and **Eastland Wood**, Fletching (Eastland 1611).

Eatenden Wood. This occupies the site of a *tūn* or Saxon farmstead owned by an early settler called Ita. The name was first recorded as Itintune, then appeared around the year 1200 as Ytenton and Itenton, becoming Itynton by 1296. Its modern spelling is obviously the result of local pronunciation.

Eatons. The land has been worked here at Eatons Farm, Henfield, since before the time of the Normans. It's mentioned in their Domesday Book as Etune, derived from *ēatūn*, 'river farmstead', describing its location beside the Adur. The final pseudo-manorial *s* of the name was added later than the 14th century, because in 1378 we find it given as Eton. **South Eaton**, near Billingshurst, is also on the site of a riverside farmstead, this one by the Arun. It was called Eyton in 1259, Little Eaton in 1618.

Ebernoe. The last two elements in this place name are *burna*, a stream, and *hōh*, a spur of land. Etymologists are undecided whether the first element is *īw*, yew-tree, or *ieg*, marshland, but they tend to favour the latter because Ebernoe lies on a tributary of the Arun. Thus we have 'the spur by the marshland stream', recorded as Iburnehew, Hybernehowe and Hiberneho in the 1270s, and Ebernowe *alias* Ibernowe in 1608. The village is famous for its medieval **Horn Fair** on July 25th, at which a horned sheep is traditionally spit-roasted and shared amongst the spectators.

Ecclesbourne Glen. See ECCLESDEN.

Ecclesden. Historic Ecclesden Manor near Angmering stands on a site first recorded late in the 12th century as Ikelesdon and Yclesdon. The name has a Saxon origin, *Eccles dūn* – Eccel's down or hill. In 1291 it's noted as Egglesdon, a form repeated in 1641, when we find it given as Ecclesden *alias* Eglesdon. Interestingly, **Ecclesbourne Glen** near Fairlight appears as Eglesbourne in 1724. Although we have nothing earlier to go on, this might possibly share the same personal name and be Eccel's bourne or stream.

Eckenfields. Between 1332 and 1386 it appears as Ekenesfelde, Eknesfeld and Ekenefeld. The second element is the Saxon word for unenclosed land, from which we get 'field'. The first element is a personal name, probably Eccen – a variant of Ecca, found connected with ETCHINGHAM – hence 'Eccen's open land'.

Eckington Corner. Scholars find this a difficult one to interpret. The name makes no less than six appearances in the 1086 Domesday Book, each with a different spelling. In the 12th century it's Achintona, Agintune and Eckentuna. Two centuries later it varies between Heghynton, Eghington and Eckyngton. There are two possibilities for its derivation, either *Hēahing tūn* – Hēaha's farmstead, or *Hēahinga tūn* – farmstead of the high(land) dwellers. Probably the latter interpretation best suits the location of the place, on the Downs next to Ripe.

Edburton. Here we have one of the handful of place names in Sussex that owe their origin to a Saxon woman. And in the case of Edburton, not just any woman but a grand-daughter of King Alfred the Great. Her name was Eadburga or Eadburh, and she's believed to have founded the parish church of St Andrew's during the 10th century, to serve her *tūn* or farmstead here. A document of about 1246 gives us the original spelling of the name, Eadburgetun. In 1296 it's noted as

Edburgeton, and in the time of Elizabeth I it's Aberton *alias* Edberton. Interestingly, 'Aberton' is still the local pronunciation.

Edgerley. Recorded as Eddeslie in 1296, the place was once a *lēah* or woodland clearing belonging to a Saxon named Eddi. Although there's no sure proof, this could well have been the same Eddi who came as a disciple with St Wilfred to convert the South Saxons in the 7th century. His companions were Burghelm, Eappa (associated with YAPTON) and Padda (associated with PADGHAM).

Edgington. Edgington Farm near Ewhurst occupies land that has been cultivated ever since the time it was the site of a *tūn* or farmstead owned by a Saxon called Ecgel. Towards the close of the 12th century the place is given as Eggingethone and Eggingheton. In 1261 it's Egelington. The same Saxon probably held more property not far away at Peasmarsh, where the curiously named **Eggs Hole** marks the location of Ecgel's *healh* or corner of land. It's recorded as Eggishale in 1366.

Egdean. See BLEATHAM.

Eggs Hole. See EDGINGTON.

Elbridge. This ancient place hasn't yet been swallowed by the encroachment of Bognor Regis only a couple of miles away. It's first mentioned in the year AD 680, appearing simply as thelbrycg – 'the plank bridge' – crossing Aldingbourne Rife. By 1274 the name had been shortened a little, to Elbrigge. We find a similar primitive plank bridge on the site of **Ell Bridge**, beside the river Ems at Westbourne. This is Elbregge in 1296, Elbrige in 1535.

Eleanor. See ELLANORE.

Elkham. The earliest recordings, Elkesham and Ulkeham, suggest Elkham Farm near Petworth came into existence as the *hām* or settlement of a Saxon called Ylca. The name first appeared in its modern form as far back as 1288.

Ellanore. This little place on the Selsey peninsula marks a stretch of shoreline once belonging to Ealda, an early settler. Originally *Ealdan ōra*, it's called Eldenore in 1327. **Eleanor Farm** here bears a late fanciful variation of the name. According to some traditional accounts, it was at Ellanore that the Saxon warrior-chief Ælla and his sons landed in AD 477 (see ELSTED) though Pevensey also lays claim to that distinction.

Elmer. now part of Middleton-on-Sea, Elmer gets its name from *æl mere*, meaning 'eel pool', reminding us that eels – whether jellied or not – have long been a favourite culinary dish. The place is mentioned as elmeres pol in a document dating to AD 953. Late in the 13th century it appears as Elmere.

Elsted. It's Halestede in the Domesday Book, Ellesteda and Elested a century afterwards. Some scholars suggest the derivation is *elna stede*, 'the place of elder-trees'. Others associate it with Ælla, first king of the South Saxons, which gives Elsted an important place in the county's history. Ælla invaded what's now Sussex with his sons

Cissa, Cymen and Wlencing in AD 477, landing at *Cymenes ōra* (Cymen's shore), an unidentified spot at the foot of Selsey peninsula now under the sea but situated roughly where the Owers Banks lie. He and his followers were Saxons from the Baltic coast, experienced fighters, yet it took eight years of bloody conflict before the native British were finally subdued. Ælla was declared king of his new territory about 480, dying at the Battle of Mount Badon in 516 when the British (traditionally led by King Arthur) avenged themselves by inflicting a crushing defeat. He was succeeded by his son Cissa, founder of modern CHICHESTER.

Ems, River. Marking the boundary between Sussex and Hampshire, the river derives its name from Emsworth just across the county border. Although it's recorded in 1577 as the Emill (from Emelesworth, an early form of Emsworth), it was probably once known as 'the west bourne', giving its name to the village of WESTBOURNE through which it flows before entering the sea at Emsworth Channel west of Chichester Harbour.

Eridge. This attractive little Wealden village occupies what was once a forest ridge that was the haunt of ernes or eagles. It's first mentioned in 1203 as Ernerigg. In 1509, when the place was a manor belonging to Lord Abergavenny, it's recorded as Ewregge.

Erringham, Old and New. Old Erringham lies beside the Adur just inland from Shoreham, while New Erringham stands above it on a steep hill. Originally this was the location of the settlement or *hām* of a Saxon tribal group called the Erringas – Erra's people. The Domesday Book records the name as Eringeham in 1086. By the mid 13th century its spelling is Eryngham.

Etchingham. A riverside village beside the Rother, Etchingham developed on the site of a *hamm* or watermeadow owned by the Eccingas, a tribe identified by the name of their leader, Ecci. In 1176 the place is mentioned as Echingehamme. In 1202 it's Echingham. And Norden's map of Sussex (1610) gives it as Itchingham. The same tribal group held more land further down the Rother at Buxted, where **Etchingwood** marks the location of their 'worth' or enclosure. This is recorded in the Domesday Book as Achingeworde, before appearing as Hechingeworth in 1327 and Itchingwood in 1563. The change of ending from -worth to -wood is quite common in the development of such names.

Etchingwood. See ETCHINGHAM.

Ewhurst. The early forms Werste (1086) and Ywehurst (1210) tell us the name originally described a hurst or wood of yew-trees. It's shared by **Ewhurst Manor**, Shermanbury, which appeared as Iwherst in 1203, and **Ewhurst Place**, Ifield, the home of William de Iuehurst – 'of the yew hurst' – in 1279.

Exceat. There's some argument about the origin of this particular name. Its second element is the Saxon word *sǣte*, meaning seat or residence (as in 'country seat'). Some etymologists think the first element could be Exe, an ancient British name for the river Cuckmere, which flows into the sea here, derived from *isca* or water. Others suggest it's a personal name, Ecci (found at ETCHINGHAM); while a third theory offers an entirely different origin, *āc scēat* – 'oak-tree corner'. The name is recorded as Essete in the Domesday Book, and subsequently appears as Exsetas and Excete during the 13th century. In the time of the Tudors it's Excett, which is how it's still pronounced. The little medieval fishing village here on the east bank of the Cuckmere was almost wiped out by the Black Death in the mid 14th century. French pirates added to its desolation, and by 1460 it was noted that only two dwellings of the original settlement were left standing.

Exfold. In 1327 this farm site was the home of Richard de Exfold, registered in the parish of Rudgwick. His surname tells us he was living 'by the oxen fold', a description that originated in Saxon times as *exna falod*.

F

Faircrouch. This means 'fair cross', probably describing a boundary or wayside cross standing here in medieval days. It's recorded as Fayercroche in 1499, reappearing as Farcrouch in 1823. The old word 'crouche' or cross derives ultimately from Latin *crucis*; while 'fair' might have been used in this case in the sense of smooth – a use that still survives in the golfing term fairway.

Fairfield. Today we would call it a fairground, but in olden times when fairs were more like markets, held for purposes other than simply amusement, a particular field would be set aside on the edge of a village or town. We get our 'fair' from the old French word *feire*, which in turn came from Latin *feria*, a holiday. The annual St Bartholomew's Fair was held at **Fairfield**, Rye Foreign, near the site of St Bartholomew's hospital. It's mentioned as Fayrefyld in the reign of Elizabeth I. **Fairfield** at Waldron, occupying a similar site, is Feyrefeld in 1437; while the oldest, recorded as Feyre feld in 1310, is now commemorated by **Fair Lane** at Salehurst.

Fairlight. This breezy clifftop village which has given its name to the little resort of **Fairlight Cove**, began its history as a fern-shaded clearing in an area of woodland. Its Saxon description *fearn lēah* developed to Farnlege by the late 12th century,

and then became Farleghe and Fairlegh. In the 1540s it appears as Ferligght and Farleght, almost certainly a reference to **Fairlight Beacon**, 'farre seene both by sea and land', which marks the first ridge of the South Downs. By 1673 the name is spelled Fairelight. **Fairlight Farm** near East Grinstead shares the same original meaning of 'fern clearing'. It's listed in the Domesday Book as Ferlega. In 1296 it's Farnlegh, then varies between Farleight (1546), Farelye (1579) and Fairly (1712). The modern name has been influenced by Fairlight itself, but the old spelling and pronunciation, Fairly, is still used locally.

Fairmile Bottom. Though there are no records to give us a precise definition, this name is either self-explanatory or may contain the element *mylde*, 'mould, soil', giving us a meaning of fair or pleasing land. There's a suggestion that Fairmile once formed part of a track called la Ruelle – 'the little wheel' (from old French *roelle*) – a circular path running round the bottom of REWELL HILL.

Fair Ridge Wood. Ferrege and Ferruge, recorded early in the 13th century, probably points us to 'the far ridge', an early description of this hilly spot above the valley of the eastern Rother. At one time there was a hatchgate in the vicinity, because we find Fairiggesgate mentioned in 1400. In 1622 the name appears in the form of Farredge, which is still its local pronunciation.

Falmer. The village pool holds the clue to this name. Once upon a time it must have made a very pretty picture in its rural setting at the head of two valleys, because it was known as 'the pleasant pool' or *fæle mere*. The Domesday Book calls the place Falemere. In 1607 it's spelled Fawmer, which is more or less still its pronunciation.

Fareham Bridge. Fareham Farm close by must lie on the site of the original *hamm* or meadow here beside a tributary of Hurst Haven. The name itself probably can be interpreted as 'ferny water-meadow'. In 1346 a John de Farham was living somewhere in the neighbourhood, while in 1404 the place is mentioned as Farhambregge.

Farthing Lane. Farthing literally interprets as a fourth-ing, or fourth part. It's a Saxon word whose original meaning has been usurped by French 'quarter', but as a place name it refers to an area of land divided up into four parcels. Farthing Lane at Ashburnham is listed as Ferthyng lond in 1361, while **Farthings**, Woolbeding, is so spelled in 1583. **Farthing Farm**, Rudgwick, was the home of Robert de la Ferthing in 1279; **Farthings**, Warnham, gave its name to Walter atte Ferthing (1327); and **Farthings Barn**, Slinfold, belonged to John atte Ferthyng (1327). Each surname tells us they lived 'near the fourth-ing'.

Fatland. It appears with this spelling in the time of Elizabeth I. Maybe its meaning lies in a later record of 1622, noting the name as Fertland *alias* Fatlands. Fertland is probably a derivation of a Saxon word meaning 'wooded' – in fact we find the same word in the name of **Vert Wood**, Laughton, listed as la Ferthe early in the 15th century, Le Verth Wood in 1524 and the Vert *alias* Olde Brouylle in 1551, with a dialectal change of initial *f* to *v*. The meaning of Brouylle is discussed under BROYLE.

Faygate. A document of 1380 contains a reference to 'terra apud Feye' (land called Feye) in this vicinity. Etymologists suggest the name is a contraction of Saxon *fēo hege*, a hedged enclosure for cattle. It appears as Fay Gate in 1614.

Felbridge. Felbridge itself lies just across the Surrey border, but the original bridge from which it gets its name was on the Sussex side. In 1255 it was mentioned as Feldbrigge – 'the bridge by the open land'. Locally the name is still spelled Fel Bridge.

Felpham. It's now become part of the coastal development stretching from Bognor Regis, but long before holidaymakers came on the scene Felpham occupied the site of a Saxon *fealh hamm* – meadowland left to lie fallow for a while after being tilled. The first record of the name is from around the year AD 880 when it appears as Felhhamme, a form reproduced as Felhham in 953. The Domesday Book gives it as Falcheham, and by 1262 it's Felkham. During the next few centuries it undergoes a slight change, becoming Phelpham in 1575,

Feltham *alias* Felgham a decade or so later.

Fernhurst. A history of Sussex published in 1870 gives the name as Farnhurst, which is how it's still pronounced, although the modern spelling is closer to the original meaning of 'fern-covered hill'. It first appears around the turn of the 13th century as Fernurst and Fernherst. In 1535 it's phonetically rendered as Farnest.

Ferring. This seaside resort just to the west of Worthing began its long history as Saxon tribal territory, taking its name from the Fēringas, the people of a leader called Fēra. Remarkably, it appears in a document of AD 765 spelled exactly the same as it is today. By the Middle Ages the settlement had grown large enough to be identified independently as Westfering (1261) and Estferryng (1379). It remained East and West Ferring till fairly recently.

Filching. The ending -ing invariably points us in the direction of a Saxon tribal name. In this case it's the Fylcingas, or Fylca's people, whom research suggests were a branch of the settlement at FOLKINGTON only a mile or two away. The site of their habitat – now occupied by 15th century Filching Manor – is recorded as Felchynge in 1288, Filching in 1302.

Filsham. Now preserved as the name of a farm a little way inland from Hastings, Filsham began its existence as the *hamm* or meadow of an early settler probably called Fygli (though there's some doubt about his exact identity). The Domesday Book lists the place as Pilesham, but

it appears more correctly as Fyleshamme in 1288 and Filsham in 1332.

Findon. Since the 12th century, the name has been spelled as it is today. Earlier, in 1073, it appears as Fintona, while 13 years later the Domesday Book notes it as Fintune and Findune. These forms point either to *fin dūn* – 'woodheap hill', referring to the steep rise behind the parish church, or *fina dūn* – 'woodpecker hill'. The village lies on the site of a 3rd century Romano-British farm which evidence suggests was probably destroyed by fire. The Roman well discovered here – almost 200 ft in depth – has yielded bones from the farm including those of sheep, horses, oxen, deer and various breeds of dog, giving us valuable clues to the lifestyle of those who once lived here.

Firle. This is a name shared by several places in Sussex. Etymologists believe it's derived from a Saxon adjective, *fierol*, meaning 'oak-covered', describing land wooded with oak-trees. Although **West Firle** lies at the foot of the South Downs, it's actually not on chalky soil but on greensand and gault, ideal for the growth of oaks. The Domesday Book refers to the place as Ferla and Ferle. By 1255 it's identified as Westferles, to avoid confusion with a now lost East Firle, possibly CHARLESTON nearby. **Frog Firle**, five miles away, also appears in the Domesday Book as Ferle. By 1288 the name had become Froggeferle. How the place got its connection with frogs is a mystery, but interestingly, there was also a now lost Pig Ferle in the county, recorded as

Pyggeferl in 1300. **Firle Place**, a Georgian house built on early Tudor foundations, takes its name from West Firle, as does **Firle Beacon** above it on the Downs.

Fishbourne. Although the village is famous as one of the country's major historical sites, a palace belonging to the peak period of the Roman occupation, its Saxon name suggests nothing of its glorious past. It's a simple, unadorned reference to the stream flowing here into Chichester Channel – 'the fish bourne'. The Domesday Book calls it Fiseborne. By 1289 it's Fyssheborne. And ten years or so later we find it described as Est Fissheburne – East or New, to distinguish it from the neighbouring settlement of Old or West Fishbourne, recorded as Westfysshburne in 1498. The Roman palace, discovered in 1960, was built around the year AD 75 on the site of a slightly earlier building. It was almost certainly intended as a residence for Cogidubnus, a client king of the Romans. Destroyed by fire between AD 270 and 300, it became a quarry for other buildings and for the fortifications of the Romano-British town of Noviomagus (modern Chichester). Excavations have revealed a number of superb mosaic floors as well as large sections of the walls, baths and heating system.

Fishersgate. Fishers' gates were a common feature of the Middle Ages, when fresh fish was brought directly from the coast to be sold at a particular gateway in the town walls. **Fishersgate** at Southwick is one, noted as Fiskergate, Fisseregate and Fisshergate between 1188 and 1341. **Fisher Street**, Lewes, is mentioned

as Fisherestrete in 1383. And **Fisherstreet**, Northchapel, took its name from the family of Will Fissere (the fisherman) of Petworth (1296). But we find an entirely different history for **Fishers Gate** at Withyham. In 1658 it appeared as Fidges Gate, belonging to a Will Fidge recorded in the parish the same year, and as late as 1823 a map of Sussex showed it still being known as Fidgets Gate.

Fittleworth. This riverside village occupies the site of a Saxon *worð* or enclosure owned by a settler called Fitela. It's given as Fitelwurða in 1168 before appearing more recognisably as Fiteleworth in 1256. According to local tradition, **Fitzleroi Farm** nearby was once the hunting lodge of a royal prince. For once tradition seems to be founded on fact, because in 1263 the place is mentioned as the home of Henry and Philip Fiz le Roy, whose surname translates from Old French as 'son of the king'.

Fitzhall. Fitteshale (1279) and Fyteshale (1398) recorded for the place suggests an origin of *Fites healh*, a nook or corner of land owned by an early settler, Fit.

Fitzleroi. See FITTLEWORTH.

Five Ashes. This explains itself, being first recorded at the start of the 16th century. The village green still has five ash-trees to perpetuate the name. Similarly, **Five Ash Down** at Buxted appears as Fyve ashen downe in 1552.

Five Lords' Burgh. One tradition suggests that five manors, or medieval boroughs, shared a common boundary at this point on the Downs close to Alciston. Another maintains the name refers to the three barrows here, all that remain of an original group of five once believed to be the burial mounds of ancient lords. 'Burgh' is probably derived from Saxon *beorg*, a mound or tumulus.

Fivens Green. The place gets its name from the family of Ann Phiuens, or Phivens, recorded in the local parish registers in the time of Charles I.

Five Oaks. It's first mentioned in 1740, and like FIVE ASHES is named after a prominent group of trees in the vicinity.

Flackley Ash. Originally this was *Flæccan lēah* – Flæcca's woodland clearing. Early spellings include Fleckelegh (1296) and Flekkelee (1337). By 1724 when the name's first found in its modern form, a large ash-tree nearby probably acted as a local landmark.

Flansham. Flansham lies a few miles from the coast on the site of an early *hām* or settlement. The 13th century records aren't much help in telling us exactly who originally owned it, but scholars suggest a Saxon personal name Flæmmi, giving us an origin of *Flæmmes hām*. Between 1220 and 1279 the place is listed as Flennesham, Flomesham and Flemesham, acquiring its present spelling in 1688.

Flattenden. It's a name that shows the influence of the Victorian Sussex dialect, because a county map of 1823 shows the place as Flottingden.

Spelled like that, it's barely changed its appearance since pre-Norman times, when it was *Floting denn*, the swine pasture of Flota. Incidentally, the personal name reveals a lot about the individual concerned – it's a nickname meaning 'the seaman', suggesting Flota may have retired from a life on the ocean wave to farm land here.

Fletching. Here is yet another example of the numerous tribal -ing names that are dotted across the map of Sussex. In this case it's the Fleccingas – the people of Flecca – who have bequeathed their identity to the site. In the Domesday Book it's recorded as Flescinges, becoming Flesching in 1249 and Fleeching in 1510. Traditionally, the name is attributed to French *flèche*, 'arrow': the village was once noted for the arrow-heads it produced during the Middle Ages.

Flexham Park. This large area of woodland sloping down into the valley of the western Rother perpetuates the name of a settlement where flax was once cultivated. It's spelled both Flexham and Flaxham during the period 1278-1335. Flax is actually the fibrous material of a plant called linum which is woven to make linen cloth, still widely used in the manufacture of clothing and napery.

Flimwell. The history of this name sheds an intriguing light on long forgotten human drama. It came into existence as *flīemena wielle* – 'the spring of the fugitives' – a place offering welcome respite to those fleeing from persecution or pursuit across the Kent county border that edges the village. The name acquired its modern spelling as early as 1409. Before then a record of 1210 gives it as Flimenwelle.

Flitteridge Wood. At some time in the distant past a ridge of land just here was the cause of a dispute of some kind. Perhaps it was over ownership, perhaps it involved a family quarrel. All we know is what the original name, *flītan hrycg* – 'dispute ridge' – tells us.

Float. The site of Float Farm, close to an inlet of the river Brede, is mentioned as Flote in both 1406 and 1553. The name comes either from *flot* – 'deep water', or *flēot* – 'creek, inlet', probably the latter.

Folkington. This little village high on the windswept Downs has its roots in a Saxon farmstead owned by a settler named Folca. Folca's *tūn* is noted in the Domesday Book of 1086 as Fochintone. In 1121 it's Fokyngton. And spanning the centuries, in 1792 it's meticulously recorded as Folkington *alias* Falkington *alias* Fowington, which gives us some idea of the pronunciation of the time. Research suggests a group from this settlement, calling themselves Fylca's people (a form of Folca) moved a short distance away to live at FILCHING. Folca himself seems to have been a fairly important figure if we assume that he was the same individual who led a tribe living at **Fulking** not all that far away. They were known as the Folcingas – Folca's people – and their territory is recorded as Fochinges in the Domesday Book, Folkinges a few years afterwards. By the 15th century the name had lost its *s* to become Folkyng then Fulkyng.

Fontwell Park. Although there's no official provenance for the name, it almost certainly originated as 'fount-well', describing the old spring-fed well near the racecourse. Horse racing was first organised here in 1924, making Fontwell the second youngest course in the country.

Footland. Footland Farm, near Sedlescombe, occupies a site being used for agricultural purposes even before the Norman occupation. Its name has the literal meaning of 'food land' – in other words, land used for the cultivation of crops. Its Saxon source, *fōda land*, is recorded in 1086 in the Domesday Book as Fodilant. Three centuries later in 1377 it's become Fodylonde. And in the reign of Henry VIII it's Fudlond, from which the modern spelling has evolved.

Forbridge. See FORD.

Ford. There's no ford here now, but at some time or other there must have been at least two in the vicinity, one across the Arun and another over Binsted Brook, because we find the site mentioned frequently in the plural form Fordes between 1190 and 1310. In 1329 its location is identified as Forde near Arundell. The medieval surname atte Forde – 'dweller by the ford' – has connections with **Fordland Wood**, Crowhurst, **Fords Farm**, Bolney, and **Ford's Green**, Maresfield. **Ford Brook**, beside the Rother at Rotherfield, is first noted as Fordbrook in 1567. And **Forbridge Farm**, Pagham, gets its name from the nearby bridge across a stream flowing into Pagham Harbour. It's recorded as le Ford-brygge in 1455, Fortebridge in 1573.

Forest Row. This is a comparatively recent development, an independent parish only since 1894 – before then it had been part of East Grinstead. The name seems to refer to a row of cottages within Ashdown Forest, variously described as Forstrowe in 1467, Forrest Rowe beside Grynsted in 1579, and Forrest row greene in 1642.

Fore Wood. Forewode, noted in 1342, is probably a reference to woodland lying to the front or fore of a parish – in this case, Crowhurst. A map of 1823 gives the name as For-ward Wood, suggesting the original had been contracted in dialect speech to For'ard by that date.

Forge Wood. The Sussex iron industry that flourished for almost three centuries, denuding large areas of the county's ancient forests, is recalled at places like ASHBURNHAM, and by local names such as Forge Wood at Burwash, marking the site of old iron works – possibly the Burwash Forge noted in the time of Elizabeth I. **Forge Wood** and **Farm** at Rotherfield mark a similar site, as does **Old Forge**, Maresfield, recorded as ye steele Forge in 1642. **Old Forge Farm** at Wadhurst is near meadowland mentioned in 1543 as Forgemede. And there are two **Forge Bridges** in the county, one at Ashburnham, the other at Westfield.

Forstal, The. This Rotherfield name is the dialect word forstall or fostal (literally, fore-stall) describing a farm with a paddock attached. It appears as le Forstalle hende, or end, in 1441.

Foul Mile. See FOULRIDE GREEN.

Foulride Green. It's Fowle Ryde in 1525, Fowle Rede green just under 30 years later. The first element is clearly the old word for a bird. The second element may be 'rid' in the sense of land cleared of undergrowth; or it may be 'rithe' – a rill or small stream. We have a similar choice for the name of **Foul Mile**, near Herstmonceux, recorded as Fowle Myle in 1643. Again the reference is probably to birds, unless it indicates 'foul' or muddy.

Four Oaks. A survey of the county made in 1795 first mentions this as Four Oaks, but some 70 years before then the name had appeared as Brownsmiths Oaks. Earlier still, in 1469, we find a local reference to the manor of Brownsmythe – to which this place must once have belonged. Interestingly, brownsmith was the medieval term for a worker in copper or brass, so presumably the old manor took its name from someone of that occupation.

Fowlbrook Wood. This name stands out from the rest not because it's especially old or even very important, but because it owes its origin to a native of Flanders who came to live in the Ewhurst area a century or so after the Norman Conquest. He was known as Fugol the Fleming, and he's recorded holding property in the neighbourhood around the year 1200. Fowlbrook Wood marks the site of his 'brook', a stretch of marshy land on the bank of the Rother, mentioned at the same period as Fugelesbroc, Fuggelsbrock and Fuggelbroc. Roughly 100 years later it's Fugesbroke, a form from which the modern name has evolved.

Foxhole. See FROGSHOLE.

Foxhunt Green. Although it has a somewhat Victorian look to it, the name is actually a good six centuries old, recorded first in 1395 simply as Foxhunt. By 1435 we find it noted a little more fully as Foxhunteslonde.

Frag Barrow. This mound, which has lent its name to **Fragbarrow Farm** near Burgess Hill, has a partner in **Frankbarrow** a mile and a half away. The two share a common origin, being originally known as *fyrhðe beorg* – 'the frith (woodland) mound' – and they're believed to have marked the limits of a sizeable tract of woodland called simply 'the Frith'. Frag Barrow is mentioned as Frekeberge late in the 11th century, becoming Frekeberwe in 1327 and Freckbarrow in 1586. Not until 1840 do we come across the modern spelling, which avoids confusion with Frankbarrow, noted as Frankbarrough in the time of the Tudors.

Framfield. The Domesday Book of 1086 records the name of this pleasant Wealden village as Framelle, which doesn't help us very much. Later forms – Fremfeld (1296) and Fremefeld (1314) – suggest its derivation is *Fremman feld*, open land belonging to a Saxon called Fremma or Fremme. Between 1673 and 1724 the name is spelled Frantfeild, showing an unexplained confusion with FRANT several miles

away – though it's interesting to note that the local pronunciation remained 'Frantfield' until very recently.

France Wood, Francis Wood. See FRANCHISE.

Franchise. Recorded as Franchis and Frenches at the start of the 17th century, the place probably acquired its name from the medieval surname Fraunceys (meaning 'the Français' or Frenchman) that we find in connection with **France Wood** at Catsfield (John Fraunceys 1296) and **Francis Wood**, East Hoathly (William Fraunceis 1327).

Frankbarrow. See FRAG BARROW.

Frankham. Originally a *hamm* or watermeadow owned by an early settler named Franca, the place appears as Fraunkhame in 1340, Franchame a generation or so later. We come across the same personal name at **Frankwell**, once *Francan wielle*, or Franca's spring. The Domesday Book records it as Francwelle, a spelling that varies only a little from Frankewelle noted in 1279.

Franklands Green. This took its name from a medieval landowner, John Fraunkelayn, registered in the parish of Ferring in 1327. The same surname is probably responsible for **East Franklands**, Wivelsfield, recorded as Francklands in 1629. In feudal times a franklin was a freeholder below the rank of nobility.

Frankwell. See FRANKHAM.

Frant. It's difficult to imagine this

pretty village was once a hub of industrial activity, it wears its scars so lightly, and yet in the year 1600 there were more than 20 ironworks in the surrounding area. Long before then however, this had been a peaceful forest glade 'overgrown with ferns' – a description rendered by the Saxons as *fearniþja*, the origin of the place name. A document dating back to AD 956 gives it as fyrnþan. At the start of the 12th century it's Fernet, and in the following century the spellings are Ferneth, Farneth and Farnth. By the Tudor period this had become Farnt – a pronunciation still in use until recently.

Freckley Wood. In 1572 this was the site of Frickleye house. Two hundred years earlier it had been the family home of Richard de Frikele. Etymologists suggest the place name originated as *Friccan lēah*, describing a woodland clearing owned by a Saxon settler, Fricca.

Frenches. Frenches at Billingshurst gets its name from the family of le Francys or Frenssh, registered in the area in the 14th century. The same surname – it meant 'the Frenchman' or someone of French descent – is shared by **Frenches**, Rotherfield (Richard Frensh 1332), **Frenches Park**, Worth (Roger le Frensh 1332), **Frenchland House**, Ashington (Freynslonde 1279) and **French Wood**, East Grinstead (Frenchelond 1574).

Freshfield Crossways. A little country crossroads, it lies on land that in medieval times had been freshly ploughed ready for sowing. Recorded as Freshfields in 1621, it had once been the home of John de Fressefeld (1296) and Ralph de

Frechefeld (1327) – dwellers 'by the fresh land'.

Friar's Bay. This coastal inlet between Peacehaven and Newhaven acquired its name from William Fryer who was living locally at Deans in 1693. The origin of his surname is obvious. It's also found associated with **Friar's Hill**, Guestling, and **Friar's Gate**, Withyham, while **The Friars** at Icklesham is Fryersland in 1569. However, **Friar's Oak Farm** near Clayton has a different source. Recorded as Fryes Oake in 1615, it originally got its name from the family of Agnes le Frye (1327) whose surname meant 'the freeborn'.

Friday Street. It's Fryday stret in 1527, Fryday streate just under 40 years later. This is a fairly common place name in southern England, indicating a small group of dwellings set apart from the main village. There's another Friday Street at Horsham, and one (now lost) at Cuckfield. These dwellings could have been isolated for some sinister reason, since Friday was regarded as a day of ill-omen during the Middle Ages. Some Friday Streets marked the way to a gallows, while unproductive field plots were sometimes called 'Friday furlongs'. **Friday's Hill** at Fernhurst probably belongs to this latter group.

Friston. Etymologists haven't quite decided about the exact derivation of this name. The spelling remains constant as Friston from 1200 right up to the early 1500s, with variants of Fryston, Freston and Freeston. It's been suggested the origin is either *Frīges tūn*, the farmstead of a Saxon called Frēo, or else *fyrs tūn*, describing a farmstead on furze-covered land. In 1610 it's noted as Frison, which is how the name is still pronounced locally.

Frith Hill. 'Frith' began as a Saxon word denoting woodland, and survived in the Sussex dialect as a description of growing wood not mature enough to be cut back. In its original sense it's given us the names of **Frith Hill** and **Copse** at Northchapel (Le Frith 1535), **Frithlands**, Cowfold (so spelled in 1682), and **Frithwoods**, Pulborough (Frythewood 1560), while **Frithfold Farm** at Kirdford is on the site of a woodland fold or enclosure mentioned as Frythfould in 1639.

Frog Firle. See FIRLE.

Frogshole. Vauxhall in 1783 and Fogs Hole in 1840, this name almost certainly began as Foxhole – in fact there's an East Foxhole Furlong just to the south. Its origin is shared by **Foxhole Cottages** at Hurstpierpoint, near 'the Fox-hole pond' recorded in 1724; and **Foxhole Farm**, Hadlow Down, which is Foxeholys in 1438. **Foxhole Farm** at Battle has a different origin, though. At the start of the 14th century it was the home of Robert de Folkeselle and William de Folksille, whose surname seems to be derived from the Saxon *Folcan (ge)selle* – 'Folc's building'.

Fulfords. The fact that there's a ford half a mile to the north-east at Broadbridge, and that the ground here is low-lying and inclined to be muddy in wet weather, are two clues indicating the origin of this name. In fact it means 'the foul, or muddy, ford', appearing as Fulford in 1357. By 1624 when the farmhouse had been built here, the name becomes Fulfords.

Fulking. See FOLKINGTON.

Fuller's Gill. This place, with **Fuller's Farm** at West Grinstead and **Fuller's Piece** at Sutton, are associated with the medieval occupational surname, le Fullere. The work of 'fulling' using fuller's earth, a clay-like substance that removes oil and grease from cloth, was carried out on the site of **Fullingmill Farm** at Ardingly, recorded as Fullinge Mylle in 1573.

Funtington. In the 12th century it's Fundintune, becoming Fontyngton and Funtington 100 years later. Despite these early spellings, research doesn't throw a lot of light on the source of the name. The second element is clearly Saxon *ingtūn* – 'farmstead of' – but farmstead of whom? One suggestion is that it belonged to a group of early settlers known as the Funtingas – 'the dwellers by the fount or spring'. But scholars say more evidence is still needed.

Furnace Green. It's near the site of a former ironworks, mentioned in 1612 as 'at the furnis'. **Furnace Pond**, Slaugham, appears as Great Furnace Pound in 1649, again with reference to local ironworks. And **Furnace Wood** marks the site of the Heathfield furnace – it still contains the remains of old iron mills, together with a sluice gate and culvert from the original hammer pond. Some idea of the scene during the county's 'Iron Age' can be found in Camden's famous survey *Britannia* (1586) where he notes that 'there be furnaces on every side... to which purpose divers brooks in many places are brought to run in one channel, and sundry meadows turned into pools and waters, that they might be of power sufficient to drive hammer mills, which beating upon the iron, resound all over the places adjoining'.

Furner's Green. The place acquired its name from a Stuart gentleman, Thomas Furnar, residing in Danehill parish in 1618.

Furzefield. This was once unenclosed land, the home of Sibil atte Ferse (1296) and Galfridus atte Furse (1332) whose surname informs us they lived 'by the furze-bushes'.

Furze Field Wood, West Chiltington, is noted as Firsefeld in 1357.

Fyning. Here we appear to have a Saxon word *finung*, used to describe a place like a clearing where cut wood was stacked. Maybe there were originally several of these sites in the vicinity, because the earliest record of the name (1230) shows it as Fininges. By 1302 it's become Fynnyng. And a Regency map of the county spells it Vining – an example of the dialect pronunciation of *f* as *v*. Interestingly, this spelling appears elsewhere in Sussex, including **Vining Rough**, a wood at Easebourne that appears as Upper and Lower Finnings in 1823; **The Vinings**, a field at Sidlesham; and a now lost place at Westhampnett recorded as Vining as early as 1279.

G

Gallows Hill. The name is a reminder that this was the site of the gallows of the old Liberty of Lodsworth where felons were brought for execution. Incidentally, galley-bird or gallows-bird is the Sussex name for the woodpecker, so called from the grisly belief that it frequented gallows and gibbets to feed on the maggots from rotting corpses. **Gallybird Hall** at Barcombe bears this dialect name, pre-

sumably for its attraction rather than its reputation.

Gallybird Hall. See GALLOWS HILL.

Gateborough. Its neighbour is **Cadborough**, the two names sharing a common derivation and development from *gāta beorg* – 'goats' mound'. During the 13th century the name is recorded as Gateberg, Gateberwe and Catisbergh. In 1514 we find a reference to Gateberghe Marsh, now the site of Gateborough Farm. Cadborough Farm, above on the hill where the goats once grazed, appears on a map of 1831 as Caresborough, possibly a misprint for Catesborough.

Gatwick. Gatwik and Gatewik in 1241, Gotewike in 1328, this was once a humble Saxon 'wick' or farm where goats were reared. Now of course its name appears in almost every corner of the globe as an international flight destination. **Gatwick Airport** was first developed on the site of an old racecourse. After limited use as a wartime airstrip, it opened for private use in 1930, remaining a private airfield until 1936 when it was used for commercial purposes. Closed in 1956, it reopened as an international airport two years later and now ranks as the eighth busiest in the world.

Gensing Wood. Its name, together with those of Gensing Gardens and Gensing Road in Hastings, preserve the identity of a now lost place in the Hastings area. Originally it had been settled by a Saxon tribe called the Genesingas – the people of Genesa – and is documented as Genesinges and Ganesing in the 12th century, Genesing in 1321.

Gentilshurst. Gentil's Farm close by is a clue that the name was first spelled Gentil's hurst, describing a wooded hill on the family property of Nicholas Gentil, registered in the parish of Lodsworth in 1334. His surname suggests somebody either well-born or known for their courtesy.

Gibbons's Mill, Gibbons Wood, Gibbshaven, Gibbs Wood. See GIB-SREED.

Giblets Lane. In spite of its Sweeney Todd overtones, the name was simply acquired from the family of William Gibelot of Sedgwick (1296), and is noted as Gyblettes in 1532.

Gibsreed. It's mentioned as Gybbysrede in 1418, a reference to some patch of 'rid' or cleared land belonging to the family of John Gybbe whom we find registered here in Ticehurst just eight years earlier. The surname Gybbe or Gibbon was a diminutive of the Norman-French name Gilbert, popular in the Middle Ages. It was also a familiar term for a tom-cat. We come across it elsewhere in connection with **Gibbons Wood**, East Chiltington, **Gibbons's Mill**, Rudgwick, **Gibbs Wood**, Lindfield, and **Gibbshaven** at Worth, which is recorded as Gybbesaven in 1582, Gibbs Aven in 1823. The original 'haven' was probably a wayside shelter like COLDHARBOUR.

Gillhope. The spelling has barely changed since 1553 when it's given as Gilhope. Two and a half centuries earlier we find a Peter de Chillehope registered in the same area. The two names are too close to be coincidental, so must share a common source. The second element is clearly hop or hope – a small enclosed valley – linked to a Saxon personal name that scholars suggest is either a feminine one, Cille, or the masculine Cilla found elsewhere in the county at CHILLEY and CHILLINGHURST.

Gillridge. It has the attractive meaning of 'golden hill-ridge', conjuring up a picture of yellow spring flowers blossoming against the bareness of the surrounding woodland. The earliest record of the name dates to 1285, when it's Golderege. After that it varies between Gelderegge and Gilderigge before appearing as Gildridge in 1627. The site, now occupied by Gillridge Farm here at Withyham, may have passed its name to **Gildridge Farm** near Herstmonceux. At the start of the 15th century this was the home of a family variously listed as Gyldrugge, Gyldregge and Gyldrygge, who probably originated from Gillridge. **Guildenhurst Farm** at Pulborough has a similar kind of derivation. Its site was once known as 'the golden wood', noted as Gyldehurste in 1301 and Gyldenhurst in 1594.

Gills Lap. In 1658, the year Oliver Cromwell died, the place is recorded as Boyletts boyes *alias* Gills lap, while **The Gill** close by is simply called Gill. Presumably Boylett was the name of a local landowner. 'Boyes' is from French *bois*, a wood; and 'lap' seems to be 'leap', a place where deer and other beasts of the chase leapt across the gill or dip just here.

Glass Eye. This droll-looking name poses a bit of a puzzle for etymologists. It's first recorded late in the 12th century as Glesye, a spelling that varies little throughout the medieval period. The second element is almost certainly -ey or -eye, meaning 'island'. The first could possibly be derived from an ancient British river-name *glas*, describing the colour of water – grey, blue or green. Significantly, Glass Eye Farm here at Beckley lies at the confluence of the river Tillingham with a tributary stream.

Glasshouse. The site is mentioned in 1640 as Glasshoyse Croft, or field, and must surely have been connected with the West Sussex glassmaking industry. **Glazier's Farm**, Waldron, was the home of Thomas Glasyer in 1445; and **Glazier's Forge**, Brightling, was similarly associated with the family of William Glasyer (1521). The glasyers or glaziers worked in 'glass houses' usually built on top of hills, where air currents could be used to create forced draughts to fan the furnaces. To date, some 27 glass house sites have been discovered in Sussex, though many more must have existed during the 15th and 16th centuries when the industry was at its height.

Glatting. Clotinga (1086), Glottinges (c.1145) and Glottyng (1314) are signposts to Saxon tribal territory. The people who lived here were the Glottingas, a group deriving their identity from their leader, Glott. His name hints at a not very likeable character, because it's a nickname meaning 'the starer, or sneerer'. At some time or other a branch of the tribe moved eastward to settle in the Robertsbridge area at **Glottenham**, a place name starting as *Glottinga hām* and developing to Glothingeham (1164) then Glottyngham (1362). The present spelling, a late corruption, is shared by the Glottenham Stream and Glottenham Manor.

Glazier's Forge. See GLASSHOUSE.

Glottenham. See GLATTING.

Glydwish. Standing on the banks of the river Dudwell, Glydwish Hall occupies land that was once a 'wish' or marshy meadow haunted by kites. The alternative name for this bird of prey is glede, derived from Saxon *glida* – literally 'glider', describing its flight. So here we have 'glede wish', a place name recorded as Gledewysse in 1296, Gledewysshe just over a century later.

Glynde. Spelled Glinde or Glynde from the early 13th century onwards, the source of the name is *glind*, a fence or enclosure – which aptly suits this little village because it was here in 1778 that a local man, John Ellman, began the sheep-breeding programme that produced the now famous black-faced Southdowns. In 1611 we find the name mentioned as Glynd *alias* Glyne – and Glyne is how it's still pronounced. **Glynde Place** here is a magnificent Elizabethan manorhouse open to the public.

Glyndebourne. Glynde Reach, a tributary of the Ouse, is the bourne near GLYNDE that gave this place its name. In 1288 it appears as Burne *juxta* (next to) Glynde. Four centuries later in 1662 it's Glindborne. The internationally renowned opera house created by John Christie has been delighting audiences here since it opened in 1934. The season runs from the end of May to early August.

Glynleigh. A document dating to the year AD 947 mentions 'to glindlea', indicating a woodland clearing containing some sort of enclosure. During the 13th century the name is recorded as Glindle,

Glindlee and Glyndele. In the year of the Restoration, 1660, it's Glinley. And around 1840 it appears romantically, if erroneously, as Green Leas.

Goatley. See GOTWICK.

Goddenwick. Goddenwick Farm near Lindfield preserves the name of a minor Saxon tribal group called the Godingas – Goda's people – who had their *wīc* or farm on this site. It's noted as Godingewyk in 1261, a spelling that changes little over the next few hundred years, appearing as Goddingeweek in 1599.

Godleys Green. It acquired its name from the family of a John Godley registered in the parish of Chailey in 1643.

Godshill. Here is a name meaning literally what it says – God's hill. It's recorded as Godeshull in 1315. Maybe somewhere beneath the foundations of Godshill Farm at Cowfold there lie the remains of a medieval house of prayer, because it's obviously a site with a strong religious association. **Godsmark's Farm** at Ashurst took its name from the family of John Godsmarke, living in the parish in the time of Elizabeth I. His surname is particularly fascinating because in those days 'God's mark' described the disfigurement of plague sores.

Godsmark's Farm. See GODSHILL.

Gold Bridge. It can hardly be the bridge itself that was gold, so originally the description must have applied to the profusion of marsh marigolds or other yellow waterside plants growing just here beside the

Ouse. We find the name mentioned as Goldebregg in 1296, Goldebrigge in 1332. **Goldbridge House** at Hurstpierpoint stands on a similar site, in this case beside a tributary of the Adur, recorded as Godebrig in 1239, Goldbrigge in 1491.

Goodsoal. The shallow dip here accounts for the -oal ending of the name. The first part is a Saxon personal name, Guðhere, hence Guðhere's *hol* or hollow, variously noted as Gotershull, Gotereshole and Gutresole between 1279 and 1347. Somewhere hereabouts we know there was a hurst or wooded hill belonging to the same person, because we find the now lost place of Guteresherst listed in the parish in 1296.

Goodwood. Everybody's familiar with the story of Lady Godiva who rode naked on a horse in the well-known Coventry legend. Her name is a Latinised version of the popular late Saxon name Godgifu, meaning 'God's gift'. In those far-off days women held a much more important status than during the Middle Ages, so it's not unusual to find one commemorated in a place name like Goodwood, which began its history as *Godgife wudu* – Godgifu's wood. The earliest records for it date from around 1200 when it's called Godiuawuda. A generation later it's Godivewod. Our Sussex Godiva also had a mere or pool somewhere locally, mentioned as Godiuemere in 1209. **Goodwood House**, which is open to the public, has been the country seat of the Dukes of Richmond and Gordon for over 300 years, while above on the Downs is the famous racecourse where the

'Glorious Goodwood' meeting, starting on the last Tuesday in July, is one of the main events of the national horse-racing calendar.

Goring-by-Sea. Garinges, recorded in the 1086 Domesday Book, is very close to the original Saxon name for this seaside neighbour of Worthing. It denotes the tribal territory of a group called the Gāringas, who were either the people of a leader named Gāra, or were identified as 'the dwellers on the gore of land'. The spelling varies little in early records. By the late 13th century it loses its final tribal *s* to appear as Goryng. The Gāringas held more land not far away at **Goringlee**, site of a woodland clearing where they probably pastured their swine. Research suggests its first mention is to be found in a Saxon charter as garunga leah. By 1249 this had developed to Garingelegh. In 1555 it's noted as Goringley *alias* Goringlegh.

Goringlee. See GORING.

Gosden Green. Recorded as Goosedowne Gate and Green in 1640, the place seems to be associated with the family of William Goseden of Prinsted, registered here about 1380. The surname tells us they lived by the goose *denn* or pasture. **Gosdens Heath** near Midhurst is mentioned as Gosedenne in 1249, giving its name to the family of Robert Goseden living here in 1425.

Gotham. See GOTWICK.

Gotwick. This name shares the same origin as GATWICK, denoting a Saxon *wīc* or farm where goats were bred.

It's first mentioned in a document dating to the year AD 834, as gata wic. In 1327 it's Gotewyke. And in 1504 its location is given as Gatwyke in Rusper. **Gotwick Farm** near Forest Row occupies the site of another goat farm, recorded as Gotewyk and Gatewyk towards the close of the 13th century. **Goatley** at Northiam was once a *lēah* or woodland clearing where goats were kept – Gatele about 1210, Gotteleye in 1279. And **Gotham**, not far from Bexhill, occupies a combe or valley where these animals grazed. The name has been contracted from 13th century Gotecumbe to Goteham, Gottham and Gottam, all recorded in the Tudor period.

Graffham. The group of early Bronze Age barrows on nearby Graffham Down shows the history of this area goes back to something like 2000 BC. Long afterwards when the South Saxons arrived to live here, they called the place *grāf hām* – 'the settlement by the grove of trees'. In the Domesday Book its name is listed as Grafham, and hardly changes at all in the next few centuries, acquiring its modern spelling in 1248.

Grainingfold. See GRAYLINGWELL.

Gravelye. Graveney in 1502, Graveligh in 1595, this was formerly the home of Thomas de Grauele (1332) whose surname translates as 'dweller by the thicket clearing'. **Gravelye Farm** at Cuckfield has a similar etymology, appearing as Graulie in 1607, Gravely ten years afterwards.

Gravenhurst. If we remember that in medieval mauscripts *v* was written down as *u*, then the forms Grauenherst and Grauehurst recorded for this spot early in the 14th century show its name originated as *grǣfan hyrst*, meaning 'the hurst of the brushwood thicket'.

Gravetye. Gravetye Manor in the village of West Hoathly occupies the site of an early 'tye' or enclosure bordered by a grove of trees. First mention of the place comes in 1279, when it's Grauetye. In 1613 it's noted as Gravety *alias* Moate House, referring to **The Moat**, a timber-framed building from around 1500 that stands below the manor on an island in a large pool. Gravetye Manor itself (now a noted restaurant) dates from the 1590s and was once used by the local 'owlers' or smugglers as a convenient place to hide their contraband.

Graylingwell. Despite the suggestion that this could mean 'the grayling stream', the name is much more likely to be a Saxon tribal one, derived from the Grǣgelingas, or Grǣgel's people, who drew their water from the Grayling Well that still rises as a spring here. During the 13th century the place is referred to as Greylingswell and Greylingewell. The same tribal group may have had an enclosure for their livestock on the site of **Grainingfold Farm** to the north-east near Billingshurst. From *Grǣgelinga falod*, the name developed in the 13th century to Grelingfolde and Grelingefold, becoming Graylingfold in 1327.

Great Cornes. In 1659 this is referred to as 'three closes (enclosures) called Corneres'. Three centuries earlier we find the name appearing as Cornore, which seems to be a derivation of *cran ōra* – a bank or slope frequented by herons.

Great Dixter. When we consider the insanitary conditions in which our forebears lived, it's hardly surprising that we occasionally come across references to sickness and disease in their place names. Great Dixter, a manor house on the outskirts of Northiam, is one such example because its name comes from *dīc steorfa*, meaning 'the ditch of pestilence'. This suggests a ditch hereabouts contained foul, contaminated water causing an outbreak of typhoid or something similar. The 13th century spellings vary from Dicdstere to Dixterve and Dyksterf. Towards the end of the Tudor period the place is noted as Dixster *alias* Dixsterne. Great Dixter was built in 1460 and restored by Sir Edward Lutyens in 1911. Both the house and its lovely gardens are open to the public.

Greatham. The pronunciation of this name – 'Grittam' – gives us a clue to its origin. The village has grown beside the river Arun on the site of a 'gritty watermeadow' – *grēot hamm* – recorded as Gretham in the Domesday Book (1086) and Gruteham in the mid 12th century. The soil locally is still coarse and sandy.

Great Ridge. Situated near the coast at Hastings, the name of this place explains itself, appearing in the plural form Rugges in 1452. Great Ridge, Ore, has the same meaning and in 1365 was the home of Reynold de Regge – 'dweller at the ridge'.

Greatwick. Between 1288 and 1332 we find a family various recorded as de Gratewyk, de Grauetwyk and de Grautewyk living here in the parish of Cowfold. Etymologists think their surname is a derivation of *grafet wīc*, indicating a farm where there was some kind of digging or excavation. The site is still a farm. The word *grafet*, stemming from the Saxon verb *grafan*, 'to dig', is the root of the medieval surname atte Grevette or de Gravette – 'dweller by the digging' – associated with several places in the county. **Gravatt's Farm**, Rudgwick, was the home of Adam de la Gravette (1256), and **Grevatt's** near Easebourne that of John atte Grevette (1288), while **Grevatt Wood, Fletchers Grevatts** and **Crabtree Grevatt**, lying together near Bury, are similarly connected with Hugo atte Greuette of Amberley (1327). The affixes Fletchers and Crabtree used to distinguish these places were added much later.

Greenden. See GREENHURST.

Greenhurst. The name hasn't changed much since 1279 when it was noted as Grenehurst – 'the green hill' – perhaps because the trees on this hill were mainly evergreens. **Greenden Wood** at Ewhurst lies in 'the green dean' or valley recorded as Grenedene in 1478, while the name of **Green Street** explains itself – the one near Crowhurst was Grenestrete in 1562, and the other, near Eastbourne, appeared as Grene Strete in 1290, later becoming a cattle droveway called Green Street Drove in 1636.

Green Street. See GREENHURST.

Gregory Lane. Recorded as Gregoryes in 1527, the place got its identity from a family once living in the Westham area. Their surname – originally adopted in honour of one of the three popular saints of that name – is also responsible for **Gregorys** near Wadhurst, and **Gregory Wood**, Chiddingly. In its diminutive form of Grig or Grigge it's associated with **Griggs Green** near Trotton, **Grigg's Farm** at Horsham, and **Grigg's Wood**, Frant.

Grevatt Wood, Fletchers Grevatts, Crabtree Grevatt. See GREATWICK.

Griggs Green, Grigg's Farm, Wood. See GREGORY LANE.

Grinses. The name of Grinses Farm is a perfect example of the double plural that occurs so often in Sussex speech. Mentioned simply as le Grene about the year 1400, before then it had been the home of Robert atte Grene – 'dweller by the green place' – registered in the parish of Bexhill in 1296. The modern spelling is a dialectal development of Green's being referred to as Greens's.

Grittenham. It's Greteham in the 1086 Domesday Book, Gretenammys four centuries later. One suggestion put forward is that the name has the same origin as GREATHAM and means 'the gritty or gravelly meadow'. Although the Domesday Book mentions a quarry here, the soil in the area is too rich to support this particular interpretation. The alternative theory is that the site of Grittenham Farm here at Tillington was referred to in Saxon times as æt þæm grēatan hamme – 'at the great meadow' – describing a large tract of land bordering the banks of the Rother at this point.

Groombridge. The medieval word for a young man or servant was *grome*, still preserved in its original sense in our modern 'bridegroom'. Only later did it come specifically to mean somebody who tended horses. So the name Groombridge refers to a bridge associated early in the Middle Ages with *gromen* – young men/servants. It's recorded as Gromenebregge in 1318, Grumbrygge about 1480, and Groomebridge in 1601; but what precise connection there was remains a mystery. A local tradition maintains the village actually owes its name to a Saxon called Gromen who built a moated stronghold where **Groombridge Place** stands. In fact the manor house dates from the late 17th century (it's been attributed to Wren) and its surrounding gardens and parkland, now open to visitors, are among the area's most popular attractions. Sir Arthur Conan Doyle renamed it Birlstone Manor House when he used it as a setting for his Sherlock Holmes novel *The Valley of Fear* (1915), describing 'the beautiful moat, as still and luminous as quicksilver'.

Guestling. Place names ending with -ing tell us at once we're on Saxon tribal territory. Guestling is no exception. It entered the county's history as the site settled by the Grystelingas, and appeared in the Domesday Book as Gestelinges before developing to Gistelyng in 1362 and Gestlinge *alias* Geslinge in 1647. The modern spelling shows a friendly confusion with 'guest'. The Grystelingas took their identity from their leader, Grystel – 'the gristly one' – an unflattering nickname for a tough character, maybe?

Guildenhurst. See GILLRIDGE.

Gumber. See GUNSHOT COMMON.

Gunshot Common. This rather sporty name belies its origin. The second element -shot is a development of *scydd*, the Saxon word for a shed or hovel, probably a swine-cot. The first element is the personal name Guma, meaning simply 'man'. Between 1279 and 1327 we find *Guman scydd* developing to Gumeshelde, Gumeshult, Guneshude and Guneshedde. By the time of Elizabeth I it's Gunsutes. The same Saxon, or at any rate another sharing his name, also had a 'worth' or enclosure on the site of **Gumber Farm** at Slindon. This appears as Gumeworth in 1251, and Gumworth on a map of Sussex printed in 1823. Over a century earlier, however, the place was already known as Gumber because we find it spelled that way in 1696 – the reason why can only be conjecture.

· · H · ·

Habin. Despite extensive study, scholars can make nothing of the etymology of this name. There are no records earlier than the Tudor period, when it appears as Habyn and Hawbyn. In 1610 it expands to Hawbedyne, then contracts again in 1684 to Haben. **Haben Farm**, opposite the hamlet on the banks of the western Rother, preserves this late 17th century spelling.

Hackenden. Around the year 1300 the name is listed as Haghindenne. A couple of decades later it's Hakendenne, and by 1591 it's just as it is today. The second element is *denn*, telling us this was once a woodland pasture where swine were kept. The first element seems to be a Saxon personal name, Haca or Hacca.

Hadfold. See ADVERSANE.

Hadlow Down. At a time when the area was covered in forest, there would have been a clearing somewhere here above the Rother valley belonging to a settler called Headda. Headda's *lēah* or clearing developed during the 13th century to Haddelegh and Hadelegh. By 1333 when 'down' had been added to describe the hill sloping to the valley, it became Hadledowne, repeated as Hadlydowne in 1543. In fact it was still called Hadley Down in 1771, so the modern spelling is a late corruption.

Hailey. See HAYLEIGH.

Hailsham. Although the 1086 Domesday Book records the place as Hamelesham, the early forms Eilesham (1087-1100), Helesham (1189) and Haylesham (1230) tell us this was originally the *hām* or settlement of a Saxon called Hægel. In the time of Elizabeth I the spelling was Heylsome, which is how the name of this small market town is still pronounced locally. The Norman forerunner of the 15th century church of St Mary's was built on the site of a Saxon moot, a meeting-place where councils were held.

Hairley. The name of this farm near East Grinstead has been altered over the years from Hedley, which in turn derived from *heald lēah*, 'the sloping clearing', describing its fairly steep site. Between 1272 and 1332 it's recorded as Haldelee and Heldele. **Hanlye Farm** near Cuckfield also lies on a slope, and shares the same meaning. For almost three centuries, until 1564, the name appears regularly as Haldelegh. Then in 1589 it's noted as Haldelegh *alias* Hanlie.

Halcombe. The early forms Horecumbe and Horcumbe, documented before 1307, suggest this name has its root in *horh cumb*, meaning 'filth combe' – no doubt a disparaging reference to the dirty, muddy state of the deep hollow in which the farm lies. In 1612 we find the name still being spelled Horcombe.

Hale Green. It must be in the vicinity of fields mentioned as Hale and Halcroft in 1433. Hale comes directly from the old word *healh*, used of a corner of land, later producing the medieval surname atte Hale, de la Hale, found associated with **Halecommon**, Rogate, **Hale Court**, Withyham, **Hale Farm**, Rudgwick and West Wittering, and **Hales Barn**, Aldingbourne.

Hale Hill. See HALLAND.

Halland. Richard atte Halle, a native of Lullington, acquired land here in the parish of East Hoathly in 1343, so giving us 'Hall land', recorded as Hallond in 1376, Hawland in 1565 and Hallandes in 1580. His surname, suggesting he or his forebears lived 'at or near the hall', is shared by **Hall Farm**, Cuckfield, **Hallgate Farm**, Petworth, **Hall's Cross**, Hooe, **Hall's Wood**, Wadhurst, and **Hale Hill**, Heathfield, listed as the home of Sileman atte Halle in 1370.

Hall's Cross, Hall's Wood. See HALLAND.

Halnaker. Although this name is recorded as Halfnaked at various times down the centuries till as late as 1624, its risqué connotation is alas illusion, because it means nothing more earthy than 'half an acre'. The Domesday Book has it down as Helneche. In 1386 it's Halfnacre. And in 1428 it's Holnaker. Interestingly, the pronunciation hasn't changed much since 1605, when the spelling is Hanycarr. **Halnaker Mill** was the subject of a poem by Hilaire Belloc, who lived most of his adult life at SHIPLEY.

Hambrook. The name hasn't changed at all since it first made an appearance in 1327. Brook is used here in its Sussex sense of marshy or well-watered land. Ham – from *hamm*, a watermeadow – produced the medieval surname atte Hamme – 'dweller by the meadow' – found connected with farms, fields and woods throughout the county.

Hamly Bridge. It began its history as the *lēah* or woodland clearing of an early settler named Eamba who owned a fording-place three miles further down the Cuckmere at AMBERSTONE. Hamly appears as Ambelegh in 1327, while the bridge itself is mentioned as Ambeleghbrigge in the middle of the following century. Greenwood's map of Sussex (1823) gives the place as Gt. Amly.

Hammerden. Hammerden is a significant place name in the county's industrial history. First recorded in 1279 as Hamerden, it suggests the old *denn* or pasture here was the site of a drop-forge where water-driven hammers were used to shape metal. If this is correct (and scholars say it's difficult to see what other interpretation can be put on the name) then here at Hammerden we have the earliest documented reference to forge-hammers in Sussex. **Hammer Wood**, Ardingly, which lies close to an old forge, is not recorded as The Hamer until 1567, while **Hammer Wood**, Lindfield, and **Hammerwood**, Forest Row, both refer to ironworks of the same Tudor period or later.

Hammerpot. The clue to this unusual name is to be found in a reference of 1703 to a Harmans or Harmars Farm in the neighbourhood. The 'pot' is the pit or slight hollow just here, so we have Harmans/Harmars Pot as a derivation.

Hammer Wood. See HAMMERDEN.

Hammingden. Hemelyngden, noted in 1296, points to a Saxon origin, *Hǣmeling denn* – Hǣmele's swine pasture. In 1327 the name is Hamelynden. By 1597 it's shortened a little to Hamyngden.

Hammonds Green. It acquired its name from the family of Thomas Hammond of Waldron, registered in the parish in 1580. Their surname – a form of Hamon, from the Norman forename Hamo – is shared by several **Hammond's Farms** and **Hammond's Woods** in the county.

Hampden Park. It's a comparatively modern district in the borough of Eastbourne, developed at the beginning of this century. Formerly part of the RATTON estate, it took its name from Lord Hampden whose family were owners of Ratton manor at the time.

Hampers Common. A map of Sussex printed in 1823 spells the place Hamphurst. Since the name originally came from the family of Elizabeth Hamper, listed here in the Petworth area in 1708, this seems to be an inaccurate rendering of Hamper's. The surname is likewise associated with **Hamper's Barn**, Washington, and **Hamper's Lane**, Horsham.

Hamsell. Ham means 'watermeadow' and Hamsell 'meadow's hill'. Recorded as Hamesell in 1261, Hammeshull in 1327 and Hamselle in 1336, the place is in an area well-watered by streams.

Hamsey. It lies in a wide loop of the river Ouse on the site of a *hamm* or watermeadow mentioned in a Saxon charter of AD 961 as æt Hamme wiþ Læwe, and Hamme *juxta* Læwes, describing its location a couple of miles from Lewes. The Domesday Book notes it as Hame in 1086. Then around the year 1222 we find a family named de Say (originating from Sai in Normandy) becoming lords of the manor of Ham, after which it is identified as Hammes Say (1306). The old name wasn't quite abandoned though, because as late as 1510 it reappears as Hamsey *alias* Hammes. The Norman church and a 16th century farmhouse, **Hamsey-place Farm**, are all that now remain of what was once a flourishing little village. Local tradition blames its demise on the ravages of the bubonic plague.

Handcombe. See HANKHAM.

Handcross. First recorded in 1617, it's been suggested Handcross refers to a 'one-handed' cross – one with just a single arm, probably used as a signpost. It's interesting to compare the name with the numerous Crosshands elsewhere in the country (all marking crossroads) which got their name from the old-fashioned pointing hand that indicated directions on fingerposts.

Hanging Hill. Known as this since the time of Elizabeth I, originally the hill could have been either an execution site where malefactors were hanged in chains, or its name could have the more wholesome derivation of 'hanger hill' from a wood on the hillside.

Hangleton. There are two Hangletons in Sussex, and both names share the same source, *hangra tūn*,

meaning 'the farmstead by the hanger or sloping wood'. Hangleton just inland from Brighton appears as Hangetone in the Domesday Book, and Hangeltune, Hangelton between 1091 and 1125. The other, on a sloping site near Ferring, is Hangleton in 1380.

Hankham. A Saxon document of AD 947 refers to the place as æt Hanecan hamme – 'at Haneca's watermeadow'. Although the personal name isn't actually on record, etymologists think it's a diminutive of *hana*, meaning 'cock-bird', used here as a nickname. The Domesday Book lists the place as Henecham. In 1293 it's Hanekeham, and just over a century later, Hankeham. Neighbouring **Handcombe Hall** is a fanciful variation of the old name, and is so spelled in 1840.

Hanlye. See HAIRLEY.

Hapstead. See HEMPSTEAD.

Hardham. Hardham lies on the site of a Roman posting station on Stane Street and its 11th century parish church of St Botolph's incorporates bricks and tiles salvaged from the ruins. For much of its history the place has had two alternative names, which accounts for a certain confusion of records – Heryngham al. dicta Herdham (1399), Hardham *alias* Heringham (1602) and Hardham otherwise Irringham (1740). The earlier of the two names seems to be from *Heregȳðe hām*, the settlement of a Saxon woman called Her-egȳð. It's in the Domesday Book as Heriedeham and is the ancestor of the modern place name. The other was derived from *Heringa hām*, denoting the settlement of the Heringas, or Here's people – Eringeham about 1150, Heringham thereafter. Because of the similarity in the two personal names, scholars think there must have been a connection of some sort between Heregȳð and Here. Here himself may well have been the same Saxon who had a 'worth' or enclosure not very far away at **Hesworth Common**, recorded as Heresworth in 1296, Hesworth meade (meadow) in 1640.

Harebeating. Sussex has some unusual-looking names, and Harebeating is surely one of the more curious. Its history is a little odd too, because it actually began as the name of a place some ten miles away at Piddinghoe, recorded during the 16th century as Harpetinge *alias* Harpingdene in Pedinghoo. The place is now lost, but it was originally the tribal territory of a Saxon group called the Herebeorhtingas – Herebeorht's people. The Domesday Book lists it in 1086 as Herbertinges, and in 1121 it's Herebertingas. By the time it became extinct, the name had become Harpingden, and the original tribal Harebeating form already transferred to what had been part of its manor lands since the Norman Conquest.

Harehurst Wood. This has nothing to do with hares, everything to do with boundaries. The place lies close to the Hampshire county border, and its name describes its location as *har hyrst* or boundary wood, recorded during the 13th century as Magna Harehurst. Similarly, a 'boundary pool' or *har mere* gave its name to **Haremere Hall**, on a riverside site near the Etchingham parish

boundary. It appears as Harmere about 1207. And **Harlands Wood**, straddling the old boundary between Lindfield and Cuckfield, is mentioned as Harlands in 1666.

Haremere Hall, Harlands Wood. See HAREHURST WOOD.

Harlot's Wood. This is the kind of name that really should have an interesting provenance – but alas, it hasn't. Research suggests it's probably associated with a Northiam man, Thomas atte Haneholte, registered in the parish in 1327. His surname describes him living 'by the cock-bird thicket'. Local imagination has obviously been at work on the spelling since then.

Harrow Hill. Harrow Hill, near Angmering, is known to have been the site of a pagan religious sanctuary or *hearg*, situated within a small Iron Age enclosure on top of the hill. Excavations have revealed hundreds of ox skulls, relics of animal sacrifices, suggesting the customary autumn slaughter of cattle took place here at the festival of Samhain (mentioned by Pope Gregory as 'sacrificing many oxen to devils'). No early forms of the name have survived, but the hill must be close to a lost Stonherie (*stān hearg* or stone harrow) recorded in 1256 on the Clapham-Findon boundary. Another harrow existed elsewhere in Sussex, because a Haregedon (*hearg dūn* or harrow hill) is mentioned in the county in 1203. Although the site can't be precisely located, the family name of Harewedon found in the parish registers of Ringmer and Stedham in the 14th century possibly gives some clue to its position.

It's very likely MOUNT HARRY was also the site of a pagan sanctuary.

Harsfold. This is called Hursefold in 1279, Haresfold in the Tudor period, and Hasfold in 1823. The second element obviously describes an early enclosure for livestock here on the site of Harsfold Manor near Wisborough Green. The first element isn't so easy to interpret but could be a personal name. The manor lies on the Arun between two other folds – **Lowfold**, so named from its situation, and **Orfold Farm**, 'the fold by the riverbank' (from *ofer falod*), recorded as Overfolde in 1347, Orfold *alias* Overfold in 1553.

Hartfield. An appealing Wealden village with an equally appealing name, Hartfield lies on what was long ago an area of open land roamed by harts or young male deer. The Saxons called it *heorot feld*. In the Domesday Book it's Hertevel. And by 1309 it's Hertfeld. A spring where the harts came to drink rose on the site of **Hartwell** in the same locality. In 1334 it was noted as the home of John de Hertwell – 'of the hart spring'. As a footnote to history, at the outbreak of the Second World War the Duke and Duchess of Windsor came to stay here at **South Hartfield House**, the first time they'd returned to England since the abdication crisis three years earlier.

Harting, East, South and **West.** Collectively these three pretty hamlets near the Hampshire border are known as The Hartings. They cover an area originally settled by a Saxon tribal group, the Heortingas – Heort's people – mentioned in AD 970 as both Heartingas and Hertin-

gas. The 1086 Domesday Book lists the name as Hertinges. By the 13th century, when four separate little settlements had developed, East, South and West appear as Esthertinge (1196), Suthertyng (1281) and Westhertinges (1296), while North Harting, absorbed into the parish of Rogate late that same century, is now **Harting Combe**, recorded as Hertyngcumbe in 1289.

Hartwell. See HARTFIELD.

Harvest Hill. Spelled Harveshill in 1602, then Harviste Hill just two years after, the place originally got its name from the family of Alexander Heruest (or Hervest) registered locally in Cuckfield in 1327.

Harvey's Cross. The cross was erected here as a memorial marking the spot where a Regency gentleman of that name fell dead while fox hunting in 1821.

Harwoods Green. It acquired its name from the family of Owen Harwood, recorded in the Petworth area in 1630. **Harwood's Farm**, East Grinstead, called Harwards in 1639, is similarly associated with the 14th century family of John Hereward, whose surname came originally from the Saxon personal name Hereweard, meaning 'army guard'.

Haselden. See HAZELHURST.

Haslingbourne. The bourne refers to a tributary stream of the western Rother which in earlier times flowed past a hazel thicket just here. From *hæseling burna*, the name developed to Haselingeburn in the 13th century, becoming Heselyngborn by

1535. The old word *hæseling*, describing a thicket of hazel-bushes, is also the source of **Hazeldean** near Cuckfield, recorded as Haselyng in 1327 and Haselinge in 1617. The -dean ending of the modern form is a late corruption.

Hassocks. Hassocks is a fairly recent development that's grown since the opening of the London-Brighton railway in 1841. It adopted the name of a field in the vicinity, called Hassocks because of its coarse, tussocky grass. In fact this is quite an old field-name in the county, because we come across a Hassoksland mentioned in Bexhill about 1370. The Hassocks railway tunnel is notable for its Gothic towers at either entrance. Originally the 1½ mile-long tunnel was whitewashed and gaslit so that passengers in 19th century open carriages wouldn't be unduly alarmed by their subterranean journey.

Hastingford. This strategic fording place near Hadlow Down was controlled by the Hæstingas, a powerful Saxon tribal group, and marked the point at which their territory was entered from the north-west. Recorded as Hastingeford in 1279, it lies at the end of a sandstone ridge that runs in an almost unbroken line from the coast to the ford here, providing an excellent line of communication between this point and the group's main settlement at HASTINGS over 25 miles away.

Hastings. Tribal settlement, Norman invasion point, Cinque Port, smugglers' base, antiques centre, and now a modern tourist resort, the story of Hastings can surely be said to encapsulate the history of Sussex as a whole. Its name, first documented in AD 790 as Hastingas, belongs to the Hæstingas, a dominant tribal group taking their identity from their leader, Hæsta, who was probably a Danish war-chief. Their territory extended over a wide area, as far north as HASTINGFORD and east to Hastingleigh in Kent. From around AD 500 to 1011 they remained a separate people from the surrounding South Saxons, appearing to co-exist with them on a peaceful basis, and at some time must have had a dynasty of their own. Their stronghold or fortified camp (referred to in 1050 as Hæstingaceaster) became the site on which Count Robert of Eu built **Hastings Castle** not long after the Norman Conquest of 1066. And it was here at Hastings that William the Conqueror mustered his army before engaging the Saxons at Senlac Moor (now BATTLE) six miles to the north-west. Together with the Kentish ports of Dover, Sandwich, Romney and Hythe, Hastings was one of the original **Cinque** (five) **Ports** – a maritime confederation, dating from the reign of the Conqueror, receiving special privileges in return for supplying the king with ships and men.

Hat Hill. Mentioned simply as 'the Hatt' in 1640, it's one of many hills throughout the country so named on account of their distinctive shape. Etymologists suggest the old French word *haterel*, meaning 'crown of the head', is also the derivation of **Hatterell**, West Grinstead, applying originally to the hill sloping down to the Adur. It's recorded as Hatherell in 1648.

Hatterell. See HAT HILL.

Hawkhurst Common. Hauekehurst (1229) and Hauckherst (1285) tell us the place was once a hurst, or wooded hill, where hawks were often seen hunting. **Hawkhurst Court** at Kirdford, noted as Hauekhurst in 1288, stands on an identical site.

Hawking Sopers. In 1624 it appears as Hawkensopers. Four years later the place is referred to as land called Sopers. Its name initially came from the family of Stephen le Sopere 'the soap-maker' (1327), one of whose members was apparently falconer to the lord of Ashurst manor.

Hawkridge. It's now a farm site near Hellingly, but in the days of the Normans Hawkridge was considered important enough to be included in their Domesday Book as Haingruge, a mangled version of the original Saxon *Heafocing hrycg*, telling us this was a ridge of land owned by a settler called Heafoc – a typically aggressive Saxon nickname meaning 'the hawk'. In the 12th century the place name is Havykynregge. Towards the end of the following century it's Hauekingeregge and Hauekerigge. And in 1444 it's Hawkyregge. We come across the same nickname attached to a livestock enclosure on the site of **Hawksfold** near Fernhurst, recorded as Haueksfold in 1296. And **Hawksden Park**, Mayfield, was either Heafoc's dean (valley) or a valley hunted by birds of prey. The name appears as Hawkesden in 1418, Hawksdene just under 20 years later.

Hawksbourne. The bourne of this particular name refers to the tributary stream of the Arun near which Hawksbourne Farm lies. In earlier times it was owned by a settler called Ealh, giving us a derivation of *Ealhes burne*, recorded in 1279 as Alkesburne. By 1572 the name had changed enough to appear as Awxburne *alias* Alkesborne, and roughly a century afterwards the transformation is complete and it's referred to as both Alkesborne and Hawkesborne. Interestingly, we find the same Saxon personal name associated with a ford at AUSTFORD.

Hawksden, Hawksfold. See HAWKRIDGE.

Haybourne. The first element in this name isn't hay/grass but the old word for a hedge or fence. So here we have 'the bourne by the hedged enclosure', a reference to the tributary of the river Arun close by. The name's spelled Heyburn in 1262, Heybourn in 1332. We also find 'hay' used in the same sense at **Hayreed**, on the Downs near Wilmington. This hasn't changed much since first recorded in 1261 as Hayrede, a name suggesting the land here was 'rid' or cleared of a hedge to enlarge it at some time.

Hayleigh. Hayleigh Farm, near Streat, stands on the site of a downland clearing that seems to have been hedged round to enclose it, probably keeping livestock secure. The source of the name is *hæg lēah*, listed towards the close of the 13th century as Haylye and Hegleghe. Around 1450 we find the mention of 'park of Haylly' – park being nothing more grand than a paddock or similar enclosure. Until very recently the name was spelled Hailey.

Hayreed. See HAYBOURNE.

Haywards Heath. Local tradition maintains that this fast-expanding town was named after a gentleman of the highway called Hayward who carried out his robberies on the heath. But it has a far older provenance than that. Long before the place separated from Cuckfield to become an independent parish, its heath was part of a small settlement known as Hayworth – 'the hedge or hay enclosure'. Our earliest records for this name date back to the middle of the 13th century. Not until the early Stuart period do we find it changing to become Haywarde (1603), Hayworths Hethe (1607) and then Heywards Hoath (1675) – hoath or hothe being the East Sussex 'heath'. The place remained open heathland until it was chosen as the compromise route for a railway line which neighbours Lindfield and Cuckfield both refused to have running through them. The London-Brighton service opened in 1841, stimulating the growth of Haywards Heath from village to modern town.

Hazeldean. See HASLINGBOURNE.

Hazelhurst. The first record of this name appears in 1018, when it's referred to as Hæselersc, the Saxon description of a stubble-field or 'earsh' overgrown with hazels. In the Domesday Book some 70 years later, the name is spelled Halsesse, becoming Haslerse a century after, and Haselhersh in 1392. The modern -hurst ending is a late corruption.

Old pasture land where hazel-bushes grew has given us the names of **Haselden** near Dallington – Heseldenne in 1200, and **Hazleden**, East Grinstead – Halseeldene in the Domesday Book, Haseldenne in 1279. **Hazelholt**, Old Shoreham, recorded as Heselholt in 1249, takes its name from a hazel thicket. And **Hazelwick Farm** at Worth has been the site of a farm since at least AD 947, when we find it documented as Hæslwic – 'the farm where hazels grow'.

Hazelholt, Hazelwick, Hazleden. See HAZELHURST.

Headfoldswood. Hudyfolde (1206) and Hudifold (1332) lead etymologists to believe this name stems from *Huding falod*, Huda's fold – a personal name also associated with UDIAM. By the mid 14th century the site had become woodland, because we find it called Hudefoldewode in 1353, Hodefoldeswode in 1380.

Heaseland. The place shares its name with its neighbour, **Heasewood Farm**, both containing the Saxon word *hēse*, meaning brushwood or undergrowth. In 1202 the area is noted as boscus (wood) de la Hese. In 1589 the two names are separately recorded as Heseland and Heyswood. Then in 1629 they come together again as Hayeswood Land. **Heaslands**, Rotherfield, is so named through its connection with the family of Richard de Hese – 'of the brushwood' – registered locally in 1296.

Heath. The Saxons described barren open countryside covered with low-growing shrubs as *hǣð*. During the

Middle Ages this became *heth* or *hethe*, producing the surname atte Huth, atte Heth and de la Hethe – 'dweller on the heathland' – associated with **Heath Barn**, Ashurst, **Heath Farm**, Plumpton, **Heath End**, Petworth, **Heath Common**, Thakeham, **Heathfields Farm**, Shipley, **Heathlands Farm**, Bepton, **Heath Mill**, Pulborough, and **Heath Place**, Hartfield.

Heathens' Burial Corner. This is probably unique in being the only place preserving in actual name the site of a pagan burial-ground. All the more pity then, that we have no firmer supporting evidence than the traditional account of a large number of urns (presumably cinerary urns of the Bronze Age) being dug up here once upon a time. As such traditions go it's very old, because the name was first recorded as long ago as 1279, as Hetheneburiels, Etenesburieles and Etheneburyles, which suggests there could well have been some truth in the story. The modern name is a slight distortion of the original, since we find it still being called The Heathen Burials in 1840.

Heathfield. This long established Wealden market town stands on the site of an area of open heathland first mentioned in the 12th century as Hadfelde. The following century (1272) it's noted as La Hethfeld, subsequently becoming Heathfelde in 1587. Interestingly, the old local pronunciation of the place name as 'Heffle' can be traced back to 1312, when the spelling is Heffeld. By tradition, the first cuckoo of each new spring was released from a basket by an old woman at 'Heffle Fair'.

Started in 1315, this famous fair was held in the town on the 14th of April, and remained an annual event for almost 550 years until it was discontinued last century.

Heene. Scholars have advanced the theory that this name stems from a lost Saxon word *hīwun* or *hīun*, meaning 'family, household', suggesting Heene developed on land originally sufficient to support a single family group. The 1086 Domesday Book gives the name as Hene, and between 1193 and 1448 it's variously recorded as Hyen, Hien and Heyn. In 1671 we find the location identified as Heene in Tarring.

Heighton Street. See SOUTH HEIGHTON.

Hellingly. The -ly ending (nearly always emphasised when pronouncing Sussex place names) tells us this was once a Saxon *lēah*, a cleared area of woodland. The first part of the name isn't quite as easy to interpret. Probably it stems from a tribal group of settlers called 'the dwellers on the *hielle* or tongue of land' – which would give us a derivation of *Hiellinga lēah* for the name. In fact this suits the site because Hellingly actually lies on a tongue between the Cuckmere and a tributary stream. Appearing as Hellingeleghe in the early part of the 13th century, it's recorded as Hellinglegh from 1316 right into the Tudor period. The same tribal group may well have had some connection with **Helling Down** a few miles away at Jevington, noted as Hellyngdowne in the time of Elizabeth I.

Hell Wood. The only record we have

of this sinister name spells it Hell-wood in 1644, a period when Puritan influence was fast gaining strength. Doubtless the description had a religiously moralistic application.

Hemingfold. This was the fold of a Saxon settler called Helm or Helma – 'the helmet' – a fitting nickname for a warrior, later coming to mean protector or lord. His property here would have been known as *Helming falod*, a name subsequently recorded as Helmefalde (1121), Helmingfelde (1414) and Helmyngfold (1460).

Hempstead. There are Hempsteads, Hampsteads and Hamsteads dotted all about the general map of England. Each one marks the site of an early homestead comprising a dwelling-house with barns, outhouses and livestock enclosures attached. The original Saxon *hāmstede* meant literally 'a settlement place'. In Sussex, three such homesteads were located at Hempstead near Arlington (Hamsted 1202, Hempstede 1325), Hellingly (Hempsted 1288) and Framfield (Hamstede c.1145, Hemstede 1325). **Hempstead Mill**, recorded as Hemstedmyll in 1543, belonged to the Framfield Hempstead. Incidentally, a family originating from this particular manor are believed to have given their name to **Hapstead** near Ardingly, which was held by Robert de Hemsted in 1332. The place itself is mentioned as Hapset in 1560.

Hendall. The name comes from *hinda dæl* – 'hinds' dale' – descriptive of a valley where female deer were often found grazing. Noted as Hindedal in 1205, Hyndale in 1509

and Hendalle in 1750, the place shares its origin with **Hendal Farm** at Withyham – Hyndedale in 1257, Hindhall bridge in 1579.

Henfield. A Victorian ornithologist once recorded 14 golden orioles perched together on a single thornbush on Henfield Common, which seems most appropriate for a place whose name means 'open land frequented by hen-birds'. The first documented mention of Henfield is found in a charter of AD 770 in which King Osmund of Sussex grants land at 'Hanefeld' to a Saxon Christian, Warbald, and his wife Tidburga, on which to build a church – probably the site of the 13th century parish church of St Peter's. The Domesday Book mistakenly spells the place Hamfeld. In 1169 it's Hanfeld, and in 1272 Henfeld.

Henfield Barn and **Wood.** See SCAYNES HILL.

Henley. In the time of Charles I this was called Hounley. Etymologists take the name to be a development of Hundligh, recorded in the parish of Easebourne in 1296. If so, its origin must be *hund lēah*, referring to a woodland clearing where hunting hounds were kept.

Henley Wood. Although it shares the same spelling as the previous entry, this particular Henley has an entirely different history. Noted in its modern form as far back as 1288, it stems from the Saxon (*æt þæm*) *hēan lēage* – (at the) high clearing. The associated medieval surname de Henlegh is responsible for **Henley's Bridge**, Ashburnham, recorded as Henlyes bridge in 1588 and earlier the home of Walter de Henlegh of Cowbeech and Herstmonceux (1327). **Henley's Down** at Catsfield is similarly connected with Alan de Hanlegh (1288) and Ancelin de Henlegh (1296), appearing as Henlydowne in 1460, Henlies Doune in 1594. And **Henley's Farm**, Itchingfield, was owned by a family called Henley or Henly registered in the parish at the beginning of the 17th century.

Hermitage. The original hermitage was a chapel built by Simon Cotes, a native of Westbourne, who refers to himself in his Will of 1527 as 'Ermyt'. A number of years earlier, in 1513, the locality is described as Ermeteslandes, suggesting it was the property of a group of monks attached to CALCETO PRIORY known as the Hermits of the Causeway.

Herrings Bridge. Noted as Herringes bridge in 1570, and Herring's Bridge 100 years later, this probably contains the same surname we find in connection with **Herring's Farm** at Mayfield, where an Edward Heryng ('herring-seller') is registered in 1296.

Herstmonceux. Pronounced 'Hursmonsoo', the name owes its history and its Gallic appearance to the intermarriage of two families. When the site was originally settled, it was known simply as the hurst, or wooded hill. The Domesday Book gives it as Herst. Late in the 13th century it's mentioned as Hesthurste and Esthurst – 'East' to avoid confusion with an identically named manor, now HURSTPIERPOINT. Then in 1304 there appears the first record of it being called Herst Munceus, a double-barrelled name that produced the alternative forms Herst Mounceux *alias* Hurstmonceux *alias* Esthurst in 1390. The Norman-French family of de Munceus, originating from Monceux in Calvados, were granted the lands and manor here at the end of the 12th century, and subsequently married into the local family of de Herst. **Herstmonceux Castle**, for many years the home of the Royal Observatory, was built in 1440 by Sir Roger de Fiennes, whose ancestor Sir John had early in the previous century married the heiress to the estates, Maud de Monceux.

Hesworth Common. See HARDHAM.

Hewenstreet. For many years a farm, it's recorded as Hewnestrete in 1405. Here we have the same Saxon word *hīwun* or *hīun* – 'family, household' – that is the origin of HEENE. By the medieval period it had developed to *hewen*, a term generally used to mean servants. We know the maintenance of this particular street was the responsibility of local landtenants because a fascinating document of the early 17th century tells us: 'The whapple way leading from Barcombe through Hewenstrete towards the restinge oak ought to be mended by the terre-tenants on both sides but in 1618 it is presented that Phillip Bennett onely is to repair the same'.

Heyshott. Hethsete, recorded around the year 1100, tells us the name is derived from *hæð scēat*, describing a corner of land overgrown with heather. In 1442 the spelling is Heyshete, and in 1675 it's Heashot.

Hickstead. The British Horse-Jumping Derby International is an annual event here every August, so in a way it's rather apt that the name should mean 'the highest place', even though the description originally referred to Hickstead's location on high ground between two tributaries of the Adur. In its medieval form it appears as Heghestede, Heghsted and Hicstede, developing to Hixted by the mid Tudor period.

Higham. There are three Highams in Sussex, and each with a different derivation. The one near Northiam stands on the site of a Saxon 'high settlement' or *hēah hām*, recorded as Hiham in the Domesday Book of 1086. Higham near Salehurst was once a watermeadow beside the eastern Rother, noted as Heghomme – 'hay meadow' – in 1279. And Higham Street is part of the promontory on which the new town of WINCHELSEA was built about 1290 after the old town had been destroyed by storms. It was initially known as 'the island meadow' because of its cliff site, mentioned as Ihamme, Iham and Yhamme during the 13th century. In 1339 we find it also referred to as Suthyhomme – 'South' as opposed to North Higham, now NORTHIAM.

High and Over. In its modern form this name is a bit of whimsy, invented to avoid confusion with neighbouring **Hindover**. The site is actually a hill above the Cuckmere originally described as (at the) high bank – (*æt þǣm*) *hēan ōfre*. In 1352 it appears as Heghenovere, then jumps 500 years or so to reappear as Hindover in 1824.

Highbrook. 'Brook' in the Sussex dialect means marshy ground, and here we have a slightly elevated site in an area well-watered by streams – hence its name, first recorded early in the Stuart period as Highbrookes.

Highden. This deep-cut valley up on the Downs may be identical with scortan dene, 'the short valley', mentioned in a Saxon document charting the bounds of Washington parish. By the 13th century however, the name had been altered to mean 'the high valley' and in this form appears as Hidene in 1288, Heydene in 1341, and Hydeane or Hyden in 1578.

Highdown Hill. How long it's been called 'the high *dūn* or hill' nobody knows, but this solitary hill rising to 266 ft a few miles inland from Ferring first became a fortified site during the Bronze Age. Something like 1,000 years later it became an Iron Age camp, and then was re-occupied by the British about the beginning of the 4th century AD. With the arrival of the Saxons, Highdown took on a special significance as the traditional burial place of their kings, starting with Ælla, war-leader of the South Saxons, who's believed to have been interred here inside the hill-fort after the battle against King Arthur at Mount Badon in 516. Halfway down the western slope of the hill are the remains of Roman buildings dating to the early 2nd century AD, while below it on its north side stands **Castle Goring**, a splendid white mansion built in the Italian style for the poet Shelley's grandfather.

Highfield. Our modern word 'field'

comes from Saxon *feld*, describing an area of open, unwooded country. Highfield therefore explains the location (Hyfeld in 1271) shared by a number of other places in the county – **Highfield Cottages**, Waldron (Hygfeld 1499), **Highfields**, Mayfield (Heghfeld 1443) and Wadhurst (Highfield 1641), **Highfields Farm**, Hurstpierpoint (Highfields 1593), **Highfield Shaw**, Burwash (Heffield 1610), and **Highfield Wood**, Ticehurst (Hye feld 1562). The place name **Highland** obviously has a very similar origin, resulting in at least seven separate places so called in the county.

Highfure. La Fure, frequently recorded in the period 1256-1380, comes from *fyrh* – '(at the) furrow or ditch', probably used to describe the shallow depression between the two hills here. At some time in its history the name seems to have become confused with 'fire', perhaps from the notion that there was a 'high fire' or beacon in the vicinity, though there's nothing to substantiate this.

Highgate. It's spelled Highegate in 1564, marking the spot where a hatch-gate led on to woodland in the Ashdown Forest. **High Hatch Lane** at Hurstpierpoint shares much the same origin. In 1296 it was the home of William atte Heghehecche, whose name tells us he lived 'by the high hatch-gate'.

High Hoad. This is noted as Hygh Hoothes in 1553, an example of the medieval East Sussex word 'hothe' being used in place of the more common 'heath'.

High Hurstwood. The forms Hay-

hurst, Heyhurst Wood, and Hyhayhurst, all recorded between 1602 and 1659, suggest the origin of this name isn't 'high' but the old way 'hay' meaning hedge – hence the hedged hurst or wood. However **High Hurst** at Newick means precisely what it looks like and is Heighherst in 1499, sharing its description with another of the same name near Nuthurst found as Highhurste in 1550.

Highland. See HIGHFIELD.

Highleigh. In Saxon times when this little hamlet on the Selsey peninsula was nothing more than a cleared area of rising ground above the marshes, it was documented as Hilegh, 'the high clearing'. The name hasn't changed very much in over 1,000 years, reappearing as Hylighe in 1332, Hylegh in 1428. It shares its origin with **Highley Manor** at Balcombe, noted as Heyley in 1566 and Highleigh around 20 years later.

Hill. The big hills of Sussex are the South Downs, but 'hill' as a name has its own independent place on the county map, appearing in connection with at least 16 sites ranging from **Hill Ash** near Harting, home of Walter atte Hulle – 'by the hill' – in 1332, to **Hill's Farm**, Wadhurst, which gets its name from the Elizabethan family of Hyll registered here in 1573.

Hindleap. Recorded in the reign of Elizabeth I as Hyndlippe, this pretty name began as a medieval term describing a low place in a hedge or fence too narrow to let cattle escape while allowing deer to leap easily across.

Hindover. See HIGH AND OVER.

Hoadley Wood. Hodleghe, Hothlege and Hadlegh, all noted during the 1280s, suggest this name shares the same origin as HOATHLEY in describing a clearing on heathland. Similarly, **Hoadley's Farm** at Withyham appears as Hodlege in 1287 before developing to Hodeleyes at the start of the 17th century.

Hoads Common. It acquired its name from the family of Robert Hode, registered in the Petworth area in 1296. Their surname, a variant of atte Hothe meaning 'dweller on the heath', is also connected with **Hoad's Wood**, Chiddingly, and **Hoath Wood**, Beckley, while **Hoad's Wood**, Warbleton, is called le Hothes in 1493.

Hoadsherf. See HODSHROVE.

Hoathly, East and **West.** These two villages lie about a dozen miles apart as the crow flies, and their names share an identical origin, hence the need to distinguish them as 'East' and 'West'. Both derive from *hǣð lēah* – a clearing on heathland – but instead of developing to Heath as elsewhere, the first element of the name became 'hothe' or 'hoath' – a word distinctive to East Sussex and often found in medieval field-names in the area. East Hoathly is noted as Hodlegh (1287), Hothlegh (1401) then Esthothelegh (1438), and West Hoathly is Hadlega (1121), Hothlegh (1327) then Westhothleg (1347).

Hobney. It lies in the Pevensey Levels, an area of marshes crisscrossed with streams called havens. Here and there stand islands of firm ground first settled many hundreds of years ago, like CHILLEY, RICKNEY, and Hobney itself, which was an island or *ey* owned by someone called Hobbe. The name first appeared in 1302 as Hobenye, but has been spelled in its modern form since the mid 15th century.

Hockham. Described as Notekynes formerly Hoccombes in 1414, Hockham Farm near Wartling occupies a site originally known as 'Hocca's combe or valley', taking its name from an early settler. In turn the place gave its name to the family of de Occumbe or de Hoccumbe, registered in the parish between 1296 and 1345.

Hodcombe. See HOLLYCOMBE.

Hoddern, Hodore. See HODSHROVE.

Hodshrove. This is spelled Hoteshrove in 1557, Hotshrove at the start of the following century. Etymologists suggest its derivation is medieval English *hothe schorve*, meaning 'steep slope covered with heathland', a fair enough description of Hodshrove's location at the bottom of a slope on the Downs. We can see an earlier development of the same place name with **Hoadsherf Farm**, Cuckfield, which lies on the side of a hill and is recorded as Hothshorue in 1289, Hothesrove in 1541 and Hodshurfe in 1612. **Hoddern** near Piddinghoe is on a similar site. Its name means 'heathland hill' – Hoddowne in 1692, the Heathdown *alias* the Hoddown in 1726. And **Hodore Farm** at Hartfield stands on a 'heathland bank' noted as Hodore and Hothore in the 1270s, and Hodower a little over two centuries later.

Hoecourt Barn. The Domesday Book refers to the name as How, indicating the Saxon word *hōh* – 'spur of land' – as its origin. In 1350 the location is given as Hoo in Launcyngg (Lancing). By the time of Elizabeth I it's called Howcourt. The same descriptive origin is associated with a number of other places in the county, including **Hoes Farm**, Petworth – le Howe in 1541 – and **Hoeland Farm**, Bury, mentioned as Hawland and Howland around the same period.

Hogs Hill. Recorded in 1795 as both Hogs hill and Hogs hole, the place gets its name from the family of William le Hog, registered in the Worth area in 1327.

Holbeanwood. Almost 1,000 years ago, somewhere in this vicinity there was once an old hollow tree used by locals as a boundary mark. We know this because a Saxon document dated 1018 records the spot as holanbeames mearce – 'the hollow-beam mark'. Centuries later in 1479 the same name reappears as Holbem Wode. Holbeanwood lies in an area long associated with iron foundries, but its own industrial history stretches back to the time of the Roman occupation, when it was the site of a bloomery, a primitive type of furnace producing iron that could be forged into tools and small weapons.

Holbrook. See HOLLYBROOKS.

Holford. This is 'the ford in the hollow' – Holeford in 1296 – referring to

a crossing-place on one of the tributary streams of the Ouse.

Holland's Barn. Recorded as Holonde in 1327, it shares its name with the country of Holland, both indicating low-lying land (Netherlands simply means 'lower lands'). The same description applies to **Hollands Coppice**, Forest Row, which is 'wood called Hollandes' in 1598; but **Holland Wood**, Petworth, was originally land attached to a hall, since we find it referred to as Hallands in 1548.

Hollgrove Wood. The original meaning of this name – 'grove within a hollow' – describes the location exactly. It's recorded as Holegraue in 1327.

Hollingrove. Here the first element is derived from the Saxon word *holegn* or holly-tree, giving us a 14th century spelling of Holyngrove for the place.

Hollington. The 1086 Domesday Book notes it as Holintune and Horintone. Between then and 1390 it's variously recorded as Holintuna, Hulingetone and Holyngton. Scholars think it originated as a Saxon tribal name indicating the *tūn* or farmstead of a group of early settlers known as the Holingas, 'the dwellers in the hollow'. Interestingly, Hollington is recorded in 1262 as the vill or holding of St Rumbold. The medieval parish church is actually dedicated to St Leonard, but there may have been an earlier building with a different dedication, unless the vill belonged to RUMBOLDSWHYKE some distance away.

Hollist Common. In 1296 this was the home of Alice de Holhurst, whose name tells us she lived 'near the wood in the hollow'. Three centuries later in 1583 the place is recorded as Hollystes or Hollyste Land.

Hollybrooks Copse. It's spelled Holebrok at the end of the 13th century, suggesting the site in those days was a boggy hollow. **Holbrook** near Horsham shares the same origin and old spelling, though it's recorded rather later, in 1504.

Hollycombe. A cartulary, or monastic register-book, of the 14th century notes this place as 'Holecumbe subtus marl. de la linche' – the hollow in the valley below the linch or boundary ridge. It's situated in a small hollow, as is **Hodcombe** at Eastdean, which is spelled Holcombe as late as 1824 and clearly has an identical derivation.

Holmbush. Holmbush – 'the hollybush' – is one of the seven 'forests' of Sussex, all that remain of the great Saxon oakwoods that once covered the entire Weald. In fact oak was once so plenteous that even until comparatively recently it was still known in the county as 'Sussex weed'.

Holmdale. The Saxon description for the holly-tree, *holegn*, developed by the Middle Ages to *holin* or *holm* – a word still used throughout Sussex to mean the holly, though elsewhere in the country it more generally refers to the evergreen oak, or ilex. Holmdale is so spelled as early as 1279, and describes a dale or valley marked by a particular holly-tree.

The similarly named **Holmesdale** near Fletching appears as Holmes Dales in 1691, taking its identity from the family of William de Holme (1296). This surname, meaning 'dweller by the holly', is likewise connected with **Holmhill**, Chithurst (Godefridus ate Holme, 1296); while **Holmsted Place** at Cuckfield stands on the site of a 'holm stead' or holly-tree place, recorded as Holmstede in 1379.

Holmhill, Holmsted. See HOLM-DALE.

Holt. Holt is a word that looks exactly the same to us as it did to the South Saxons. Even its meaning is unchanged – it's simply 'thicket of trees'. During the Middle Ages it gave rise to the descriptive surname atte Holte – 'dweller by the thicket' – that we find associated with **The Holt** at Pyecombe, and **Holt Farm**, Clapham - this is called the Holte next Passyng (Patching) in 1322. **Holt Bottom** on the Downs at Jevington is similarly referred to as the Holt in 1516, while **South Holt Farm**, Compton, marks a thicket south of the parish, described between 1279 and 1303 as Suholte, Holte Comptone, and Suttholte *juxta* Cumpton.

Holtye. Holeteye, Holetye (1279) and Holetegh (1332) tell us this was once the site of a tye or enclosure near a hollow. From Saxon *tēag*, tye has passed into the local dialect as a description of a large open field such as a common.

Holywell. The place is now in danger of being engulfed by the southward spread of Eastbourne, but at the beginning of the 14th century when its name is noted as Holy-welle, there was very little here apart from a spring of clear water bubbling up from the turf just below an ancient burial mound on the cliffs. Why 'holy' isn't known, but as the Saxon word was *hālig*, a deriva-tion of *hǣl* meaning 'omen', perhaps the spring was an early sort of wish-ing well.

Holywych. The first element of this name has less to do with 'holy' than with 'hollow' – it's recorded as Holewyche in 1229, Hollewych and Holwych in 1555. Not until the clos-ing years of the Tudor period do we find it rather charmingly given as Hollywitch. It means 'the wych-elm in the hollow', a reference to the def-inite hollow in which Holywych Farm at Hartfield lies. Incidentally, the wych-elm doesn't get its name from witches but from a Saxon word meaning pliant, describing its flexi-ble branches.

Homestall. In the early Stuart period (1613) the spelling is Hom-stall, and has its origins in the old word *hāmsteall* indicating a dwelling or abode.

Homestreet. Between 1485, when it appeared as Holmestreke, and the present day, this name has under-gone a total change of meaning. Research suggests its medieval derivation *holm streke* should be interpreted as 'the strip of land by the holm or holly-tree'. Streak or strake is a dialect word quite com-mon in Sussex field-names, a devel-opment of *strēac* meaning 'stripe'.

Home Wood. Noted as Homwode in 1296, this was initially a term for woodland lying close to a manor or similar estate, in contrast to the Out or Outer Wood. **Homewood** at Wal-dron appears as la Hamoda (a con-traction of Hamwoda) in the 12th century. **Home Wood**, Worth – Homwude in 1244 – may have belonged to the manor of Burleigh Arches. And late 14th century **Homewood House** at Bolney, called Holmewoods in 1558, was earlier connected with the family of Simon atte Homwode registered in the area in 1296.

Honer. Some 1,300 years ago a Saxon document records Honer in its full original form as holan horan fleot, 'the hollow bank creek', a ref-erence to what's now known as Pagham Rife. Although we have no later records to chart its develop-ment, it's easy to see how the name has been honed down over the cen-turies to its present form.

Honey Bridge. This is noted as Hol-ney Bridge in the mid Tudor period. Before that it was Hony in 1332, and earlier still in 1290, Holenye. It lies in what originally must have been marshy land bordering the Adur, so its derivation is very probably *holan ēg*, describing an island of firm ground marked by a dip or hollow.

Honeypools, Honeycrock. See HON-EYWICK WOOD.

Honeywick Wood. In earlier times, before the advent of sugar cane and sugar beet, honey was the only available sweetener for food and drink, so it's not surprising to come across at least one place name refer-ring to a honey 'wick' or farm where hives were kept. The place was originally the home of Walter de Honewyke or Hunewyk, whose family name appears in the parish records of Chiddingly between 1285 and 1327. By 1580 the place itself is mentioned as Honywyke. **Honeypools Farm**, Shipley, has a less easy name to translate. It was actually first called Honeypots, having been Hunypoute in 1308, Honypottes in 1549, and Honypooles otherwise Honeypottes in 1576. Scholars have suggested its origin may well be found in the old Sussex expression 'a regular honeypot lane' describing one ankle-deep in mud. On the other hand, **Honeycrock** at Hailsham – mentioned as Honey Crocks in 1829 – is almost certainly a reference to honey pots as such.

Hooe. The Domesday Book spells it Hov. Throughout the Middle Ages it's Ho or Hoo. And in 1611 it's called Hoo *alias* Howe. The name comes directly from *hōh*, a Saxon word meaning 'spur of land' describing Hooe's location on a ridge above the marshes of Hooe Level draining into Norman's Bay.

Hook Green. Called Hokegrene in 1547, the year of Henry VIII's death, the place acquired its name from the family of Letitia atte Hoke, natives of Wadhurst recorded in the parish in 1296. Their surname, informing us they lived 'by the hook of land', came from the Saxon word *hōc*, the source of 20 or so other Sussex place names, ranging from **Hook Barn**, Balcombe (atte Hoche 1332, Hooke 1592) to **Hook Wood**, Warbleton (le Hoc 1202).

Hope. This isn't our modern 'hope' but Saxon *hop*, a word once used to describe a small enclosed valley. **Hope Farm** at Beckley acquired its present spelling by 1262, while Hope Farm, Rudgwick, followed it as la Hope just under 100 years after. **Hophouse Farm**, Catsfield, is called Hopeland in 1401, being land owned by the family of John atte Hope registered here later the same century. In 1543 it reappears as Hopelandgate, and is subsequently recorded as Hoophowse in 1609.

Horam. There's no doubt about the meaning of this name because we find it documented around the year AD 950 as Horham, the unflattering Saxon description for a dirty settlement. Probably it was noted for the muddy condition of its site, made worse in bad weather by overflowing streams in its vicinity. During the period when the Wealden iron industry was at its most productive Horam was a major centre, with at least eight blast furnaces and five power forges, plus the sites of seven primitive forges called bloomeries, all lying within a four-mile radius of the village.

Horleigh Green. Like HORAM, Horleigh Green lies in an area where there are several streams, so we can hazard a guess that the same muddy conditions applied in wet weather to give it the name of *horh lēah* – 'the dirty clearing'. Between 1288 and 1332 the spelling is Horleye, Horle and Horlegh.

Hornbrook. During the 13th century this was the family home of William le Fullere de Hornyngebrok – 'the fuller of Horningbrook' – giving us the place name at that date. It seems to have originated in Saxon times as *Horninga brōc*, describing an area of marshy land owned by a tribal group called the Horningas, 'the dwellers on the horn or spit of land'. Hornbrook Farm lies in the parish of Horsham which began its history as a swine pasture belonging to Washington, referred to in a Saxon charter as horninga dene – 'the pasture of the Horningas'. It seems likely then that both Hornbrook and Horsham were once part of the same tribal territory.

Horn Combe. See HORNS CROSS.

Horney Common. The common, together with the hatch-gate that used to lead to it, are recorded as le Herney common and Herneygate in 1564, Hornay Common in 1613, and Horny gate in 1658. Etymologists think it's a name derived from *hyrne hæg*, the Saxon description for a hedged enclosure lying in a corner of land.

Horns Cross. In 1271 this was the home of Roger de Horne, whose surname means 'dweller by the spit of land'. We find the same word used to describe the site of **Horn Combe**, West Hoathly – 'the horn-shaped valley' – recorded as Hornecumbe in 1279. And **The Horns**, a low hill jutting into the Pevensey Marshes, appears as Orne in the 1086 Domesday Book, and Horne two centuries later.

Horns Hill. Scholars conclude that the early forms noted for this name – Hornesele (1327) and Hornesell (1370) originated as *Hornes hyll*, the hill owned by a settler called Horn. Unusually, the personal name here is Anglo-Scandinavian rather than Saxon.

Horsebear. From *hors bær*, the name is descriptive of a woodland pasture used to graze horses. In 1279 the spelling is given as Horsebere.

Horsebridge. For much of its early history this hamlet on the banks of the Cuckmere was called Hurstbridge – 'the bridge by the hurst or wooded hill'. It's found as Herstbregge in 1279. Then in the Tudor period it changed slightly to Horstbridge (1553), and later still lost its middle *t* completely to give us the modern form of the name. The same sort of change has happened with HORSELUNGES.

Horse Eye. Horse Eye is part of the flat tidal marshlands called the Pevensey Levels intersected by a network of streams, with here and there areas of higher, firmer ground that became the sites of early settlements. The Saxons called these islands *ēg*, a word responsible for the common name-ending -ey or -eye. Horse Eye was where they kept their horses corralled. A document of AD 947 refers to it as 'to horsiges gemæro' – 'to the boundary of the horse island'. In the 12th century its name is spelled Horsia, with subsequent variants of Horsie, Horsye and Horseye. We also find it called Nordhorseya – 'North' to avoid confusion with **Horsey** a few miles south at Eastbourne, which was the site of another 'horse island' recorded as Horsea about 1054, Horsie in 1198.

Horselunges. This is what's known as a manorial name, one that's identified by the name of the lord of the manor – HERSTMONCEUX and HURST-PIERPOINT are other examples. Horselunges began its history early on in the 14th century as Hurstlyngever, when the estate of Hurst – 'the wooded hill' – was owned by the French-descended family of de Lyngyver or Lyngevre. By 1459 the name had been contracted a little to Horselinger, but then a century later we find it referred to more fully as Herstlongever *alias* Herstlonger *alias* Horselunger. As an interesting footnote, in 1318 Agnes, wife of William de Lyngyver, released the estate to Philip de Herst, whose surname tells us he was a native of the place.

Horsey. See HORSE EYE.

Horsham. This fast-expanding market town first came into existence as a swine pasture belonging to Washington about a dozen miles south. By the start of the 10th century the land was being used to provide grazing for horses from the *hām* or settlement that by now had developed on the site. It's first recorded as Horsham in AD 947, and its spelling has remained pretty constant through the intervening centuries – although interestingly, we find it called Horsom in 1657, a pronunciation still in use until recently. It was once quaintly thought the name referred to the notorious condition of the town's streets, with mud so deep it reached the horses' hams or flanks. A different belief claimed Horsham was so called because many of the horseshoes for the army of Edward I were made in local smithies. Horsham is the only place in the country apart from Oxford to have a CARFAX.

Horsley. The name hasn't altered at all since first recorded in 1273, when it described a cleared area of woodland where horses were put to graze.

Horsmanshoad. Early on in the Stuart period (1610) it appears as Horsemanhodes, confirming that the second element is the old East Sussex word hothe/hoath, meaning heath. The whole name could therefore be 'heathland used by horsemen'. Alternatively it could share much the same origin as **Horseman's Wood**, Westfield, which gets its name from the family of Robert Horsman registered in that parish early in the 14th century.

Horsted Keynes. Until shortly after the Norman Conquest the settlement here was known simply as Horsted – 'the horse place' – referring originally to a place where horses were kept for breeding. Interestingly, around 1190 the spelling is Horsestud. After the Normans came to power Saxon manors such as this found themselves with new masters, hence the affix Keynes, acquired from William de Cahainges (his family came from a place called Cahagnes, between Vire and Bayeux) who was presented with Horsted by William de Warenne, son-in-law of the Conqueror, for the role he played at the Battle of Hastings. In its Anglicised form, the name is recorded as Kaynes or Keynes from the 13th century onward, appearing in 1721 as Hosted Caines, as it's still pronounced. Two centuries or so earlier it's mentioned as Grethorsted – 'Great' in contrast to **Little Horsted**, which was also once a 'horse place', listed as Horstede in 1086, Lytel Horstede in 1355.

Houghton. It's one of Sussex's oldest surviving place names, dating as far back as AD 683, which is only two centuries after the Romans departed. A Saxon charter of that year refers to it as Hohtun – 'the farmstead on the spur of land' – describing the settlement's location on a headland jutting into the Arun valley. During the Middle Ages the spelling varies between Hottone (1210), Houton (1263) and Hoghton (1327). **Houghton Green** near Playden has an entirely different origin. It gets its name from a family called Horton who were living in the neighbourhood in 1683 – in fact there's still a Horton field here to preserve the old spelling.

Houndean Bottom. The early forms Hundeden (1230) and Houndedene (1347) suggest the derivation is either *hunda dene* – hounds' valley, or *Hundan dene* – the valley of an early settler nicknamed 'the hound'. By the late 15th century the spelling had developed to Hunden and Hownden, with 'Bottom' added much later to describe Houndean's location at the foot of the Downs.

Hounster Lane. This isn't an easy name to interpret. It's recorded as Hundestorr in 1296, Houndestorre just over a decade later, then as Houndhurst *alias* Hounster in 1620. We can't say with any certainty whether the original 'hound's tor' was an outcrop of the local sandstone resembling a dog in some way, or whether it was associated otherwise with dogs. On the other hand it could have been Hunda's tor, belonging to an early settler nicknamed 'the hound'.

Hove. Until comparatively recently it used to be considered quite the thing to pronounce it 'Hoove' – in fact it's spelled that way in 1675. Rather earlier, we find it recorded as Houve (1302) which is the same as the medieval word for a hood or similar covering. Etymologists think the name originally applied to a small dwelling – a hovel – maybe one like COLDHARBOUR that was used as a wayside shelter for travellers. Nowadays Hove is better noted, of course, for its comfortable seaside hotels and classical architecture set amid attractive parks and well-kept public gardens.

Howbourne. This could well be 'the crooked stream' or *wōh burna*, a name given initially to the winding tributary of the Ouse on which Howbourne Farm, near Hadlow Down, is situated. It's called Owborne *alias* Woborne in 1591, Houghborne in 1701.

Howick. Its early appearance as Howicke (1327) tells us this name is derived from *hōh wīc*, 'the farm by the spur of land', perfectly describing Howick Farm's situation at the foot of a hill near Lodsworth. The county's other Howick Farm, in a similar location close to Rudgwick, is recorded as Howich in 1166, Howyke in 1279.

Hucksteep Wood. Late in the 12th century this is given as Huckelstepe. A century or so later it's Hocstepe, Hukstep and Houcstepe. The derivation is most likely *Hucceles stēap*, describing an area of sloping ground owned by an early settler named Huccel.

Huddlestone. Somewhere in the vicinity of Huddlestone Farm here on the Selsey peninsula there may still lie buried some trace of the early medieval farmstead on which it stands. More than 600 years ago, in 1373, it's named as Houdeleston, 'Hūdel's *tūn* or farmstead', becoming Huddleston by the late Tudor period.

Huggetts Furnace. Site of an early bloomery or furnace where iron was being worked as far back as the 1st century AD, the place acquired its present name from the family of John Hoget, registered in the Hadlow Down area in 1333. Their surname, also found spelled Hugot, Hughet, Hogelot, Hughelot, is nothing to do with 'hog-herd' but began as a diminutive of the old French personal name Hue, itself derived from the even older German Hugo. It's connected with a number of other places – all in the eastern half of Sussex – including **Huggett's Wood**, Danehill, **Hugletts Stream**, Wartling, and **Huggett's Pit**, Maresfield, which is given as Haglotts in 1546, and must be near a now lost Hogeletisbrige (bridge) recorded here in 1333.

Hundredsteddle. Hundredsteddle Farm, at Somerley on the Selsey peninsula, marks the site of the meeting place of the old Manhood Hundred whose boundary lay at MANHOOD END. 'Steddle' is the Sussex dialect word for the wooden framework on which cornstacks used to be built, probably used in this case to refer to a wood-framed building where the meetings actually took place.

Hungerhill Barn. Hungerhulle, recorded in 1359, tells us this is a type of name typically referring to barren land, so we can only suppose that poor soil on the cultivated slopes of the hill produced equally poor crops, leading inevitably to hunger. Similarly, **Hungry Hatch** near Fletching is Hungerhacche in 1386 and Hungers Hatch in 1691, describing a hatch-gate leading on to an unproductive field plot.

Hungry Hatch. See HUNGERHILL BARN.

Hunston. A name that hasn't changed much since it was recorded in the 1086 Domesday Book as Hunestan – 'Hūna's stone'. Local research has failed to identify any particular feature that might account for the description, so it probably refers to an old stone or rock used in Saxon times as a boundary mark. The spelling has been Hunston since 1332.

Hunter's Burgh. This is one of a number of similarly-named barrow sites on the South Downs, Burgh developing from the Saxon word *beorg*, meaning hill or (burial) mound. The long barrow here is recorded as Hunters burg in the days of Elizabeth I, though why 'Hunter' we don't know. It may have the same association as **Huntsland Farm** on the Selsey peninsula, where the land was originally owned by the family of John le Hunte (1369). His surname – it meant 'the huntsman' – also occurs in connection with **Huntland** near Worth (Robert le Hunte 1296), while **Hunter's Hall**, Wadhurst, stands on land called Hunters in 1652.

Hurchington. Etymologists suggest the Saxon whose *tūn* or farmstead produced this name was called Hererīc. In fact the same personal name has been found in connection with the now lost place of Herchingeland, recorded in 1215 not far away at Folkington, although we can't say for sure that it was the property of the same individual. From *Hererīcing tūn*, Hurchington developed to Herchinton, Irchinton and Herchington, forms all recorded in the latter half of the 13th century.

Hurst Green. It appears as Hurst in 1342, Herst grene in 1574. The name (from *hyrst*, a wooded hill) is one of the most common elements in English place names, reflecting the rural landscape of earlier times. By itself it accounts for a dozen or more different places in Sussex alone, some of them owing their origin to the associated medieval surname atte Hurst – **Hurstland** and **Hurstwood** fall into this category. Others, like HERSTMONCEUX and HURSTPIERPOINT, are distinguished by the addition of feudal Norman-French affixes; while one or two more, such as **Hurston Place** at Storrington (the *tūn* or farmstead by the hurst) have disguised their roots only a little. Most of these hursts were woods from which timber was taken to feed the furnaces of the Sussex iron industry.

Hurstland, Hurston. See HURST GREEN.

Hurstpierpoint. The Saxon manor of Hurst, spelled Herst in the Domesday Book, passed into Norman hands after the Conquest. Its new lord was Robert de Pierpoint, a native of Pierrepont – 'the stone bridge' – near Falaise, who held the manor as a tenant of William de Warenne, administrator of the Rape of Lewes. The Pierpoint family connection was to prove a long one, lasting until 1431, but its most enduring memorial is the place name, recorded first as Herst Perepunt in 1279. After this date its development tends to ring the changes, sometimes reversed (Parpoynthurst 1439), sometimes contracted (Harstpount 1520), and occasionally charmingly expanded (Hurst upon ye point 1722). In 1261 it's also mentioned as Westherst, to distinguish it from HERSTMONCEUX which conversely appears as Esthurst in 1302.

Hurstwood. See HURST GREEN.

Hurtis Hill. This once formed part of the family property of John le Hurt of Mayfield, who's registered in the parish in 1327. Instead of becoming Hurt's Hill, the place name has kept its medieval genitive form, an abbreviation of 'Hurt, his hill'. His surname means 'the hart or stag', either from resemblance or association.

Hydneye. As a rule, names ending -ey or -eye have the Saxon word *ēg*, 'island', as their derivation. Sometimes the sites were true islands, others were areas of firm ground surrounded by marsh, and a few like Hydneye, near Willingdon, were places watered by streams. This particular 'island' belonged to an early settler called Hidda, and it's recorded as Hidenye in 1200, Hydenye in 1332.

Hyffold. See IDEHURST.

Hylters. At some time this little place, perched on the side of a valley above the course of an old Roman road, was known intriguingly as 'the hiding place'. Why it should be called so is a mystery. Maybe its location provided a safe refuge, or maybe it was simply hidden out of the way. The Saxon origin of the name is *heolstor*. By 1310 this had developed to la Hulstre. During the Tudor period it's mentioned as land called Hulsters at Bowehill, a reference to Bow Hill just to the south. And in 1676 it's given as Hulters *alias* Hilters. Incidentally, our modern word 'holster', a pistol case, has the same derivation.

$$\bullet \ \bullet \ \mathbf{I} \ \bullet \ \bullet$$

Ibrook Wood. Ibroke and Ybrok, recorded during the 14th century, suggest the name comes from $\bar{\imath}w$ $br\bar{o}c$ – 'marshy ground by the yew-tree' – a somewhat puzzling description since this is an area of well-drained land standing some 400 ft above sea level.

Icklesham. Originally the site was a *hamm* or watermeadow belonging to a South Saxon called Icel who chose to make his home here beside the river Brede. In the 8th century AD, when Icklesham was part of lands granted by royal charter to the Bishop of Selsey, we find the name given as Ikelesham and Icoleshamme. During the period 1195-1494 it appears as Ickelesham, Ykelesham and Ikeleshamme. And in 1603 it's Icklesome, which is how it was still being pronounced until recently.

Idehurst. In Saxon days Idehurst was one of several swine pastures belonging to Felpham. A document of AD 953 refers to it as Hidhirst – 'the wooded hill on the hide of land'. In 1262 the name is given as Hydehurst. Neighbouring **Hyffold** began as a fold or enclosure on the same hide (a measure of land of roughly 120 acres), being recorded as Hydefold in 1296 and Hyfold a couple of decades later.

Iden. Where this pretty village now lies, above a bend of the eastern Rother, was once a *denn* or swine pasture bordered by yew-trees, a spot known in Saxon times as $\bar{\imath}w$ *denn*. The Domesday Book lists the name as Idene in 1086, a spelling that remained virtually unchanged for the next 500 years, varying only as Idenne.

Ide's Common. It gets its name from the family of Sarah Ide of Upwaltham, recorded in the area in 1666.

Similarly, **Ide's Barn**, East Dean, has associations with the family of Daniel Ide, registered slightly earlier in 1641. Their surname derives from an old word meaning 'labour'.

Idolsfold. Etymologists think the spelling Islesfold, given for this farm at Kirdford in documents of the 14th century, comes originally from *Īseles falod* – 'Īsel's fold or enclosure'. Possibly this was the same early settler owning a watermeadow at the site of the now extinct parish of Ilsham, at Climping to the south, recorded as Iselesham in 1321. **Isling Bridge**, on a tributary of the Arun close to Idolsfold, was originally 'Īsel's land' – interestingly, despite its modern spelling, locally the name is still pronounced 'Island'.

Ifield. The old village of Ifield has shared the same fate as THREE BRIDGES and been swallowed up by the development of Crawley New Town. Ironically, in 1279 we find the situation reversed and Crawley mentioned as Croule *juxta* (near) Hyfeld, proving it to be the less important of the two settlements at that time. Ifield began its history as an area of unenclosed land distinguished by some prominent yew-tree, hence *īw feld*. The Domesday Book refers to it as Ifelt. In 1210 it's Yfeld, becoming Iffelde by 1432. Ivel, recorded for the place in 1726, quaintly preserves the old pronunciation.

Ifold. It's been Ifold ever since the late 13th century, taking its name from *ēg falod* – 'the island enclosure' – referring to an area of firm ground in a boggy area by the stream just here. Late in the reign of Elizabeth I the place is mentioned as Ifold *alias* Ivold, giving us the dialect pronunciation of the day.

Iford. Iford lies at the foot of the Downs in an area known as The Brooks where numerous streams flow into the Ouse, though we don't know which one was the original 'yew-tree ford' that first gave the village its name. In the 1086 Domesday Book it's called Niworde, but slightly later records from the Norman period give it more accurately as Yford and Iforde.

Inchreed. Hyntesrede (1296), Inchered (1304) and Encheredd (1332) point to an early medieval origin of *Intes rede*, describing a plot of cleared (literally 'ridded') land belonging to a settler named Inte. *Rede* or *rude* is an element often found in Sussex place names, significantly in areas of ancient woodland that were opened up for habitation.

Ingrams Green. The place was originally connected with a family called Ingelram, recorded in the neighbouring parish of Trotton between 1296 and 1332. **Ingram's Farm**, Bexhill, is mentioned as Ingrams in 1655, possibly taking its name from the family of Ingelrannus who owned land at Barnhouse in the 12th century. And **Ingram's Farm**, Ninfield, was the home of Andrew and Robert Ingeram in 1265. These places all share the same surname, derived from the old German *Ingelramnus*, meaning 'Angle raven' – the Angles were a German warrior people who settled in Northumbria, Mercia and East Anglia.

Inholmes. It's called Inhomes in 1593, The Inholmes in 1659, stemming from Saxon *innam*, a piece of land taken in or enclosed (the word actually comes from *nam*, meaning 'seizure'). This derivation is also the origin of **Inholms Copse**, Stedham, **Inholms Farm**, Plumpton, **Inholms Gill**, Lower Beeding, and **Inholms Wood**, Cuckfield, which is recorded as Homehill *alias* Inholmes in 1591, Inums in 1606.

Inlands. An Anglo-Norman estate was usually divided into two parts – the 'inland', occupied by the lord and his household, and the 'utland' or 'outland' given to his servants in return for rent and service, or as a means of support for those who weren't freemen. Inlands once formed part of such an estate, being noted as Inlonde in 1199.

Innerwyke. Innerwyke Manor and its neighbour **Outer Wick Farm**, near Felpham, originally formed one property, referred to as Wyke in 1623 and Weeke in 1640. Four centuries earlier the place had been the home of William de Wik, whose name – meaning 'of the farm' – came from Saxon *wīc*.

Iping. In early Saxon times this was the territory of a tribal group distinguished as the Ipingas, the people of a leader called Ipa. The Domesday Book gives the name as Epinges, and during the 13th century it develops from Ipinges to Iping and Yping. **Iping Bridge**, spanning the western Rother, is described as pontem de Ipynge in 1398. Along with the changes to its spelling the pronunciation of the place name has likewise altered, from short-vowelled 'Ipping' to modern 'Eye-ping'. The tribal leader Ipa – or another Saxon of the

same name – owned land south of here at Chichester, where a now lost Ipthorne – 'Ipa's thornbush' – is recorded between 1291 and 1428.

Iridge. Somewhere in the vicinity of Iridge Place, near Salehurst, stands a ridge of land once identified from some prominent yew-tree as 'the yew ridge'. In 1248 the spot is called Yrugge. In 1316 it's Iwrugge.

Iron River. The most likely explanation for the naming of this tributary of the Ouse is the rusty brown chalybeate deposit it leaves on its banks.

Isenhurst. It's hard to credit that the rolling Wealden landscape of Sussex was ever an industrial 'Black Country', its ancient oak forests denuded to feed the fires of countless furnaces. The iron industry reached its height during the 16th and 17th centuries, but its roots went back much earlier, as names like Isenhurst attest. The place lies in an old iron-smelting area, and the first documented references to it date from the second half of the 13th century when it's recorded as Hysenherst and Isenherst – 'the iron wood'.

Isfield. Isefeld, noted in 1215, suggests the village developed on the site of open land belonging to an early settler called Īsa. We come across the same personal name associated with the now lost place of Iscombe – 'Īsa's combe or valley' – near Forest Row. Interestingly, a marriage register of 1711 gives Isfield as Isvill, which is more or less how the name is still locally pronounced.

Isle of Thorns. In the time of Elizabeth I the name appeared as Ile of

Thornesgill, suggesting the gill or dip where thornbushes grew formed a little island of firm ground surrounded by well-watered land. A century later, in 1658, it was referred to more briefly as Ile of Thornes.

Isling Bridge. See IDOLSFOLD.

Itchenor, East and **West.** There's no longer an East Itchenor as such (it's become an extinct parish) but its neighbour West Itchenor is still very much on the map, a popular waterside village lying on Chichester Harbour. This area was one of the first to be colonised by the invading South Saxons, so it's hardly surprising that Itchenor's recorded history dates back over 13 centuries to the year AD 683, when it's referred to as Iccanore – 'Icca's shore' – a stretch of shoreline to which one of those Saxons, Icca, had laid claim. In the Domesday Book it appeared as Icenore. A hundred years later, in 1187, it was Ichenore, becoming Westichenor in 1243. During the period of the Napoleonic Wars the village was the site of a large shipyard and dock, which has added to its character.

Itchingfield. This was originally an area of open land belonging to a tribal group known as the Eccingas, whose main settlement was at ETCH-INGHAM. Surprisingly for this type of place name, Itchingfield isn't recorded before the 13th century when its spelling is Ecchingefeld and Hechingfeld. In 1541 it appears rather charmingly in the Horsham parish register as Hedge and Fylde. Forty years afterwards it's Itchingfeeld.

Itford. Itford Farm lies beside the Ouse below the steep slope of Itford Hill, and marks an ancient crossing place owned by a Saxon called Itta. For some reason the Domesday Book records the place as Litelforde, but its name is more accurately given as Iteford in 1242.

Iwood. The late medieval forms Ewode (1317) and Iwode (1332) tell us this particular name began its history as $\bar{\imath}w$ $wudu$, 'the wood of yew-trees'. Apart from the many superstitions once surrounding it, the yew was (and still is) greatly valued for its elasticity, making it an ideal wood for longbows.

Jarvis Brook. Mentioned in the time of Elizabeth I as Jervys Brook, this little village took its name from the family of Priscilla Jervis, whom we know were natives of nearby Mayfield. **Jarvis Lane**, Steyning, is similarly associated with the family of Robert Gerveys (1340), appearing as

Gervases in 1403; while **Jarvis's Wood**, Hellingly, owes its name to the family of Thomas Gervays (1331). The surname in its various forms developed from an old Germanic forename meaning 'spear servant'.

Jay's Copse. The land originally belonged to the family of Thomas le Jay, registered in the parish of Lurgashall in 1312. Also found spelled le Jai or le Gai, their surname came from French *gai*, the jay-bird – maybe used initially as a nickname for somebody who chattered a lot, or else behaved in a mischievous manner. We find it elsewhere associated with **Jay's Furze**, East Lavington, **Jay's Farm**, Bignor, and **Jay's Farm**, Wisborough Green, which is called Jeyeslond in 1369.

Jenkins Green. It's Jenkins' Green in 1720, deriving its name from the family of Thomas Jenkin of Hailsham, recorded just eight years earlier. **Jenkin's Wood** at East Grinstead is likewise connected with an Elizabethan landowner, Thomas Jenkins, listed in 1592. Although it's now regarded as thoroughly Welsh, the surname is actually Flemish in origin, a diminutive form of John.

Jenners. Jenner is a surname we come across frequently in Sussex and Kent. It began as an old French occupational description of an engineer or architect, and was the family name of Ann Jenner, resident in the Slaugham area early in the 18th century, from whom Jenners gets its identity. Similarly, **Jenner's Lane** at Plumpton was originally the property of a family recorded during the Tudor period as Jenner, Gynner and Jayner.

Jevington. The group of South Saxons who first settled this downland village chose to build their *tūn* or farmstead in the shadow of a Neolithic causewayed camp close by on **Combe Hill**, in an area of ancient burial mounds. They've been identified as the people of a leader called Geofa, and the name they gave to their home, *Geofinga tūn*, had developed to Govingetona by 1189, appearing as Gevyngton 100 years later, and becoming Jevingtone by the end of the 15th century.

Jolesfield. Records are limited for this particular place name and that of its neighbour, **Jolesfield Common**, but research has uncovered a William Jolle registered in the county in 1327, so it's possible, though not provable, that a member of the same family owned land hereabouts, giving us a medieval origin of *Jolles felde*.

Jordans. There are two Jordans in Sussex, at Ardingly and Willingdon, and two **Jordan's Farms**, at West Chiltington and Udimore, as well as a **Jordan's Barn** at Lindfield. Each of them bears the name of a previous owner whose surname can be traced back to the Knights Crusaders and their custom of bringing back water from the river Jordan with which to baptise their children, resulting in this being used initially as a font-name.

Jugg's Road. 'Jug' was the nickname once commonly given to the fishermen of Brighton, and it was along this road – formerly known as Juggs borstal – that the fishwives travelled into Lewes to sell their husbands' catch. It's interesting to note that 'borstal' or 'bostal' is still used in Sussex as a dialect term for the steep paths on the slopes of the South Downs.

Juniper Wood. Noted as Jennepers late in the Tudor period (1591), the place probably gets its name from a family we find recorded as Jenefer in 1554, and Junipher in 1691. Their surname had its roots in the Anglo-Norman Guinevere (a version of the old Welsh personal name Gwenhwyvar) which developed to modern Jennifer.

Jupp's Barn. The place acquired its identity from the family of Richard Juppe of Steyning, who appear in records of 1670. Their surname is an occupational one, denoting somebody who made jupes, the long woollen garment worn like a close-fitting coat by men during the Middle Ages. Variously spelled Juppe, Jupe or Joup, we also find it associated with **Juppsland** near Billingshurst and **Juppshill Shaw**, Cuckfield.

Jury's Gap. The name of this section of the coastline just east of Camber may share a similar kind of origin with **Jury Farm** at Donnington, recorded as le Jury in 1535. Research suggests it had some connection with Richard ate Jewerye (1327), who came from the Jewry, or Jewish quarter, five miles away in Chichester.

· · K · ·

Kemp Town. Now a district of Brighton, Kemp Town derived its name from Thomas Read Kemp, responsible for developing the area during the 1830s, when Brighton was still enjoying something of a boom in the afterglow of its Regency years. The family name Kemp – from Saxon *cempa*, 'warrior' – is also to be associated with **Kemp's Hill**, Easebourne, **Kemp's Wood**, Sedlescombe, and **Kemps Farm**, Balcombe.

Kent Ditch. Recorded as Kent Dyke in 1610, this stream forms part of the boundary between Kent and Sussex before flowing into the eastern Rother. In 1526 we find it mentioned by its earlier name as 'the stream called Mylryve' – the mill rill or brooklet. **Kent Water**, a continuing stretch of the county boundary, appears in 1288 described as 'water called the Bloke', a name most likely derived from *blāc*, meaning pale or white, with reference to the clarity of the stream.

Ketley. Its spelling hasn't altered

since 1548, the year we first find this name on record. Etymologists think it probably has its roots in medieval *kete legh*, describing a cleared area of woodland scavenged by kites, carrion-eating birds of the hawk family.

Keyfox. See KEYMER.

Keymer. In Saxon times one of the tributary streams hereabouts formed a pool that seems to have been used as a watering-place for cattle, giving us *cȳ mere* or 'cow's pool' as an origin for the village's name. The Domesday Book (1086) calls it Chemere, but just a few years afterwards it appears more accurately as Kymere. In 1677 we find it mentioned as Keymer *alias* Kymer, giving us some idea of the pronunciation. A similar history is shared by **Keynor Farm** on the Selsey peninsula, close to the site of a 'kine bank' or *cȳna ōra* where cattle grazed above the flat marshland. Around 1187 the name is noted as Kyenora. Six centuries later, in 1784, it's given as both Kenor and Keynor. **Keyfox** may well have been another place where cattle or kine were kept, but the precise meaning of its name escapes definition. It first appears as Keyfaux, before being recorded as 'land called Keyfoxer' in 1504.

Keynor. See KEYMER.

Keysford Bridge. As late as 1724 this was spelled Carsford, a development of Caseford noted in the reign of Elizabeth I, and Carlesford recorded much earlier in 1332. The original bridge spanned a tributary of the Ouse at a spot where a medieval owner, identified as Carle, gave his name to a crossing-place

just here. It's more than likely the same individual owned a water-meadow not very far away at CALEM.

Kidbrooke. Kidbrooke Park near Forest Row occupies a site that was once an area of marshy ground where the rapacious scavenging birds called kites were frequently seen. We can trace the development of the name through the forms Kete-brokebregge (1438), Kydbroke Gate (1531) and Kid Brooke Gill (1658), with 'bridge' and 'gill' showing the topography of the place, close to the river Medway and the Weir Wood reservoir.

Kilsham. Now preserved as a farm name, Kilsham began its history as *Cylles hamm*, a watermeadow owned by an early settler, Cylli, bordering a loop of the western Rother just south of Petworth. It was recorded as Kelesham around the year 1280, and continued to be spelled Kelsham till quite recently.

King's Barn, Kingsfield Wood. See KINGSFOLD.

Kingsfold. It's difficult to know whether the numerous King- place names in Sussex applied originally to royal estates, or to property owned by families bearing the surname King – first given to 'king's men' attached to a royal household, or else bestowed as a nickname for a boastful swaggerer or somebody playing the role of king in medieval pageants. **Kingsfold** near Billingshurst (Kingesfolde 1279) and **Kingsfold** near Warnham (Kyngesfold 1296) both probably fall into the former category, as most likely does **Kingsfield Wood**, Maresfield (Kyngesfelde 1333). And we know for certain that **King's Barn**, Upper Beeding (Kingesberne 1281) was part of an estate recorded as Grangie Regis – 'the King's grange' – at the start of the 13th century. **King's Well** (Kyngiswell 1553) takes its name from a spring rising in the Wartling area on land called Kyngwellelond in 1307; while **Kingswood** at Findon is given as Kingeswode in 1330, and **King Wood**, Brede, as Kyngwode in 1362. On the other hand, **King's Wood** at Worth got its identity from the family of John le Kyng, recorded in the parish in 1296.

Kingsham. Traditionally the capital of the South Saxon kings, Kingsham lies near Donnington on the historic Selsey peninsula. First mentioned as Kingesham in AD 930, it was the *hām* or manor of Æthelwalch (c.660-686) and his queen, Ebba, a Christian princess of the Hwicce dynasty whose kingdom covered the south-west midlands. Incredibly, it was to retain its importance as a royal residence for almost 1,000 years, only relinquishing it in the reign of Elizabeth I. **Kingsham Wood**, on the Hammer Stream north of Chithurst, marks the site of a *hamm* or water-meadow forming part of another royal estate, being noted as Kyngesham in 1285.

Kingsley Hill. The modern name is a development of Kentchley Hill, which is how it was spelled in 1840. Long before this, in 1296 we find it documented as Kentesle, a develop-ment of the original *Centes lēah*, denoting a cleared area of land owned by an early settler called Cent.

Kingstanding. 'Standing' is the Sus-sex dialect term for a market stall, but it's probably not used in that sense here. Given the site's well-wooded location near Buxted, it's more likely the word referred to a place where huntsmen stood to shoot game, though whether they were royalty or commoners can be judged by the fact that first mention of the name – as Kings Standing – appeared in 1658, the period of Cromwell's Commonwealth.

Kingston. This was a royal estate as long ago as the 9th century AD, when a law enacted during the reign of Alfred the Great required that any person breaking a solemn pledge should suffer 40 days' imprison-ment at the cyninges tun – the king's manor. By 1312 its name had devel-oped to Kyngeston, and just a few years afterwards we find it referred to as Kingston *juxta* Arrundell, to distinguish it from KINGSTON-BY-SEA and KINGSTON NEAR LEWES.

Kingston-by-Sea. Like KINGSTON in the previous entry, this popular coastal resort began its history as a Saxon royal manor or *cyninges tūn*, noted in the Domesday Book (1086) as Chingestune. For centuries it bore the alternative name **Kingston Bowsey**, a feudal relic of its connec-tion with Robert de Busci, a native of Boucé in Normandy who was granted the manor in 1199. Thus we find it called Kyngeston Bouci in 1315, Kyngeston Bowsey in 1608, and Kingston Bowsey *alias* Kingston by Sea in 1730. The place remained in the possession of the Bowsey fam-ily until the 18th century, an associa-tion lasting more than 500 years.

Kingston near Lewes. First recorded in 1340 as Kyngeston *juxta* Lewes, the village has a slightly later history than the county's other two Kingstons, though like them it was founded as a royal manor. It lies a couple of miles south-west of Lewes, where two royal mints were established in the first half of the 10th century by King Æthelstan, so possibly we can date its foundation to the same period.

King's Well, Kingswood. See KINGS-FOLD.

Kipson. The name is shared by Kipson Bank and Kipson House, near Hunston on the Selsey peninsula, preserving the site of a *tūn* or farmstead owned by a Saxon called Cyppi. By 1187 the name had developed to Keppeston, becoming Kipeston in 1279, and Kepston in 1554.

Kirdford. Just to the south of the parish church we can still find the same ford that gave this pleasant village its name in Saxon times. In those days it was part of the possessions of a lady we know was called Cyneðrȳð – clearly a person of some importance because she also owned property at the now lost place of Kynridehurst nearby. In 1228 Kirdford appears in records as Kinredeforde. Later the same century it's Cunredford, becoming Kurdeford by 1438. And 200 years after, the name is noted as Kirdford *alias* Kirford, which is how it's still pronounced.

Kitchenham. There are two Kitchenhams in Sussex, both in the eastern half of the county and sharing their history with a further three places in roughly the same area. The oldest is **Kitchenham** near Peasmarsh, marking the site of a Saxon *hām* or settlement owned by an individual called Cycci. The Domesday Book refers to it as Checehā, an abbreviated form of Checeham. In 1279 the spelling is Checenham or Kecenham, developing to Kechenham by 1327. **Kitchenham Farm**, near Ninfield, owes its name to Cycci's *hamm* or watermeadow on the banks of the river Ashbourne, recorded as Cechehamme in 1332, Kechenham in 1396. And close to the Peasmarsh Kitchenham we find **Kitchenour**, where the same Saxon owned a bank of land identified originally as *Cyccen ōra*. In the latter half of the 12th century the place is noted as Chekenora and Kechenore, subsequently becoming Kychenor in 1477. A second *hām* or settlement associated with Cycci lay on the site of **Kitchingham**, recorded as Kechenham in 1242. By 1606 the spelling had altered to Kechingham, but a map of 1823 still referred to it as Kitchenhams, so it looks as though the modern name has kept the slightly older spelling to avoid confusion with the other two Kitchenhams.

Kitchenour, Kitchingham. See KITCHENHAM.

Kithurst, Kitford Bridge. See KITS BRIDGE.

Kits Bridge. The old bridge, spanning a stream that eventually flows into the river Mole across the Surrey border, seems to have been a regular haunt of kites, because in 1332 we find it described as Ketebrugge – 'the kite bridge'. The name was still

Kyte bridge in 1600. Most likely the stream was used as an open sewer, a common practice in medieval times. A ford where these birds gathered is probably the origin of **Kitford Bridge**, for the same insalubrious reasons; while **Kithurst** lies on the site of a wooded hill where they were seen in numbers, being recorded as Kitehurst about the year 1340. At one time the red kite was a common scavenger, even on the streets of cities, but with the improvement of sanitation, loss of suitable habitat (especially the old oakwoods where they nested) and persecution by man, they're now in danger of extinction in this country.

Knelle. See KNOWLE.

Knepp Castle. Its site on a knoll above the river Adur accounts for its name – *cnæpp* or 'hill-top', recorded as Knepp about 1145. The original castle was built here late in the 11th century by William de Braose, who as administrator of the Rape (county division) of Bramber was also responsible for building Bramber Castle. All that remains now is a fragment of the Norman keep surrounded by the outline of its moat beside the Worthing-Horsham road close to West Grinstead. The present Knepp Castle, built in 1809 in a separate location nearby, was destroyed by fire in 1904, but rebuilt in exact detail soon afterwards. Below the castle lies **Kneppmill Pond**, fed by the Adur – in fact one of the early names for the river was aqua de Cneppe – 'Knepp Water'.

Knightsbridge. It seems odd to find a little place in deepest Sussex sharing its name with the area of Lon-

don's most fashionable department stores. But Knightsbridge Farm, lying beside the Cuckmere north of Hellingly, has its foundations buried in the 13th century, when the site was recorded as Knytebrigge. To begin with, 'knight' (from Saxon *cniht*) simply described a young man or servant, but later in the Saxon period it developed to mean a feudal tenant retained by his lord or king to serve him as a mounted warrior. We don't know whether the original bridge here was part of the possessions of such a retainer, or whether it had some connection with the Knights of St John of Jerusalem who owned extensive property in Sussex between the 12th and 14th centuries.

Knockbridge. In 1306 the spelling is given as Knockebregge. The fact that Knockbridge stands on a small hill close to a bridge spanning the Pannel Sewer, tells us all we need to know about the origin of its name, because *knocke* is simply the medieval word for a hillock or hump.

Knole House, Knowlands Wood. See KNOWLE.

Knowle. Saxons used their word *cnoll* to describe a rounded hill-top, thus giving us modern 'knoll'. In time the description produced the medieval family name atte Knolle, and together they're found associated with a dozen or so places in Sussex. **Knole House**, Fulking, shows a variant spelling, as does **Knelle** (Cnelle c.1190, Knolle 1288) and **Knell House**, Goring (la Cnelle 1230), while **Knowlands Wood**, Barcombe, appears as la Cnollond in 1247.

Knucker Hole. According to old Sussex legend, this pool at Lyminster was once the home of a water-monster that terrorised the neighbourhood, devouring the inhabitants along with their cattle and sheep. In despair, the king offered to give the hand of his daughter in marriage to any man who would slay the creature. Eventually the deed was accomplished – some versions of the legend give the credit to St George – and the 'Tombstone of the Slayer', a coffin slab in Lyminster church, is still pointed out to visitors. The fact that the Saxon term for a water-monster was *nicor*, the origin of Knucker's name, gives us some idea how far back into folk tradition the theme of this well-worn story must reach.

· · L · ·

Lackenhurst. Now a farm at Shipley, the site is recorded as Lotenherst in 1285, suggesting its name originated as *Lottan hyrst* or 'Lotta's hurst', a wooded hill belonging to an early settler. In 1511 the spelling was still virtually unchanged as Lotenhurst; but by 1823 it had altered to Lackners, giving us a good idea of its pronunciation in Regency days.

Lagness. Lagness has the distinction of being one of the county's oldest Saxon names, first found in a charter of AD 680 which refers to it as langan ersc – 'the long stubble-field'. In 1179 it reappears as Langeners, and a century after as Lagenersh, then in 1650 it's noted as Langnersh *alias* Lagmarsh.

Lampham. It means 'the water-meadow of the lambs', conjuring up the image of a medieval springtime day here on the Pevensey Levels. Originally *lamba hamm*, the spelling appears as Lampeham, Lempham and Lambham during the period 1252-1335, and Lamppam in 1486. We know there was once a pool where lambs came to drink somewhere in the neighbourhood of **Lampool** near Maresfield, because the place is recorded as Lampol in 1295, later becoming Lampole Green in the time of Elizabeth I.

Lampool. See LAMPHAM.

Lancasters. This was formerly the home of a Stuart gentleman, John Lancaster, residing in the parish of Henfield in 1641. In the same year we find a Richard Lancaster living at **Lancaster's Farm**, a few miles away near West Grinstead. They must surely have belonged to the same family, and could probably trace their name to an ancestor in service to John, Duke of Lancaster – Shakespeare's John of Gaunt – who was granted the Ashdown Forest by his father Edward III in 1372, renaming it Lancaster Great Park.

Lancing. Lancing stands with its face to the sea and its back to the Downs, between Worthing and the mouth of the river Adur. The river, the sea and the Downs made the site a particularly attractive one for settlement by the South Saxons, presenting both a good defensive position and a base from which to launch incursions inland along the river valley. The area's strategic importance to them can be gauged by the fact that it was the tribal territory of Wlencing, son of Ælla, the warrior-chief who spearheaded the Saxon invasion of Sussex in AD 477. While Wlencing's elder brother Cissa established himself at CHICHESTER, the Wlencingas, Wlencing's followers, settled here beside the Adur. In 1086 the Domesday Book records the place name as Lancinges. By 1361 it's Lanceyng. One of the town's most distinguished features is its public school, **Lancing College**, founded in 1848 by the Revd Nathaniel Woodard, curate of New Shoreham, and transferred to its present site on a spur of the Downs above the river ten years later in 1858.

Landhurst. In 1579 the name was Lanehurst, describing the hurst or wood that still lies at the end of the lane here. But its history goes back much earlier than that, because we find the place mentioned as Lanherst in 1107, proving, incredibly, that its topography has hardly

changed at all during 900 or so years.

Landport. The site (now a farm) lies close to Lewes, which provides a clue that the name's second element isn't 'port' as in harbour, but as in portal or gateway. The word came originally from Latin *porta* or gate, and during the Middle Ages developed to mean a town with market privileges, whose leading citizen was called the portreeve. In an associated sense it also described the market-place itself, which is how Landport – 'the long market' – must have got its origin. The earliest reference to it is Lamporte in 1296. We can see the development of its spelling rather more clearly in connection with the now lost place of Lamport near Eastbourne, listed as Langport in 1107, Lamport in 1567, and Landport in 1838.

Langham, Langhurst. See LANGLEY.

Langley. Mentioned as Langele in the mid 15th century, the name means 'the long clearing', a description shared by **Langley Green**, which appears as Langeley slightly earlier in 1296. Similarly, both **Langham** and **Langham Wood** mean 'the long *hamm* or watermeadow', having been spelled in their modern form since 1332 and 1420 respectively. **Langhurst** near Horsham (Langeherst 1327), **Langhurst** at Rusper (Langenhurst 1327) and **Langhurst Farm**, Kirdford (Langehurst 1230) all mark the sites of long wood-covered hills, as does **Lankhurst** at Framfield (Langherst 1296) and **High Lankhurst**, Ore (Langeherst 1296); while **Langridge** – 'the long ridge' – is Langeregge in 1327.

Langney. The village of Langney that has given its name to **Langney Point** on the coast above Eastbourne, came into existence as a long strip of ground standing high and dry in the Pevensey marshes. The Saxons who first settled this area referred to it as *langan ēg*, 'the long island'. In 1086 the Domesday Book listed it as Langelie, and in 1121 it was Langania, reappearing more recognisably as Langeney in 1396.

Langridge, Lankhurst. See LANGLEY.

Lashmar Wood. Its name was adopted from a family called Lashmer whom we come across in 1630 recorded in Wivelsfield parish register. As Lechemere or Lachemer, their surname had already made an earlier appearance in the 14th century, when it was affixed to a *hale* or corner of land on the site of **Lashmars Hall**, not far away at Henfield. In 1327 the place was mentioned as Lechemereshale. Some 50 years later it was Lachmereshalle, from which the modern name has developed.

Laughton. Many centuries ago there was little of importance here at Laughton apart from a simple plot of garden where an anonymous Saxon worked on his vegetable patch while his wife no doubt tended to her herbs and other medicinal plants. They knew the spot as a *lēactūn* – literally 'plant farm' – a description that eventually was entered in the Domesday Book as Lestone before being recorded more accurately as Lectone in 1291. A generation later the spelling had altered to Leghton, becoming Laughton by 1338. The Saxon word for plant, *lēac*,

is clearly the forerunner of our modern 'leek', but in its original sense it's also preserved in words such as charlock, garlic and hemlock.

Lavant, East and **Mid.** Located just to the north of Chichester, these two hamlets lie beside the river Lavant to which they owe their identity. The original South Saxon *tūn* established on the site took the description 'the farmstead by the Lavant', appearing in the Domesday Book (1086) as Lovintune. By 1314 this had been shortened to Lovente, showing obvious confusion with the river-name itself. Early in the Norman period the settlement split into three small sites which were to become the nuclei of two later parishes, one comprising East and West Lavant (Estlovehunte 1288, Westlouinton 1239), the other Middle or Mid Lavant (Mydloventon 1264). West Lavant no longer exists, but research suggests it was probably situated where **Lavant House** now stands.

Lavant, River. In 1225 we find this west Sussex river described as la Lovente. Scholars believe its name originated as a British river-name, that had in turn come from the Romans and their word *labor*, meaning 'to glide'. Interestingly enough, in the western half of the county 'lavant' is a term used of streams that are liable to flood without warning – in fact there's an old dialect expression, 'How it did rain! It ran down the street in a lavant!'

Lavington, East and **West.** For centuries East Lavington bore the alternative description **Woolavington**, a name still preserved by Woolavington Down just south of the hamlet.

The place came into existence as the main *tūn* or farmstead of a Saxon tribal group called the Lāfingas – Lāfa's people – who had a second settlement a mile or so away at BARLAVINGTON. Just as Barlavington was where they grew their barley, so Woolavington seems to have been where they reared their sheep, giving us *wull Lāfinga tūn* – 'the wool farm of the Lāfingas' – as an origin of the place name. The Norman Domesday Book notes it simply as Levitone, but it's recorded more fully in 1243 as Wullavyton, and just under a century after that as Wollavyngton. The site was already identified by its alternative name as early as 1288, when we find it mentioned as Estleuyngton – 'East' to avoid confusion with its daughter settlement at West Lavington a short distance away near Midhurst.

Laybrook, Lay Green. See LEIGH.

Lea Bridge. The place appears in 1288 as 'the bridge of the Leghe', describing its original location in a medieval *legh* or cleared area of woodland bordering the river Cuckmere. Similarly, **Leeford**, recorded as Leyford around the year 1220, marks the site of a clearing near a fording-place across the river Brede.

Lealands. See LEAMLAND.

Leamland. Lemelond (1437) suggests to etymologists the name is probably a contracted derivation of *læge hamm land* – 'the fallow watermeadow'. *Læge*, used of fallow land left untilled or unsowed for a time, has given us one of the alternative meanings of our modern 'lea', found in connection with **Lealands** near

Hellingly, which appears as Layland in the time of Elizabeth I. However **Lealands**, Rotherfield, and **Lea Farm**, Rye Foreign, both take their names from the old word *lēah* – 'clearing' – discussed more thoroughly under LEIGH.

Leap Cross. First mention of this name appears half way through the 15th century, spelled Lepecrouche. Then much later, in 1724, it's Lip Cross. *Crouche* is simply the medieval word for a cross, and in this case probably applied to a wayside preaching cross or boundary mark. The place may well share the same site as Lepeland, recorded with Lepecrouche about 1450 before reappearing as Lype land in 1557. Both names are most likely a reference to the 13th century custom of 'lep', allowing tenants to pasture their cattle on common land between Michaelmas (September 29th) and Martinmas (November 11th).

Leasam. Leasam House, a handsome Georgian building dating from around 1800, is all that now preserves from extinction the name of an early settlement here at Rye Foreign. It originated as *Līefeles hamm*, the watermeadow of a Saxon called Līefel, appearing as Leueleshamme in 1288. Late in the Tudor period it reappeared with the alternative spellings Levelysham *alias* Levesham, which by 1675 had been contracted to Lesam.

Leeford. See LEA BRIDGE.

Leggatt Hill. The neighbourhood is recorded as Ligit heath in 1740, taking its identity from the family of ate

Lidgate or atte Lythegate, registered in the parish of Lodsworth in 1312 and 1363. Their surname tells us they or their predecessors lived 'by the swing-gate' or *hlidgeat*.

Legsheath. Spelled Leggesheath in 1564, the site was formerly the property of a family named Leggy – maybe used as a nickname meaning 'long legs'. Geoffrey, Robert and Walter Leggy were all registered locally in 1296.

Leigh. Leigh, together with its variant forms Lea, Lee, Ley, Lay, and corresponding ending -ly, -ley and -lie, are practically all derived from the Saxon word *lēah*, one of the most common elements in place names. It's found especially in areas of ancient forest like the Weald, and simply indicated a glade originally; but later in the Saxon period it acquired the meaning of 'cleared area of woodland', and then 'cultivated clearing', and finally 'meadow' or lea. In records compiled during the Middle Ages, when more and more families had settled in these areas, we come across the surname atte Lee and its variants de Legh or de la Lye, meaning 'dweller in/near the clearing'. These occur, for example, in connection with **Lay Green**, **Lee Bank** and **Leigh Manor**, while places like **Laybrook Farm** (Leybrok 1268) and **Leythorn Park** (Laythorn 1527) are distinguished by having the additional description 'marshy ground' and 'thornbush' attached.

Leithe, The. In 1296 it was the family home of Thomas and Richard de la Lythe, whose surname, describing them living 'by the *hlið* or slope', is a reference to the geography of the site.

Lentridge. See LINTHURST.

Lewes. A thousand years of history have shaped Lewes into one of the most attractive little county towns in England, a place where past and present meet in a happy relationship appreciated by all who visit it. It takes its name from *hlǣw*, the Saxon word for the 'low' or hill above the Ouse on which it first developed, recorded as Lǣwe in AD 961. Then as the early settlement expanded to cover the surrounding downland slopes, the name acquired a plural form, appearing as Lǣwes in 1065 and Lewes in 1086. By 1675 its spelling was Lewis – still the correct pronunciation. The town's importance to the Saxons is demonstrated by the fact that King Æthelstan (925-940) established two mints here which continued issuing silver coinage right up until the Norman Conquest. It's probable there was a Saxon stronghold on Brackmount, one of the two mounds protecting **Lewes Castle** – built by the Conqueror's son-in-law, William de Warenne, at the end of the 11th century to guard the river valley. According to local tradition, the town actually received its name in honour of a god of the British, Llwy, Lord of Light, whose symbol was fire and whose worship involved sacrificial burning. The tradition is maintained to a less extreme degree by the town celebrations on November 5th, marked by some of the biggest bonfire and torchlight processions in the country.

Leythorn Park. See LEIGH.

Lickfold. Noted as Lykfoldbrigge in 1347, the hamlet lies on a tributary of the western Rother, marking the site of an early 'plant fold' or *lēac falod* – an enclosed piece of land where plants were cultivated. Perhaps like LAUGHTON the description applied originally to a garden. Nearby is **Lickfold Farm**, listed in 1332 as the home of Walter de Lykfold. Another early garden enclosure has likewise given its name to **Lickfold** at Wiggenholt, recorded as Lekefold in 1509.

Lidham Hill. The hill preserves the name of an ancient *hamm* or watermeadow that once lay below it on the banks of the river Brede. Known as *Hlȳdan hamm*, 'Hlȳda's meadow', after the Saxon settler who'd owned it originally, the site was noted as Ledhamme in 1288, and Lideham around 50 years later.

Lidsey. Lying only a couple of miles inland from Bognor Regis, Lidsey can date its history equally as far back as its better-known neighbour. In fact its name has altered very little in the 13 centuries since AD 683, when it was documented as Lydesige, the 'island' of a Saxon called Hlȳdi who'd chosen to make his home here on a piece of land rising above the surrounding stream-fed marshes. Almost 300 years later in 957 the site was recorded as Hlidesya, becoming Lydeseya in 1229, then Lidesey in 1412.

Limbo Farm. See POLING.

Limbourne. Now a farm name, Limbourne began as a description originally applying to the Rother tributary on which it lies. In 1288 it's

called Lymburn – 'the stream overhung with lime-trees' – reappearing as Lymeborn in 1528. **Lime Park**, close to Herstmonceux, likewise owes its name to a lime-tree or linden. Known until recently as **Lime Cross**, the place was first recorded in 1335 as Lym, taking its identity from a prominent tree in the vicinity. By 1466 it seems to have acquired a wayside or preaching cross, because it's mentioned in that year as Lymecrouche, becoming Lyme Cross in 1517.

Limden, River. It bears the old identity of the eastern ROTHER, known to the Saxons as the Limen, a name derived from the ancient British word *lem*, meaning 'elm-tree'. The Limden flows into the dean or valley of its parent river, and appears as Limundene in 1180, Lumendenne in 1332. Its wide estuary is now covered by the Romney marshes.

Lime Barnetts. See LIMEKILN BOTTOM.

Limekiln Bottom. This is one of the 'bottoms' of the south Downs, and as its name implies, was once used as the site of a kiln where calcium carbonate or limestone was calcined by prolonged heating to produce lime. In 1640 we find it described as Limekill hurst – 'kill' showing the old dialect pronunciation of the word. Those working in such kilns were known as lime-burners, one of whom had his home at **Lime Barnetts** near Ripe. The modern name is a corruption of Lymberneres, recorded in 1365, and its Tudor form Lymeburners (1562).

Lime Park. See LIMBOURNE.

Limmer Pond. We don't know why Limmer Pond, at Aldingbourne, was originally known as 'the leap pool', but that's how it's recorded in AD 680, as hleap mere. Probably the explanation must be that it was small enough for deer to leap across. By 1471 the name had contracted slightly to Lypmere, a form from which Limmer later developed, with the unnecessary duplication of 'Pool' added for good measure.

Limney. In 1453 the spelling is Lymney. A century earlier the place had been the home of Gilbert ate Lymene (1327) whose surname informs us he lived near the Lymene or Limen – the old name for the eastern ROTHER, on one of whose tributary streams Limney lies.

Linch. This is the Saxon word *hlinc*, denoting a bank or rise, applied here as a description of the original site. In the Domesday Book of 1086 the name's spelled Lince, reappearing as Linche or Lynche in the mid 13th century. **Linch Farm**, Bepton, lies on a similar rise, recorded as Linces in 1190 and Lynche in 1387; while **The Links** at Folkington is referred to as 'pasture called the Linckes' in 1625. The word eventually came to mean a stretch of flat or undulating ground by the seashore, hence 'golf-links'.

Linchmere. The mere or pool is probably Linchmere Marsh, to the south of the parish church. It was originally the property of a South Saxon named Wlenca, whom some scholars suggest could have been a tribal member of the Wlencingas based at LANCING. Welenchemere or Lenchemere, recorded for the place in 1428, was a development of the Norman spelling, Wlenchemere. Towards the close of the Tudor period (1582) it was listed as Wyllynchemere *alias* Lynchmere.

Lindfield. Lindfield is one of the best-kept villages in Sussex – a fact officially recognised by the number of times it's been awarded this much-coveted title. Even the Saxons seem to have found it an attractive place because they named it *linda feld* – 'linden land' – describing an unenclosed area where lindens or lime-trees were growing. It's mentioned in a charter of AD 765 as Lindefeldia. During the 13th and 14th centuries the manor of Lindfield was owned by the Bardolf family, hence we find its name recorded as Lyndefeld Bardolf in 1327. In 1675 it appears in a fresh disguise as Lindfeild Dorchter, the affix being a corruption of 'd'arches', which in turn was a scribal contraction of 'archiepiscopi' – telling us the place had at some time been part of the diocese of an archbishop.

Linfold. Linfold Farm, just south of Kirdford, lies on the site of an early *līn falod*, a fold or enclosure where flax was grown. It's recorded as Linfaud in 1239, Limfold just over 30 years later. Unlike FLEXHAM PARK, where the main element of the name is *fleax*, here we have *līn*, the forerunner of 'lint' and also 'linen' – the cloth that's made from flax. Incidentally, the linnet bird gets its name from the same source, because of its habit of feeding on flax-seed.

Links, The. See LINCH.

Linthurst. Lindhurst, recorded for

the place in 1220, suggests it was the site of a wooded hill where lindens or lime-trees once grew. Towards the end of the same century the spelling is given as Lentenhurst. Similarly, **Lentridge Farm** near Plumpton lies on a ridge of land where lindens were a dominant feature. It's called Lynderugge in 1327, and Lentrege or Lynteridge around 1500.

Lion's Bank. It's simply Liones in the year 1400, taking its name from the family of Richard de Leons, registered in the parish of Wiston around 1260, whose Norman ancestors originated from Lyons la Forêt, in Eure. As a forename, Leon or Lyon was fairly common in this country during the Middle Ages, especially for Jews. In its variant forms as a surname – Lyon, de Lyuns, de Lyons – we find it associated with **Lions Farm**, Ifield, **Lyons Clump**, Warnham, **Lyons Farm**, Sompting, and **Lions Green**, Waldron, which appears as Lyons Grene in 1679.

Lippering. The place name is the only memorial we have of a minor tribe of South Saxons called the Liperingas, or Lipera's people, whose territory was just here on the history-rich Selsey peninsula. Their little settlement is mentioned as Liperinges around the year 1200, a spelling that hardly changes in the course of the next six centuries, reappearing as Lyprings in 1823. Now even the settlement has gone, and only Lippering Farm remains to save the name from total extinction.

Lisburn. The most feasible suggestion on record is that Lisburn and its neighbour **Londonderry**, first noted

in 1822, were named by an Irish landowner who'd come to live here in the Maresfield area.

Lithersgate Common. The fact that the land just here is fairly steep lends credence to the theory that the name originated as *hliðes geat* – 'the slope's gate' – describing a feature of the place, referred to as Lydesgate in 1296. In 1795 the spelling had contracted to Lizgate, and a generation later it was Lysgate, both forms showing a pronunciation that has persisted up to the present day.

Litlington. The village lies beside the Cuckmere a couple of miles from the sea, surrounded by the slopes of the South Downs and the grass-covered remains of ancient burial mounds. In the Saxon period it was the site of a *tūn* or farmstead owned by a settler called Lȳtela, whose nickname 'the small one' suggests he was of a diminutive stature even for those times. From *Lȳteling tūn*, the place name had developed to Littelington and Litlintone by the end of the 12th century, appearing in its modern form in 1548.

Little Bognor. See BOGNOR REGIS.

Littlegreen. The name explains itself. It's given as Littlegreen in Compton in 1695, referring to its position just north of its larger neighbour.

Littlehampton. Not much survives of the old town on the east bank of the Arun to remind us this was once a busy medieval port, where vessels unloaded stone from the quarries of Caen and sailed out again laden with good English timber. But Littlehampton still keeps up its boating connections, with a popular yachting centre and motor-launch trips up the Arun among the attractions it offers as a lively all-round holiday resort. It began its long history as a Saxon *hāmtūn* or home farm, indicating one that was close to a settlement – maybe the old Romano-British village that had been here before the Saxons invaded. The Domesday Book records the name as Hantone in 1086, and it's still Hampton in 1230. However by 1482 it had acquired its prefix, appearing for the first time as Lyttelhampton, probably to distinguish the port here from that at Southampton further along the coast.

Little Horsted. See HORSTED KEYNES.

Little Park. Called le Lytill Parke in the time of Henry VIII (1539), we come across the place a century and a half earlier mentioned in connection with 'the park of the abbot called le Plashet', which seems to be a reference to PLASHETT PARK some distance away at Ringmer. Since Little Park is close to Battle, this suggests both properties formerly belonged to Battle Abbey. **Littlepark Farm**, Hurstpierpoint, is called Herst Park *alias* Little Herst Park in 1582, preserving the parish's original name; while **Littlepark Farm**, Ifield, is noted simply as Litill Parke in 1549. All three places would have been enclosed areas of private land where deer and other beasts of the chase were hunted for sport.

Littleworth. This isn't the traditional field-name 'little worth', a derogatory reference to poor-quality soil. Instead it's the description of a small 'worth' – an enclosure in the vicinity of a homestead. In 1439 the name is Lytulworth. Just over 40 years later we find it called Lytelworth Parcus, or parkland.

Locksash. See LOXWOOD.

Locks Green. It acquired its name from the family of a John Locke, living in Albourne during the Tudor period. Similarly, **Lock Farm**, Ashurst – noted as Lokkys in 1447 – originally had connections with a Richard Loc, registered in the parish in 1327; while in 1725 **Lock's Farm**, Washington, was the home of Henry Locke and his family. Their surname is derived from *loca*, 'enclosure', a word that developed to medieval *loke* used of a barrier, particularly a river lock.

Lods Bridge. See LODSWORTH.

Lodsworth. The Domesday Book documents the name as Lodesorde, but just under a century later in 1165 it's recorded in a form that virtually duplicates its Saxon original, Lodeswurða, denoting the enclosure of an early settler called Lod. After this the name develops via Loddesworth (1272) to Ludsworth (1627), a pronunciation that's still in use today. The village has given its name to the river Lod, a tributary of the western Rother flowing through it. In turn, the Lod passed its name to **Lods Bridge** not far away, where the family of Richard atte Brugge – 'by the bridge' – were living in 1327. It's given as Lodsbridge in 1795.

Londonderry. See LISBURN.

Loneham. The name of Loneham

House, at Udimore, is the only trace we now have of a little settlement here between the rivers Tillingham and Brede. It marked the site of a watermeadow owned by an early settler called Lāfa – a Saxon personal name we come across elsewhere associated with BARLAVINGTON and EAST LAVINGTON. By 1288 the place name had evolved from *Lāfan hamm* to Louenham. Slightly later records give it as Lounhamford (1381) and Louenhammesbrokes (1403), the latter denoting an area of water-logged land in the vicinity. In 1621 the place is called Stonehams *alias* Lonehams.

Loose. In 1649, the year of Charles I's execution, the name was noted somewhat equivocally as The Loose Farm. In fact it had a perfectly ordinary down-to-earth origin as *hlōse*, the Saxon word for a pigsty. At the start of the 13th century the place (still a farm) was the home of a family variously listed in Battle parish records as de Loses, de Lose and de Lhoses – 'of the sty'.

Lordine Court. See LORDINGTON.

Lordington. The earliest known record of this name appears in 1086 in the Domesday Book, where it's given rather inaccurately as Harditone. Documents of the medieval period list it more reliably as Lerdington (1229) and Lurdyngton (1368), suggesting to etymologists that its origin was almost certainly *Lēofrǣding tūn* – the farmstead of Lēofrǣd. The spelling had hardly changed at all three centuries later in 1684, when it appears as Lordington *alias* Lurdington. We come across the same late Saxon personal name – possibly even the same individual –

associated with **Lordine Court** at Ewhurst. Here Lēofrǣd owned a stretch of the old Roman *strǣt* or road that ran along the valley of the eastern Rother. This time the Domesday Book is less hit-or-miss, recording the place as Lordistret, but the original name, *Lēofrǣding strǣt*, is shown better by the forms Lurdingstrate (1210) and Lourdyngstrete (1342). The modern name has been deliberately gentrified at some time or other by a change of suffix.

Loudwell. Within living memory, there used to be some rural areas still relying for their water supply on the old parish pump, or on wells that were fed by natural springs. The further back in history we go, the more we realise how precious these sources of fresh, clean water must have been, and why so many early settlements are found in their vicinity. The spring on the site of Loudwell Farm, Hadlow Down, obviously bubbled up from the ground in a particularly vigorous fashion because it was known as 'the loud spring' or *lude welle*, a name documented as Ludwelle, Lowdewell and Luddewell in the period 1327-1437. The same description clearly also applied in the case of **Ludwell**, Horsted Keynes, since we find it mentioned as Ludwell Spring as late as 1668; while **Ludwell** at West Hoathly – given as Lidwell in 1823 – was originally the home of Osbert de Ludewelle, living near another 'loud spring'.

Lovehill. It's Love Hyll in 1540, the time of Henry VIII, painting a rosy picture of young Tudor lovers plighting their troth on its slopes. More prosaically however, it's just as likely the place came by its name in the same way as **Lover's Farm** near Chalvington, which was the home of John and Margery Loverd (meaning 'love hard') in 1521. Similarly, **Loves Farm**, Easebourne, was formerly associated with a family called Luffe (1641); and **Loves Farm**, Wisborough Green – called Lovis in 1410 – with Henry Loue or Love, registered in the parish in 1298.

Lovel Barn. This is one of those names smoothed down by centuries of dialect use. Initially it was Lotfeld (1296), denoting an area of unenclosed land divided into strips allotted or apportioned for specific cultivation. But only 20 years afterwards we find the spelling has already altered to Lovelde, a form from which the modern name has evolved. Much the same kind of change has been at work in the case of **Lovell's Farm**, Cuckfield, marking the site of another 'lot field'. It's recorded as Loffeld in 1288, Lofield in 1629, and Lowfield in 1823, so the dialect pronunciation of *f* as *v* has clearly affected the name much later than it did Lovel Barn.

Lowfold. See HARSFOLD.

Loxwood. Lokeswode, recorded for this north Sussex village in 1288, suggests to etymologists a derivation of *Locces wudu*, describing a patch of woodland once owned by an early settler called Locc. Its spelling had changed very little by the Tudor period, being noted as Lowkswode in 1520. We come across the same personal name connected with **Locksash**, where Locc owned an 'earsh' or stubble-field, mentioned as Lokesers around the year

1230, and Lokeshassh in 1307. And Locc's ford crossed a stream in the vicinity of **Luxford Farm**, Crowborough, where its name is given as Lockesford in 1327, Luckesford in 1587. It could well have been someone originating from this place who later passed on their name to **Luxford's Farm** not far away at East Grinstead, because we find a Richard Loggesford living at that site in 1387, and his surname is almost identical in spelling to Luggesford, a form that had been recorded for Luxford itself a century earlier in 1279. Incidentally, Luxford is now a fairly common Sussex-Kent surname.

Luckhurst. The development of Luckhurst shows the not infrequent corruption of final -ers to -hurst in place names. A map of the county issued in 1823 showed it as Luckers Crouch, and in Tudor times it had been Lukkars Croche – the medieval word *crouche* (cross) probably referring to some old boundary or preaching cross hereabouts. Rather earlier we find the place associated with the Mayfield family of Henry Luggere (1296) to whom it clearly owes its original identity.

Ludlay. Here we meet one of the handful of Saxon women who have bequeathed their names to the property they once owned. She was called Lēofgȳð, and had a cleared area of woodland somewhere on this site, hence its original description *Lēofgȳðe lēah*. Between 1287 and 1457 the place name is recorded as Louethelee, Leuythele and Leuedele, forms easier to understand if we remember that medieval *u* represented *v*. By 1530 it had become

Lewdelay, and a decade after that had contracted even further to Ludley.

Ludley. The name may look virtually identical to that of the previous entry, but it has a different history and development, originating as *Loddan lēah*, the woodland clearing of somebody called Lodda. The spelling is Lodelegh in 1296, Loddelegh in 1320. At the start of the 17th century it's found as Ludleys *alias* Ludleys Yeard (yard), reappearing on a map of the county a century later as Ludlow.

Ludwell. See LOUDWELL.

Lulham. See LULLINGTON.

Lullington. A place name that's hardly changed its appearance since Saxon times, it originated as *Lulling tūn*, telling us there was a farmstead here belonging to an early settler called Lulla. In 1192 it's recorded as Lullintun. Four hundred years or so later, in 1608, it's Lullington *alias* Loynton, giving us some idea of its pronunciation. The same personal name reappears in connection with LYMINSTER, and also with **Lulham**, where we find Lulla's *hām* or settlement mentioned as both Lolleham and Lulleham towards the close of the 13th century.

Lumley. It's first identified in a survey of 1786, acquiring its name from the family of Lord Lumley of Stansted.

Lunces Common. Research suggests the site was probably connected at some time with a medieval landowner, Osbert de Luns. It's noted simply as Lunces in 1580.

Lundsford. The earliest forms we have – Lundredisford, recorded around 1220, and Lundresforde, 1296 – point in the direction of *Lundrǣdes ford*, a name originally describing the fording-place of a South Saxon, Lundrǣd, across one of the many tributary streams in this area. In 1308 it's called Lonesford. Towards the end of the same century it reappears as Lunceford. Although there's nothing to prove a definite connection, it's possible a native of Lundsford gave his name to **Lunsford's Cross**, south-east of Ninfield, because we find a John de Lunnesford – 'of Lunnesford' – living there in 1340. The place name first appears in its modern form in the mid-Tudor period.

Lunsford's Cross. See LUNDSFORD.

Lurgashall. With old half-timbered houses overlooking its green, Lurgashall is a picturesque north Sussex village lying below the slopes of Black Down at the head of a wooded valley in which the river Lod rises. The site must have been pleasing even in Saxon days, when it was known as *Lutegāres healh*, taking its name from a corner of land owned by one of the early settlers, Lutegār. The original spelling is reflected in a document of 1224, giving the name as Lutegareshal. Half a century or so later it alters, to Luttegershale, and then in 1529 reappears as Lurgarsale – a form that until recently remained the correct pronunciation.

Luxford. See LOXWOOD.

Lychpole. Every so often we come

across a place name offering tantalising hints of some long forgotten human tragedy. Lychpole Farm, lying at the foot of Lychpole Hill north of Sompting, marks the site of a pool in which it's quite possible a corpse was once discovered centuries ago. The fact that Lychpole is recorded as Licchepol in 1268 and Lychepol in 1296 lends support to this story, because the Saxon word for a corpse or body was *līc* – it survives in our churchyard 'lichgate' where biers were rested. On a slightly less lugubrious note, some scholars consider an alternative origin of the name to be *læce pōl* or 'leech pool' – it's mentioned as Leechpool in 1747. The argument has some credibility, since leeches live in water-holes and the like, and were commonly used as a primitive medical aid, applied to suck blood from infected wounds or to bring down a fever. In fact the old word 'leechcraft' once denoted the art of medicine.

Lydford. This probably has a medieval origin as *lode ford*, 'the track to the ford'. It's spelled as such in 1373, becoming Lidford just under 300 years later in 1636. Interestingly enough, it's still possible to see what may be the actual cart track leading down to a tributary of the Adur.

Lydwyke. There can be no argument about the derivation of this particular name, because a Saxon charter of AD 956 records it clearly enough as hliþwic – literally 'slope farm', describing a small farm standing on the slopes of what was then a swine pasture belonging to the manor of Annington. In 1483 the name

appears as Lytewyke.

Lye Green. This is a variant spelling of LEIGH, a derivation of the Saxon word *lēah* signifying a cleared area of woodland. In fact the name is spelled Leighgreen in 1627. **Lyecommon** shares the same origin – in 1414 it's referred to simply as the Lye.

Lyford. In 1332 it's called Lyghtford, probably a description of the bright, sparkling water of the western Rother flowing over the pebbles of the old ford. The site is now occupied by Lyford Farm, while **Lyford's Bridge** nowadays provides a drier means of crossing the river.

Lyminster. Lyminster has a significant ecclesiastical role to play in the history of Sussex. Lying just south of Arundel, not far from CALCETO PRIORY, it marks the site of a minster or monastery founded by a Saxon Christian named Lulla, being first documented around the year AD 880, as Lullyngmynster. Two centuries later its name appeared in the Domesday Book as Lolinminstre, contracting slightly to Liminstere by 1244. At the start of the 17th century we find it recorded as Limster *alias* Lymister – and 'Limster' remains the correct pronunciation. The place is believed to be identical with the manor of Nonneminstre, held by Earl Roger de Montgomerie for the Norman abbey of Almenêches in 1086. Although the earliest definite reference we have to any religious house here is from a later date, 1263, Nonneminstre is mentioned several times in records of Sussex properties conferred on Almenêches. In fact there's every reason to suppose Lulla's Saxon monastery became a nunnery after its foundation, since Nonneminstre is evidently a derivation of *nunne mynster*, 'the minster of the nuns', and we know that the farm by the Saxon church of St Mary Magdalene occupies the site of a Benedictine nunnery established during the reign of Æthelstan (AD 925-940) and subsequently suppressed by Henry V early in the 15th century.

Lymley. This is almost certainly 'the clearing by the Lymene' – the old name for the eastern ROTHER on whose banks Lymley lies. In the 13th century it would have been called Lymenelegh, developing to Lymlegh in the 16th century, though we have no records that could give us specific dates for these forms.

Lynwick. It's spelled Linnick in 1844, which is how the name is still pronounced, though in its modern form it first appears rather earlier, in 1628. The clue to its origin lies further back still, because in 1279 the place was recorded as Lyndewik, telling us it began its history as *lind wīc* – 'the farm by the lindens or lime-trees'.

Lywood Common. During the 30 year period between 1559 and 1589, the place name is variously recorded as Liode, Lyod, Lyoth and Leyhoth. Its second element is 'hothe' or 'hoath', a word peculiar to East Sussex, once used instead of the more common 'heath'. So here we have not woodland but an area of heathland, originally owned by a family whose surname – meaning 'dweller at the clearing' – shows a similar number of variant spellings, appearing as de la Lehe, atte Legh and ater Leghe between 1271 and 1327.

· · M · ·

Mackerels Common. Although there are no old forms of the name on record, it most likely shares the same origin as **Mackrell's Farm** at Cuckfield, which is known to have been owned by a family registered as Mackerel or Mackril in 1646.

Madehurst. At the northern end of the parish lies a spot known as No Man's Land, mentioned in 1361 as Nonemanneslond. It was here that the district moot or court assembled to hear pleas and dispense justice (hence 'a moot point') and no doubt deliver speeches besides. In fact Madehurst owes its name to these old meetings, because it originated as *mæðel hyrst* – 'the speech wood' – appearing as Medliers in 1188 and Medhurst in 1255 before acquiring its present spelling in 1423.

143

Magham Down. The place was known as Magham as long ago as 1261, being noted thereafter as Mekham (1339) and Megham Downe (1582). The name and site both owe their origin to a South Saxon nicknamed Mæcga – 'the warrior' – who built his *hām* or settlement here on the edge of the marshes near Hailsham. His property extended a few miles north to **Magreed** where an area of land he'd cleared of undergrowth and brushwood was later recorded in 1409 as Magerede.

Magreed. See MAGHAM DOWN.

Maidlands. Maydenlonde, noted in 1326, tells us the first element in this name comes from the Saxon word *mægden*, denoting a maiden or virgin. Here the reference is either to property once given as part of a marriage dowry, or to land that was literally virgin territory, yet to be cultivated. The place was still known as Maydenlands 200 years later in 1527.

Main Down. Rising above the South Downs Way just below South Harting, Main Down probably takes its name from an early settler called Mǣga who'd staked his claim to the *dūn* or hill here. It's noted as Mayndon in 1350.

Malecomb. In the year 1200 the spelling is given as Mailecumbe, suggesting to scholars that it originated as *Mǣglan cumb* – the combe or valley of an individual called Mǣgla, just one of the many Saxons who make no more than a solo appearance in the county's place names.

Males Burgh. This is one of a dozen or so ancient burial mounds in an area of the Downs below West Firle. The second half of its name is from *beorg* or 'barrow', while the first commemorates Godfrey le Merle (1327) who presumably owned the land on which the barrow stands.

Malham. The hamlet is situated on the banks of the Arun, marking the site of a watermeadow once identified by some kind of cross. Maybe it lay near one used as a wayside Calvary, since the Saxon word *mǣl* referred specifically to a rood cross. The earliest record we have of the name is Maleham, noted in 1230. Its modern spelling had already appeared by 1296, but the place is also mentioned in 1353 as Malhammeswode.

Malling Hill. See SOUTH MALLING.

Mallingdown. Noted as Maulyngestone in 1285, Malingstone in 1442, Mallingdown Farm originally derived its name from an old boundary stone belonging to one of the manors of South Malling. Its change of ending from -stone to -down is reflected by neighbouring **Down Street** on the hill-slope here.

Manhood End. The place came by its somewhat ambiguous name because it marked the limit of the Manhood Hundred, whose meeting place was at HUNDREDSTEDDLE. This particular Hundred – one of 67 such county divisions in Sussex – had been a liberty of the Bishop of Chichester, consisting of lands formerly granted by King Cædwalla to St Wilfred in AD 683. In fact Eddi, a companion-disciple of St Wilfred, is traditionally associated with Manhood End and may have built a small chapel here. The original meaning of Manhood seems to have been 'common wood' or *mǣne wudu*, referring to woodland held in common by the community. It's recorded as Manwuda in 1170, la Manwode a century later, and The Manhode in 1610.

Mansbrook Wood. Mannesbroc, listed in the year 1200, is identical to the original Saxon form of this name, describing an area of boggy land owned by somebody called Mann – a personal name that initially meant nothing more than 'man, male person' but later came to signify a servant, vassal or bondman.

Mansers Shaw. It's been identified with a family living in the Battle area during the 13th and 14th centuries, variously documented as Manasseh de Herst, William Fitz Manser of Herst, and Manserus de Scotegny. The name is from Hebrew *Manasseh*, 'one who causes to forget', and was only used by those of the Jewish faith. The family probably originated from nearby Herstmonceux, although Manserus de Scotegny could well have been born at Scotney, just across the Kentish border.

Manxey Level. The Level – part of the flat expanse of Pevensey marshes – preserves the name of a now lost place recorded during the 13th century as Manekesie and Mankeseye. It marked the site of a marsh 'island' originally owned by some early settler called Mannoc, thus giving us *Mannoces ēg* as its derivation. The Level itself is first mentioned as Manxey late in the reign of Elizabeth I.

Maplehurst. See MAPLESDEN.

Maplesden. Mapelesden (c.1190) and Mapelesdenne (1325) prove beyond doubt that the place was once a *denn* or woodland pasture identified by a particular mapletree. Similarly, **Maplehurst** occupies the site of a 'maple-tree wood', its name showing unnecessary duplication as Mapelhurst Wood in 1485. In the case of **Maplehurst Wood** at Ore the process is reversed however, because that place is called simply Mapelherst in 1296.

Marden, North, East, West and **Up.** Up Marden seems to be the oldest of this triangle of hamlets lying close to the Hampshire county border. It's the earliest to be recorded, appearing in a Saxon charter of the year AD 931 as Upmerdon, describing its location 'up above the *mǣre dūn* or boundary hill'. The hill referred to is probably Telegraph Hill. In the Domesday Book of 1086 the name is listed without any prefix as Meredone. East Marden is subsequently mentioned around 1175 as Estmeredun, while a century later we find North Marden abbreviated to Northm'den.

Marehill, Mareland. See MARESFIELD.

Maresfield. Despite appearances, the name of this pretty village near Uckfield has less to do with horses than with pools, especially shallow ones. 'Mare' is the Sussex dialect word responsible – it's a variation of the more common 'mere'. So Maresfield actually means 'open land where there are pools', still a fairly good description of the surrounding

145

area. Originally it was recorded as Meresfeld (1293), but less than half a century afterwards the spelling was already being influenced by the dialect speech of the time, altering it to Maresfeld (1340). The same old Sussex word is also responsible for the names of **Marehill** and its neighbours **Middle** and **West Mare**, as well as **Mareland Farm** at Nuthurst; while **Marlands** near Itchingfield shares the same origin, being recorded as Marelands in 1579.

Mark Cross. There are two places in East Sussex with this name. The first, near Wadhurst, is mentioned as Markecross in 1509; the second, further south, is Mark Crosse in 1580. Their location offers some clue to their meaning – the one lying on the boundaries of Rotherfield, Mayfield and Wadhurst, and the other on the parish boundary of Ripe – because Mark comes from *mearc*, the old Saxon word for a boundary. We find the same term applied to **Mark Dyke**, the great drainage channel that originally acted as a boundary line between the Norman Rapes (county divisions) of Pevensey and Hastings, and nowadays separates the parishes of Pevensey and Wartling. Similarly, **Marker Point** on Thorney Island was once *mearc ōra*, 'the boundary shore', forming part of the border between Sussex and Hampshire. **Markly**, 'the boundary clearing', lies close to the edge of Heathfield parish, being noted as Merkelegh and Markeleye during the 13th century. And **Mark Street**, dividing Maresfield and Fletching, is Markestrete in 1546.

Marland Bridge. For centuries, before the advent of more modern methods, Sussex farmers used the rich chalky clay known as marl to spread on their fields as a natural fertiliser. Marland Bridge owes its name to this practice, because in 1296 it was recorded as Marledelonde, 'the marled land', becoming Marland bridge long afterwards, in 1703. **Marles**, near Rudgwick, lies in an area where deposits of marl were once excavated, mentioned as Littlemarles, Midlemarle and Marlepitfeld in 1455; while **Marlpits** and **Marlpit Shaw** are clearly names that share the same origin. **Marline Wood**, Hollington, lies near a Hyghmarlynggate noted in 1562; **Marling Place**, Wadhurst, marks a site called le Marlyng in 1333; and **Marling Shaw**, Hadlow Down, similarly appears as Marlyng in 1499 – all three being places where marl was readily available.

Marley. The Saxons used several different words for a boundary or border in order to delineate their territorial areas. One was *mearc*, which we find associated with places like MARK CROSS; another was *mǣre*, connected with MARDEN, and also with Marley here at Peasmarsh. The place lies close to the parish boundary, on the site of an old clearing or *lēah* once marking its perimeter, recorded as Merelege in 1275. A different origin, however, is shared by the county's two **Marley Farms** – at Battle and at Brede. They are on what once had been cleared areas of woodland containing pools, hence *mere lēah* as their derivation. Both appear as Merle in the 14th century, and as Marle or Merley the century after.

Marline Wood, Marling, Marlpit.
See MARLAND BRIDGE.

Marlpost Wood. During the Middle Ages the land here was part of the property of the Benedictine nunnery at Rusper. Its name would seem to be a poor reflection on the quality of the nuns' cooking, because it originated as the Latin term *malus repastus*, or 'ill feeding' – in other words, a bad meal! It's first mentioned in 1274, as Maurepast. The following century we find the spelling changing to Malrepast and Marlepast, developing to Marlepost by 1638.

Marringdean. Marringdean Farm, on the edge of Billingshurst parish, occupies an area of old pastureland that once contained what was probably the actual boundary stone. It's recorded as Merehonedene in 1288, a derivation of *mǣre hān denn*, 'the boundary-rock pasture'. In 1618 the name reappears as Maryngedene.

Marsham. It's spelled both Mersham and Meresham at the end of the 13th century, giving us the choice of either *mersc hām* – 'marsh settlement', or *meres hām* – 'pool's settlement' as its origin, both suggesting the site must have been pretty water-logged. Aptly, the name is now preserved by Marsham Sewer, a stream rising at Batchelor's Bump and draining the countryside between Fairlight and Pett. **Marsh Hovel**, at West Chiltington, likewise marks an area of old marshland, called Mershe and le Mersch in 1361. The 'hovel' refers to a shelter of some kind, perhaps like COLDHARBOUR, a wayside shelter. **Marsh Peak** at Elsted lies on a site referred to in 1538 as le Marshe de Elstede, 'peak' probably describing a copse at the fork of two roads here.

Marsh Hovel, Marsh Peak. See MARSHAM.

Martinland. Called Martensland in the time of Elizabeth I, the place gets its name from a family living in the parish of East Hoathly at that period. The surname Martin or Marten – originally adopted in honour of one of the most venerated saints of the Middle Ages, Martin of Tours – remains a common one in Sussex and Kent.

Maudlin. Maudlin occupies the site of a medieval leper hospital, described about 1275 as 'Hospitale Sancte Marie Magdalene de Loddesdoune *juxta* Halnaked' – the Hospital of St Mary Magdalene at Lodsdown near Halnaker. The place had earlier been recorded around the start of the same century as Loddesduna, denoting the down or hill of an early settler, Lod – probably the same Saxon who'd already given his name to LODSWORTH some miles to the north. Maudlin, a contraction of Mary Magdalene, appears as Maudelayn in 1412. In 1823 a map of the county shows it as Maudling.

Maxfield. Mexefeld (1368) and Mexfeld (1535) are early forms of this name suggesting it began as *meox feld*, describing an area of unenclosed land that had been spread with dung to fertilise it. The Saxon word *meox* survives still as 'mixen', a midden or dunghill.

Mayes. Noted in 1352 as Mayeslond, originally it had been the property of William le May, living in the Forest Row area just half a century earlier. His surname, from medieval *may*, 'maid/youth', is also associated with **Mayes** at Waldron, and **Mays**, Selmeston, which appears as le Mase in 1532.

Mayfield. Its popularity with visitors hasn't in any way affected the charm of this attractive Wealden village, overlooking unspoilt countryside from its ridge above the eastern Rother. The original little settlement here developed on open land overgrown with the camomile-scented plant called mayweed, known to the Saxons as *mægða*. In 1086 the Normans recorded *mægða feld* as Megevelle in their Domesday Book. During the medieval period it changed from Megthefeud (1279) to Magefeld (1340) and Maughfeld (1438). Then towards the end of the 16th century it appeared as Mavell *alias* Mayfyld. The village actually owes its origin to St Dunstan (AD 909-988) who, as Archbishop of Canterbury, was responsible for building a palace here, the remains of which are now part of the Convent of the Holy Child Jesus. The simple wooden church he raised to serve the needs of the swineherds living in the surrounding forest is now the site of the parish church of St Dunstan's. As well as being a principal adviser to all the Wessex kings of his time, the saint was also skilled as a blacksmith. Traditionally, he had his own forge in Mayfield – though whether it was here he tweaked the Devil's nose with a pair of red-hot tongs is another matter. Tradition also ascribes the village name itself to 'maiden field', a claim supported by its High Street sign, showing a group of jolly maids.

Maynard's Green. It gets its identity from the Maynards of Mayfield and Rotherfield, a medieval family also responsible for the name of **Maynard's Gate Farm** at Rotherfield, noted simply as Maynards Gate in 1567.

Meads Place. This old site, formerly a farm, has bequeathed its name to **The Meads** district of Eastbourne. Fittingly, it began its history as an enclosed area of parkland known to its earliest residents as *æt þæm edisce*, 'at the enclosure'. By 1196 this description had fused to produce Mades, a form later altering to Medese (1316) before reappearing as Meedes in the mid 16th century.

Medmerry. This attractive place name is first recorded in a Saxon charter of AD 683 as Medemenige, 'the medium island', which etymologists take to be a reference either to its size or to its position in relation to the larger island of Thorney and the smaller one now occupied by the village of Selsey. Like Selsey, Medmerry was never a true island as such, but an area of dry higher ground surrounded by marshland. Its name had contracted to Medmeny by 1296, but then expanded again to Mydmeneye in 1409 before reappearing as Medmery in 1724. Medmerry Farm now marks the original site.

Meeching Court Farm. See NEWHAVEN.

Merrieweathers. See MERRYFIELDS.

Merryfields. Merryfields near Cuckfield (Merifeelds 1606) and Merryfields, Wivelsfield (Meryfeilds 1595) lie on the border of their respective parishes, suggesting their name is a derivation of *mǣre feld*, 'the boundary land'. Alternatively, they may be sites once regarded as particularly attractive, since an old but now obsolete meaning of the word 'merry' signified 'pleasant', as in the phrase Merrie England. **Merrieweathers** at Mayfield acquired its identity from the local family of Gilbert Meryweder (1296) whose surname – actually a nickname for a cheerful, lively fellow – in turn came from a common medieval term for pleasant weather.

Mersham. Mersham lies in an area of ancient marshlands between Hurst Haven and Wallers Haven. A Saxon charter dating to around AD 800 mentions it as mereshamm, 'the watermeadow of the pool', giving us a fair idea of its original site. The name had altered very little by the middle of the 12th century, when it was Meresham.

Merston. The Domesday Book lists the place as Mersitone, but its derivation is more faithfully reflected in 1274 as Mershtone – 'the marsh farmstead'. There are a number of streams in the vicinity, so the land must have been water-logged when the site was originally settled in Saxon times. By the Tudor period, 1569, Mershtone had become altered to Marston.

Methersham. Dialect speech has shaped the spelling of the modern name, because as late as 1617 it appeared as Mardersham, a development of Madreshamme (1288) and the earlier Maderesham (c.1185). These forms point etymologists to a Saxon origin, *Mǣðheres hamm*, denoting the watermeadow

of an early settler called Mǣðhere.

Michelgrove. The place lies in an area of ancient woodlands between the sea and the Downs, on the site of a *micel grāf* or 'great grove' mentioned in 1193 as Muchelegraua, and as Michelgrave in 1320. Early in the 18th century its location is given as Mitchellgrove in Clapham. That old word *micel*, 'great, much', survives still in the thrifty expression 'many a little makes a mickle'.

Michelham. This historic spot began as 'the great watermeadow' or *micel hamm*, bordering a large bend in the river Cuckmere. Medieval documents record it as Mykeleham in 1279, a spelling that changes to Michelham by 1325. It's thought the Saxons had a settlement here before the Norman barons of Pevensey built a hunting lodge on what was to become the setting of **Michelham Priory**, founded as an Augustinian house in 1229 by Gilbert de Aquila, Lord of Pevensey. The priory was dissolved in 1536, but subsequently has been restored and now belongs to the Sussex Archaeological Trust. It's surrounded by some 6½ acres of lovely grounds enclosed within a river moat which is one of the longest in the country.

Mick's Cross. Together with the curiously-named **Mick Mill's Race**, this little place at Lower Beeding was originally connected with the family of Ada Mychel (1296) and John Michel (1327), the 'race' being a channel of water working the millwheel. According to local tradition however, the two places were actually named after Mick Mill, a notorious smuggler who challenged the Devil to a race here, gambling his soul as the prize. Although Mick managed to out-run the Devil and save himself from Hell, he was considered much too wicked for Heaven; and since neither side would take him, so the story goes, the old reprobate became immortal.

Middleham. It's called Middelham in 1248, a name describing its position as the *hām* or settlement that lay on the Downs between one just to the south-west at SOUTHERHAM, and another about a mile north at NORLINGTON.

Middleton-on-Sea. This sandy seaside resort is first mentioned in the Domesday Book (1086) as Middeltone, 'the middle farmstead'. In Saxon days its site would have been a little further inland, so the description probably refers to its location between the settlements of Felpham and Flansham. **Middleton** near Westmeston shares the same history, from its position between its own parish and Streat, appearing as Midelton around the year 1093; and **Middleton Farm**, Chailey, lying between Newick and Lindfield, is mentioned as Middelton in 1288.

Midhurst. A sturdy old market town full of history and character standing at the junction of the A272 and A286, Midhurst must get its identity as 'the middle wood' from its position midway between the South Downs and the wooded hills around Black Down to the north. Records spell the name Middeherst in 1185, Midherst in the 1450s. Its many handsome buildings include two old inns, the Spread Eagle, parts

of which date from the 15th century, and the Angel, where the Pilgrim Fathers are said to have stayed on their way to join the *Mayflower* for passage to New England in 1620. To the west of Market Square is land that once formed part of the 100-odd acres known as the Liberty of St John of Jerusalem, which from the time of Edward II was vested in the Knights Hospitallers, who held jurisdiction over this area.

Midwyn Bridge. See OUSE, RIVER.

Milkhurst Wood. Melkherst and Milkeherst are 13th century forms of this name giving it a Dylan Thomas-sounding origin of 'milk wood'. The most likely explanation is that milch-cows were once pastured on its slopes.

Mill. There are almost 40 different places in Sussex bearing the name Mill or one of its numerous variations. They range from **Millbrook** via **Milland** to **Mill Wood**, and the majority of them clearly mark the sites of either watermills or windmills, some of which are still standing as attractive features of the landscape, memorials to a bygone age.

Milton Street. The downland hamlet of Milton Street lies beside the lane leading to its neighbour **Milton Court Farm**, from which it takes its name. The farm itself occupies the site of an early medieval farmstead recorded as Middelton in 1332, Myddelton *alias* Milton in 1535, a description referring to its position halfway between Wilmington and Lullington on this side of the Cuckmere river. Milton Street is first noted in 1589, as Mylton Strete.

Interestingly, it's thought the old-time 'owlers' or smugglers bringing their contraband up the Cuckmere used an underground tunnel running from here to Wilmington Priory.

Minnis Rock. This feature of Hastings is mentioned as le Menewes in 1500 and Mynnis in 1657. Etymologists take the earlier spelling to be a clerical error for le Menennes, a name they derive from *menesse*, 'jointly-owned property', suggesting Minnis Rock was originally in the common ownership of the burghers of Hastings.

Minsted. Mintestede, recorded in 1169, tells us here was a place where mint could be found growing in profusion. The village lies in a well-watered area close to the western Rother, so its soil would have provided a suitably moist habitat for this aromatic plant. During the Tudor period the place name was spelled Mensteds and Mynsted.

Miswell Wood. Somewhere in this vicinity a spring bubbling out from a mossy bank identified the site as 'the moss spring' or *mēos wielle*. It's mentioned as Mesewell in 1344. Similarly, **Mizbrooks Farm** at Cuckfield occupies marshy ground grown over with moss, noted as Mesbroke in 1296, and Misbrookes in 1503.

Mitchborne. This began as a rivername, *micel burna*, 'the great bourne or stream', once used locally to describe the tributary of the Adur on which Mitchborne lies. We find it called Mucheleburne in 1332. Two centuries later the Tudor spelling is Michelbornes.

Mizbrooks. See MISWELL.

Mizzards. It's recorded in 1386 as Musardes, taking its identity from the family of William Musard, described as 'of Ipynge' in 1327. Their surname came from the old French word *musard*, meaning absent-minded or vague.

Moat. Moats are generally associated in the popular imagination with medieval castles, but they were frequently used as a dry ditch to provide security for manor houses and the like. Moat at Hadlow Down – called Mott in 1547 – marks the site of one of these defensive ditches, as does Moat at Pulborough, described as le Mote and Moteland in 1500. **Moatcroft Road**, Eastbourne, preserves both the name and location of an ancient fortified peel or small tower that was replaced in Norman times by the manor house here. During the 15th century it was recorded as Mote *sive* (or) Pele, le Moyte, and the Motte, reappearing as Mottdowne in 1574.

Mock Bridge. The name is a derivation of *Moccan brycge*, denoting the bridge of an early settler called Mocca spanning a tributary of the Adur at this point. It was spelled Mokebrugge in 1296. By 1638 it had become Mokebridge, which is how it's pronounced still. The author Michael Fairless (Margaret Fairless Dowson) who lies buried nearby at ASHURST, spent the last two years of her life at Mock Bridge House writing her classic story of Sussex folk, *The Roadmender*, published posthumously in 1902.

Molecomb. Molecumbe (1284),

Mollecombe (1301) and Moulecombe (1640) are forms of this name suggesting it started as *Mollan cumb*, 'the combe or valley of Molla', one of the many individuals we encounter only once in the place names of Sussex.

Mole, River. Recorded as Moule in the time of Elizabeth I, the name is simply a back-formation from that of Molesey in Surrey.

Monks. See MONKYN PYN.

Monkyn Pyn. Lying just north of Wilmington, this curiously-named place was the site of a livestock enclosure owned by monks attached to the 12th century priory. The old *monken pond* or 'monks' pound' was noted in 1393 as Munckenepende. By 1541 the spelling had changed to Monkyn Pynde, and its present form has been in use since 1673. Several other places in the county also have former connections with monks, or with the associated medieval surname Monke, le Monek and Mooncke. They include **Monks Common**, Nuthurst, **Monkshill**, Forest Row, and **Monk's Gate**, Lower Beeding; while **Monks** at Rudgwick, mentioned as Knights Hatch *alias* Monckes in 1605, had earlier been identified with Robert le Monek de Rugwyk (the monk of Rudgwick) recorded in 1344.

Moonhill. This isn't an easy one to decipher. It's called la Monhell in 1279, so its description 'the moon hill' is clearly an ancient one. Interestingly, we come across a number of Rainbow Fields mentioned in old records, so maybe Moonhill falls into the same category and came by its name simply because the full moon rose above it. It was spelled Moonehill in 1603. **Moon's Wood**, near Sedlescombe, has an entirely different origin however, taking its name from the family of Ada la Mone of Senlac (1296). Their surname – still quite common in Sussex – has a Norman-French derivation, either *moun*, 'monk', or Moyon, a place in La Manche.

Moor. The Saxon word *mōr* signified a tract of wasteland where the soil was poor and not much good for tilling. In the medieval period the word became *more*, giving rise to the associated surname de la More, atte More or atte Moure, describing someone living on such land. There are almost 20 different places in the county identified by this name or one of its variations, ranging from **The Moor** at Ambersham, via **Moorhead**, Horsham, to **Morelands** at Rudgwick.

Morgan's Green. The hamlet takes its identity from the family of Agnes Morgan, whom we find registered locally in 1605, two years after the death of Elizabeth I.

Morgay. This is a name with a pretty history, because it means 'morning gift', describing a piece of land customarily given by a husband to his new wife the morning after their wedding day. There must have been many such properties in the county, but Morgay Farm at Ewhurst is the only place actually preserving the name of this old custom. Originally *morgen giefu*, it's recorded as Morgtheve and Morgheyve in the mid 13th century, becoming Morgewe in 1554.

Morley. There are three places in Sussex sharing this name, each of them marking the site of a *mōr lēah* or cleared area of wasteland. Morley Farm, Westmeston, is the oldest of the trio. It's listed in the Domesday Book (1086) as Morleia, but its modern form is first noted in 1266. Morley Farm, Shermanbury, is Morle in 1309, a spelling shared by Morley Farm, Northiam, at the slightly later date of 1429.

Morners Barn. It took its name from a Stuart landowner, John Marner, registered in the parish of Yapton in 1641.

Morning's Mill. Spelled Moryngemyll, Moryngesmyll and Mornyngsmill between the years 1504 and 1598, the land here was originally the property of a Richard Moryng who appears in the Lay Subsidy Roll of 1296.

Moseham. A name that hasn't altered at all since its first appearance in 1531, it's probably from *mos hamm*, 'the boggy watermeadow', a reference to overflowing streams in the vicinity.

Motcombe. This was considered an important place in Saxon times, because it was in the downland combe here that meetings of the Hundred moot or local council were held. The origin of its name, *gemōt cumb*, literally meant 'the moot valley', noted as Motecumbe in 1219. The route to the old meeting place is still marked by **Borough Lane** in Eastbourne. There were similar sites at MADEHURST, and quite probably QUEDLEY, and on land now occupied by **Moustows Manor**, Henfield,

which gets its name from *gemōt stow*, 'the moot place', described as la Mostowe in 1343.

Motts Mill. See BROAD OAK.

Mottynsden. This may look a typically Saxon name but it's actually medieval, originating as Motyn's *denne*, woodland pasture owned by a John Motyn who's recorded locally in 1332. It's spelled Mottensden in 1613, and Mottingsden as late as 1930.

Moulsecoomb. Downland neighbours Moulsecoomb and **North Moulsecoomb** have now been virtually absorbed by the inland expansion of Brighton, but they were once the site of an early settlement that had developed in the combe or valley just here. The place had been the territory of a South Saxon called Mūl – a nickname suggesting he was known as an obstinate character, because it meant 'the mule'. Mūl's combe is recorded as Muliscumba around the year 1100. By the close of the following century this had altered to Molscumb. And in 1610 it was Mulscombe, which is how Moulsecoomb is pronounced still. The border of the Mule's territory lay within a short distance at Falmer, where **Moustone** marks the location of a boundary stone recorded around AD 765 as Mulestana. In 1203 the place reappears as Muleston, and towards the end of the Tudor period it's Mulston *alias* Mowlestone, becoming Lower Mousestone in 1631. A corner of land that may or may not have belonged to the same early settler has given us the name of **Mousehall**, near Mayfield. Stemming from *Mūles healh*, it's noted as Muleshale

153

in 1315 and Mowsale in 1438. The modern spelling has been in use since the time of Henry VIII.

Mount Caburn. Although there's no actual evidence of the name before the late 18th century, when it's given as Mount Carbone and Mt Caburn, in its pre-Saxon form it must have been very similar to modern Welsh *caer bryn*, sharing the same meaning – 'the stronghold hill'. Rising to 150 ft on the Downs just below Lewes, it still bears traces of the ramparts of an Iron Age hill-fort some 2,000 years old, believed the last one in Sussex to be abandoned. As with CHANCTONBURY and CISSBURY, legend attributes the formation of Mount Caburn to a clod of earth dropped from the Devil's shovel as he excavated DEVIL'S DYKE.

Mountfield. This East Sussex village is listed as Montifelle in the Norman Domesday Book of 1086. It was originally an area of unenclosed land owned by an early settler called Munda – a personal name we encounter elsewhere in connection with NORTH and SOUTH MUNDHAM. *Mundan feld* or Munda's land had become Mondefeld by 1340, and Montfeld two centuries after that. Munfield, noted in 1724, gives us its pronunciation.

Mount Harry. There's nothing recorded earlier than 1610, when Speed's map of the county shows the site as Mountharry. Traditionally, it was named after the unfortunate King Henry III who was defeated by the army of Simon de Montfort in 1264 at the Battle of Lewes, fought on Offham Hill close by. However, it's more likely Mount

Harry has the same origin as HARROW HILL and was once the site of a pre-Christian *hearg* or pagan sanctuary.

Mousehall, Moustone. See MOULSECOOMB.

Moustows Manor. See MOTCOMBE.

Muddles Green. This was the property of a Tudor landowner, Nicholas Moodell of Waldron, recorded in 1547; while **Muddleswood** at Newtimber is thought to take its name from William de Methelwolde, a native of Methwold in Norfolk, who settled in that parish at the start of the 14th century.

Mundham, North and **South.** The two lie just over a mile apart from each other in the county's oldest area of Saxon colonisation, the Selsey peninsula. North Mundham seems to be the original site, marking the *hām* or settlement of a warrior-farmer called Munda. It's identified as Mundhame in a document of AD 683. The Domesday Book gives it as Mundreham, but the Saxon form is repeated as Mundehame in 1270, and the place distinguished as North Mundham eight years later. A slightly earlier document, dated AD 680, refers to it as other Mundan ham, 'Munda's other settlement'. Scholars think this is probably with reference to **Muntham** not far away at Findon. Despite the fact that they share exactly the same origin, it's interesting to note the Domesday Book gives the Findon *Mundan hām* a different spelling – Moham. But it's Mundeham a century and a half later, and Mundham in 1296. Although the village here has now disappeared, its name was preserved by Muntham Court, built about 1850 and demolished in 1961. **Muntham** near Itchingfield was originally part of the manor estates.

Muntham. See MUNDHAM, NORTH and SOUTH.

Muslins. Noted as Muslondes in 1560, this most likely described a piece of land infested with field-mice.

Muster Green. It was here that Royalist and Parliamentary troops mustered before engaging each other at the Battle of Haywards Heath in 1642. The Royalists suffered a heavy defeat, with the loss of more than 200 men.

· · N · ·

Nash. This is a name that started in the medieval period as *at them asch*, referring to somebody living 'at/by the ash-tree". Towards the end of the same period it had evolved to *atten asshe*, which, shortened in everyday speech to *'n asshe*, in time produced modern Nash. We find it associated with half a dozen or so places in Sussex, including Nash itself, **Nashland Farm**, Slaugham, and **Nash Street**, Chiddingly.

Nate Wood. It has the rather more homely spelling of Gnat Wood in 1861, having earlier been Natewode (1673) and before that Natwode (1285). The earliest reference occurs around 1145 when the place is mentioned as Natawuda, a derivation either of *Natan wudu* – 'Nata's wood', or *nēata wudu* – 'the cattle wood'.

Navant Hill. In 1540 it's given as Novetthall, possibly in error for Novetthill. Records for the years 1296, 1327 and 1332 list the place as the home of Gocelin ate Onelte and Richard ate Ouelte or atte Noueld. Since the land rises fairly sharply here, scholars suggest these various name-forms have a common root in the Saxon word *of-hylde*, meaning 'steep slope'.

Naylands. Although the place lies well inland at Balcombe, it had been identified early in the Middle Ages as *at them eyland*, 'at the water-land', probably because it's surrounded by lower ground once subject to flooding. In time the name was altered to *atten eyland*, then *'n eyland*, appearing as Neyland in 1313. The same derivation is shared by **Neyland Farm**, Forest Row – it lies in an area well-drained by streams, which in 1387 had been recorded as the home of William atte Nelonde – 'dweller at the water-land'.

Neatenden. This began as "the nether farmstead', a small settlement lying in a nether or lower position to some 'upper farmstead' that has long since disappeared. It's noted as Netherton in 1220, Nytherton in 1296, forms from which the modern name has developed.

Nepcote. Nepcote is known for its famous Sheep Fair, established in 1790, which is nowadays held on the second Saturday in September and includes the annual Southdown Sheep Society show. The village itself appears on Greenwood's map of Sussex (1823) as Nob Gate. Research suggests it possibly came by its name through some early connection with the families of Philip le Nulp and John le Nolp, who are registered in the Findon area in the second half of the 13th century. However it's interesting to compare this place name with **Nep Town**, Heathfield, and **Nepland Pit**, Burwash, which share the dialect word 'nep' used of the catnip or catmint plant.

Nepland Pit, Nep Town. See NEPCOTE.

Netherfield. It looks as if it should mean 'the nether or lower land', but Netherfield actually has a rather more interesting derivation, because it preserves intact the old word 'nadder' from which we get modern 'adder'. So this was originally a piece of land infested with adders, described by those who first settled nearby as *næddre feld*. In 1086 the Domesday Book records it as Nedrefelle, and it's Nadrefeld in 1225, Nedderfelde in 1332. By 1469 we find the name changing to something like its modern form as Nethir-

feld. Incidentally, 'adder' isn't the only word in the language to lose its head: 'apron' and 'uncle' are other examples that once began with *n*, whereas 'newt' demonstrates the process in reverse, having started as 'ewt'.

Nettlesworth Place. Nettlesworth Place, situated between Heathfield and Warbleton, marks the site of an early settlement last recorded in 1332, when it was mentioned as Nedelesworth. It had come into existence as *Nēðeles worð*, the enclosure of a South Saxon called Nēðel, whose property had also included a wooded hill close by at a place known as Nedleshurst, now likewise lost.

Newbridge. A self-explanatory name, it occurs three times in the county. Newbridge near Hartfield is so called in 1564, and **New Bridge**, Alfriston, shares its spelling a little later, 1618; while **Newbridge Wood**, Billingshurst, the oldest of the three, is described as la Nieubrugge in 1317.

Newelm. It's still possible to find the small downland spring that gave this hamlet its original description of *æwielm*, 'the welling-up place'. It's recorded as Ewelm in 1296, Ewelme just under a century later. By the Tudor period though, the name had altered to Newhelme, and in 1795 it's given as New Elm.

Newham. See NEWICK.

Newhaven. This busy cross-Channel port became the 'new haven' or harbour in the 1580s, after severe storms had diverted the course of the river Ouse from its outlet at SEAFORD. **Meeching Court Farm**, on the cliffs above Newhaven, preserves the name of the old village of Meeching that once stood here – last mentioned in 1729, it was to remain independent of the port until 18th century development finally engulfed it. As a settlement it had had a long history, marking the territory of a South Saxon tribe called the Mēcingas, the people of Mēce (a warrior nickname meaning 'the sword') who laid claim to an area already containing fortified camps dating as far back as 250 BC. Documents record the place as Mecinges in 1091, Mechinges in 1272. In 1587 a survey of the Sussex coast gives village and port separately as Michin and Newehaven, but by 1685 they're combined into one as Meetching *alias* Newhaven.

Newick. Once this pleasant mid-Sussex village was simply the *nīwe wīc* or 'new farm' that had come into existence at a later date than other places nearby. It's noted as Newik in 1218. Similarly, **Newham Farm** at Steyning occupies the site of a new *hām* or settlement recorded as Neweham in 1267. And **Newnham Park**, Buxted, dating from the same period, is Newenham in 1266, subsequently appearing as Newnam parke in 1564.

Newman's Barn. See NYMANS.

Newnham Park. See NEWICK.

Newpound Common. The Lay Subsidy Roll of 1296 records the place as the home of Richard atte Punde, whose name tells us he lived close to a pound or livestock enclosure.

Obviously there was a new one built here at some later date.

Newtimber Place. See NYETIMBER.

Ninfield. Lying just a few miles inland from Bexhill, Ninfield began as a small settlement that had developed on what its earliest inhabitants described as *nīwnumenan felda* – 'the newly-taken land'. The Domesday Book inaccurately records it as Nerewelle in 1086, but the old Saxon spelling shows up again in the 13th century forms Nimenefeld, Newenefeld and Nyneynefeld. By 1400 it had become Nenefelde, shortening to Nindfeild in 1672.

Nobies. According to local tradition, the name of this little place near Fittleworth began as 'Nobody's'. If tradition is right, it shares its origin with other tracts of ownerless land including **No Man's Land**, Madehurst, lying on the border of three separate parishes and called Nonemanneslond in 1361; and **Nomanswood**, Wadhurst, which we find described as such in 1610.

Nore Hill. Nore is a name that's had its initial letter tacked on. It began in medieval days as *atten ore* – 'at the bank or slope' – which got shortened to *'n ore* in everyday speech. In 1353 Nore Hill was the home of Richard atte Noure, whose surname illustrates this confusion. Likewise, **The Nore** at Sompting came by its spelling in the same way.

Norlington. This was known as the *northling ton*, 'the northerly farmstead', because of its position in relation to neighbouring settlements at MIDDLEHAM and SOUTHERHAM. It appears as Northlingeton in 1296, becoming Norlyngton two centuries later.

Norman's Bay. This is a fairly modern name for the holiday village that's starting to develop between Pevensey Bay and Bexhill. Its only connection with the conquering Normans is that it lies just a short way along the coast from their landing point in 1066.

Norrups Barn. It's on land recorded in 1482 as Northuppe, its position being 'up north' of the parish of Bersted.

Northbrook. There are two, one near Funtington (Nortbrok 1273), the other near Goring (Northbrok 1279), both indicating old areas of marshy ground to the north of a settlement. The Funtington Northbrook had its counterpart in **Southbrook**, 'the south marshy land', recorded as Sotbrok in the same period.

Northchapel. Lying close to the Surrey border among the wooded hills of the western Weald, Northchapel marks the site of a medieval chapel standing to the north of Petworth. It was probably built as a chapel of ease, used by worshippers living at some distance from their parish church. In 1514 the place is mentioned as North-Chapell.

North Down. This is a late name for what used to be rather more picturesquely known as **Horeappletree Common**, near Heathfield, a place taking its description from an old apple-tree marking the *har* or boundary between the Hundreds of Hawksborough and Dill. There are two other North Downs in the county, at Singleton and at Ferring, their name – from *dūn* or 'hill' – being self-explanatory.

Northease. See SOUTHEASE.

Northiam. In Saxon days this was 'the high meadow' or *hēah hamm* lying above the shallow valley of the eastern Rother. The Domesday Book (1086) records it as Hiham, a spelling also used by the Normans for 'the high settlement' nearby at HIGHAM. In fact Northiam and its neighbour confusingly shared the same name until the beginning of the 13th century, when one is Hyham and the other Higham. But then in 1288 we find Northiam described for the first time as Northeham, a form repeated in 1588 as Northyhamme – 'North' to distinguish it from HIGHAM STREET, site of the new town of Winchelsea, which is mentioned as the 'South' or Suthyhomme in 1339. A document of 1675 spells the name Nordiam, a pronunciation that remained in local use till only recently.

Norton. Norton indicates the location of an early *tūn* or farmstead lying to the north of its neighbouring settlement. There are three such places in Sussex: Norton, Aldingbourne, so spelled in 1279; Norton, Bishopstone, recorded as Northetone late in the 13th century; and Norton on the Selsey peninsula, which appears around 1300 together with a now lost Suthton, or 'south farmstead', thought to be the site of the present village of Selsey.

Novington. See OVINGDEAN.

Nunningham. Nunningham Farm near Herstmonceux shares its name with **Nunningham Stream**, draining into the Pevensey marshes. The farm itself lies on land once occupied by the settlement of a Saxon tribal group called the Nunningas, or Nunna's people. Originally *Nunninga hām*, the place name developed via Unnyngeham to Noningham and Nonnyngham between 1296 and 1332. We come across Nunna again in connection with an early farmstead on the site of **Nunnington Farm**, across the county at West Wittering. Nunna's *tūn* is recorded as Nunyngton around the year 1275, becoming Nonyngton in 1334, and Nonongtons two centuries later in the time of Henry VIII.

Nunnington. See NUNNINGHAM.

Nutbourne. One of the streams feeding into the river Chilt between Nutbourne and its neighbour **Nutbourne Common** was known to the South Saxons as *hnutu burna*, 'the bourne or stream overhung with nut-trees'. In time it gave its name to the little settlement lying on its bank, recorded in the Domesday Book (1086) as Nordborne. In 1274 the place is noted as Nuteburne, and 30 years later its location is given as Notbourne by Pulberwe (Pulborough). The same derivation is also shared by **Nutbourne** near Southbourne. It too lies on a stream, this one emptying into Thorney Channel, appearing as Notburn in 1277, Nutteburne in 1307. And **Nutbourn** near Billingshurst is similarly mentioned as Notburne in 1288.

Nutham Barn, Nuthurst. See NUTLEY.

Nutley. Nutleg, Notley and Nutteley, forms recorded between 1249

and 1333, tell us Nutley began as *hnutu lēah*, literally 'the nut clearing', describing a cleared area of woodland where nut-trees could be found. But **Nutley Wood** at Hellingly originally must have been 'the cattle clearing' or *nēata lēah*, because it's recorded as Natelegh in 1285. We find an early *hamm* or watermeadow shaded by nut-trees at **Nutham Barn**, Horsham, whose spelling hasn't changed since 1261; while **Nuthurst** was once a wooded hill where these trees used to grow – it's called Nothurst in 1228, Nuttehurst in 1342.

Nyetimber. The Saxon word for 'new' was *nīwe*, but in place names such as Nyetimber we find a variant form, *nige*. Here it was used to mean 'new-timbered', though scholars aren't sure whether the description originally applied to a building construction or to land newly-timbered with trees – the origin of **Nyewood**, which is described as la Nywode, 'the new wood', in 1337. Nyetimber itself appears in the 1086 Domesday Book as Nitinbreham, suggesting it might have been a *hām* or settlement; but by 1283 its name is simply Niutimbre, repeated as Nytimbre in 1327. The same description gives us the origin of **Newtimber Place** at Hassocks (open to the public), occupying a site recorded as Niuembre in 1086 and Nytimbre in 1248, before altering its spelling to Newetymber in 1270.

Nyewood. See NYETIMBER.

Nymans. Owned by the National Trust, these 30 acres of beautiful gardens near Handcross take their name from a family recorded in the

159

Lay Subsidy Roll of 1296 as le Nyman – 'the new man, or new-comer'. The same Roll also provides us with the name of Robert le Nyuweman or Nyman, whose home was on the site of **Nymans Farm** not far away at Henfield. And we find this surname similarly connected with **Newman's Barn**, Patcham, where a William Nyman is registered in 1327.

Nyton. Nyton lies just a couple of miles inland from Bognor Regis in an area fed by a number of streams. In medieval days the surrounding land was probably heavily water-logged, because the little settlement here was referred to as *atten eyton* – 'at the island farmstead'. In time this description got shortened to *'n eyton*, and by 1327 the place name was already appearing as Nyton.

O

Oakendene. See OCKLYNGE.

Oakhurst. The dense oak forests that once covered much of Sussex north of the Downs have dwindled now to patches of woodland scattered across the basin of the Weald (a name, incidentally, we owe to the Saxons, for whom it meant 'forest'). But at one time, before the depredations of the local iron industry, the oak still grew so plentifully as to be known throughout the southern counties as 'the Sussex weed'. **Oakhurst** simply means 'the oak wood'. Situated near Kirdford, it's recorded as Okhurst in 1395. **Oke-hurst** just a few miles away is Ochurst earlier that same century; and **Oakhurst Farm** down at Sidlesham is spelled Okehurst and Oke-hurst in the time of Henry VIII. **Oakleigh** marks the site of a clearing in the oakwood, described as Oclegh in

1279. **Oakreeds Wood** at Linchmere has a similar origin, but here the site had been cleared of oaks in the sense of being rid of them, appearing as 'the wood called Okeredes' in 1536. Where **Ockham** now stands beside the river Rother, there once lay a watermeadow bordered by oaks, called Occham around 1205, Ochammeswode some 70 years later; while its neighbour **Great Ockford** records 'the ford by the oak' that provided a crossing over the river in earlier times.

Oakleigh, Oakreeds Wood, Ock-ham. See OAKHURST.

Ockenden, Ockenden's Shaw. See OCKLYNGE.

Ocklynge. Ocklynge marks the end of a linch or ridge of high ground carrying the main road between

Eastbourne and Willingdon. It was known originally as *Offan hlinc*, or 'Offa's linch', later changing to Oke-lyng (1167) and Okelinge (1332). In 1627 it was spelled Ocklinge, which is still how it's pronounced. Occa – or more likely another of the same name – was the leader of a small group of Saxons who took their identity from him as the Occingas, owning land to the north-west at Cowfold on the site of **Oakendene Manor**. This was their *denn* or wood-land pasture, its name evolving from *Occinga denn* to Okyngedenn in 1279 and Okindenne in 1327, before becoming Okendeane in 1754. It's possible Occa had his own pasture-land about six miles away at **Ock-enden**, near Cuckfield, but records of this place name are so late – Okendenes in 1547, Oakendean in 1692, and Ockenden in 1716 – that it could just as easily have been 'the oaken pasture'. However, there's an interesting earlier reference to the site in 1480, when we find **Ock-enden's Shaw** just south at Clayton described as Okynden lond, appar-ently land belonging to Ockenden at that period.

Offham (Hamsey). Offham lies close to a pronounced bend in the Ouse, taking its name from some old watermeadow beside the river known as 'the crooked meadow' or *wōh hamm* because of its irregular shape. It's mentioned as Wocham around the year 1092, and Wogham in 1296. Then for some reason the initial *W* was dropped – possibly the result of local usage – and in the early part of the 14th century we find the name recorded as Ofham and Offam. But the old form wasn't quite abandoned, because in 1609

Wogham surfaces again side by side with Offam, suggesting the name was still being pronounced 'Woffham' at that date.

Offham (Arundel). As well as shar-ing the same spelling as the previous entry, this particular place name has a very similar history, both describ-ing watermeadows lying on the bends of rivers. In the case of this Offham however, the river is the Arun and the derivation *Offan hamm*, 'Offa's meadow', named after an early settler. The Domesday Book records the place as Offham in 1086. The personal name Offa was a pop-ular one in Saxon times (it was the 8th century King Offa of Mercia who built Offa's Dyke to keep out the Welsh), so it's not surprising there's also another place in the county, **Offington**, where it's found. This hasn't changed much since it was *Offing tūn*, 'Offa's farmstead', although in the Domesday Book its Normanised spelling is Ofintune.

Offington. See OFFHAM (Arundel).

Old Buckhurst. See WITHYHAM.

Open and Closed Winkins. See WINKENHURST.

Ore. The village appears as Ora in 1121, preserving the Saxon word *ōra* meaning 'the bank or border'. In fact the original settlement developed on the hill forming the south-eastern termination of The Ridge, a prehis-toric track running inland to Bald-slow, a couple of miles away. Many relics of ancient British occupation have been uncovered in the area.

Oreham Common. Lying on the

161

slope of a hill just south of Henfield, Oreham was once *ōra hām*, 'the bank settlement', descriptive of its location. It appeared as Erham in 1199, Orham in 1310. **Little Oreham Farm** and **Oreham Manor** probably occupy the original site.

Orfold. See HARSFOLD.

Orznash. The second element in this name is the dialect word 'earsh' used of a field of corn-stubble. Such a field belonged here at one time to somebody called Ōsa, giving us *Ōsan ersc* or 'Ōsa's earsh' as the derivation of the name. It's noted as Osenerse in 1200, Osenersh in 1327, and then changes very little before 1628 when it's Osnersh.

Otteham. An early 14th century chapel at Otteham Court, near Polegate, is all that now remains here of a grange run by Premonstratensian monks before they left to found a new community at BAYHAM ABBEY. It had been built on a Saxon site originally called *Ottan hām* – 'Otta's settlement' – mentioned as Hotteham, Otteham and Otham between 1154 and 1230. We find this same Otta (or at least another Saxon sharing his name) owning a *healh* or corner of land at **Ote Hall**, Wivelsfield, noted as Ottehale in 1279; as well as a *hæg* or hedged enclosure not too far away at **Otye Wood**, Horsted Keynes, called Otehye in 1437.

Ote Hall, Otye Wood. See OTTEHAM.

Ouse, River. This is a comparatively late name, mentioned first in Michael Drayton's topographical work *Polyolbion* (1622). Originally the river had been known as the Midewinde or 'middle winding', because it divides Sussex in two. That old name still survives as **Midwyn Bridge** at Lindfield. Another early description, recorded about 1270, was aqua de Lewes (water of Lewes) which scholars think could have been mistakenly copied as aqua del Ewes, later corrupted from Ewes to Ouse. An alternative theory, hinging on the fact that the river once had an extremely wide, marshy estuary, points to the Saxon *wāse* or 'ooze' as its derivation. By the medieval period this word had developed to *wos*; and in 1288 we find the river-bridge at Lewes actually referred to as pontem de Wos.

Outer Wick. See INNERWYKE.

Oving. The village lies on the outskirts of Chichester in one of the oldest Saxon areas of Sussex. Its name was first recorded in AD 956 as Uuinges, identifying the site as the territory of a tribal group known as the Ūfingas, or Ūfe's people. An earlier document, dated AD 669, also mentioned a river-crossing hereabouts called ufes ford. By the start of the 13th century the place name had become Huvinges, changing to Ouvinge in 1282. And in the time of Elizabeth I we find it spelled Ooving, a pronunciation still in use.

Ovingdean. Ovingdean has no connection with OVING, despite the apparent similarity of name. It's in a little dip of the Downs above Rottingdean, overlooking the sea, on land once owned by the Ofingas, a Saxon tribe taking its identity from its leader Ofa. *Ofinga dene*, 'the dean or valley of the Ofingas', appeared in the Domesday Book of 1086 as

Hovingedene, but by 1255 its modern form was already recognisable as Ovingdene. Ofa possibly had his own *tūn* or farmstead just a few miles north on the site of **Novington Manor**, near Plumpton. Although this is recorded as Nouinton in 1261 and Nouyngton in 1327, it's Offyngton in 1515, and etymologists think the earlier forms owed their initial *N* to the medieval *'n Ofington* – 'at Offington'. In 1579 we find **Drews Farm** here described as Drews in Plumpton sometimes (ie formerly) Offingtons.

Owlscastle. According to legend this place at Horsham gets its name from the Sussex 'owlers' or old-time smugglers who used it as a hiding-place for wool being shipped illegally to France. They acquired their description from the owl-hoots they used as a warning signal.

Oxenbridge. Oxen were still used as draught animals in Sussex well into this present century, many farmers in fact preferring them to horses because of their greater strength and endurance, and value as meat at the end of their working life. Oxenbridge, on the Rother near Beckley, was obviously a crossing-place once associated with these beasts, being recorded as Oxenebrigg in 1279. Similarly, Oxenbridge at Iden appears as Oxenebrigge at the same period. A dean or valley where they were put to graze has given its name to **Oxendean** just below Jevington, called Oxendeane in the time of the Tudors; while another downland valley, **Oxteddle Bottom**, was also associated with them but at a much earlier date. Around the year 1100 it's mentioned as Oxenesetene, from *oxena seten*, a description that translates literally as 'the oxen property' and probably applied to an old earthwork where they were penned. In 1581 the name was still virtually unchanged as Oxensetten, becoming Oxsettle Bottom in 1799.

Oxendean, Oxteddle Bottom. See OXENBRIDGE.

· · PQ · ·

Padgham. St Wilfred came to Sussex as a refugee from Northumbrian persecution, and stayed to convert the South Saxons to Christianity before departing again in AD 686. With him came four companions including Padda, who traditionally owned land here at Padgham. Padda's *hamm* or watermeadow was first mentioned around 1245 as Padihamme. A century later the spelling was Padchamme – more or less how the name's still pronounced. A possible alternative derivation has nothing to do with Padda however, being simply *padde hamm*, 'toad meadow', describing the habitat of paddocks or toads.

Pagham. This historic village on the edge of Pagham Harbour was originally documented in AD 680 as Pecgan ham, the settlement of a South Saxon named Pæcga. Nearly 300 years later, about AD 975, it was recorded as Pacganham, becoming Paggaham by the middle of the 12th century. The harbour itself – once known as Selsey Haven – was formed around 1345 when the sea swamped a large area of land here to create an estuary a mile wide stretching inland almost as far as Sidlesham.

Pallingham. Pallingham Manor Farm, lying in a bend of the Arun just south of Wisborough Green, occupies the site of a Saxon settlement belonging to a tribal group called the Pællingas, or Pælli's people. From *Pællinga hām*, its name evolved to Pallingeham, Palingham and Pallyngham, forms noted during the period 1233-1329.

Pangdean. The old country word 'pink' used as an alternative name for the chaffinch, came directly from Saxon *pinca*, imitating the bird's distinctive note. Pangdean began its history rather delighfully as 'the chaffinch valley' or *pinca denu*. In the Domesday Book it's recorded as Pinhedene, returning to its older form as Pynkeden around the year 1300, then becoming Pyngden in 1454 and Pingdeane in 1609. A hurst or wood where chaffinches were also frequently heard gave its description to **Pinkhurst**, mentioned as Pinkeherst

in 1228, Pynghurst in 1319.

Pannelridge Wood. See PENHURST.

Parbrook. Although the actual name isn't on record before 1740, it probably began in medieval times as *pere brook*, indicating marshy ground where pear-trees grew, because in 1195 we find a now lost place nearby called Perregate, 'the gate by the pear-tree'.

Parham House. Just over 100 years before the Norman Conquest in 1066, the place was recorded as Perham, 'the *hām* or settlement by the pear-trees', a name subsequently noted in the Domesday Book as Parham. Until the suppression of the monasteries in the reign of Henry VIII, Parham had belonged to the Manor of Westminster, supplying it with venison from the great deer park that still exists here. But the Dissolution of 1537 ended its ecclesiastical tenure, and in 1540 the estate was granted to Robert Palmer of London, whose son, Sir Thomas Palmer, commenced the building of Parham House, a beautiful Tudor mansion nowadays open to the public. Its east wing incorporates part of the monastic grange founded here by Westminster Abbey in the mid 14th century.

Park. The name comes from medieval *parrok*, which in turn originated as *pearroc*, the Saxon word for a small enclosure or paddock. During the later Middle Ages it referred more specifically to an area of enclosed land, often attached to a manor, stocked with deer and other beasts of the chase. With its associated surname atte Parc, le Parker and de Parco, it occurs as the name of some 30 or more places in Sussex, from **Parker Corner** via **Parkgate** to **Park Street**. **Parkhurst**, near Lurgashall, was 'the park wood', recorded as Parckehurst in 1279, an origin shared by Parkhurst at Buxted (Perkehurst 1439) and Parkhurst Farm, Tillington (Pyrkhurst 1296). And we find medieval *parrok* surviving almost unchanged as **Parrock**, a place name listed in the Domesday Book as Apedroc in 1086, but spelled in its modern form since the mid 13th century.

Parkminster. The original form of this name was *pytt cnoll*, 'the knoll by the pit or hollow' – it's noted as Pyteknolle in 1296, then reappears as Picknoll around 1655. By the middle of the 19th century Picknoll had further developed to Parknole, a name that was subsequently altered to Parkminster by the Carthusian monks who built **St Hugh's Monastery** here between 1875 and 1883.

Parrock. See PARK.

Partridge Green. This hamlet near West Grinstead takes its name from the family of John Partrych, registered locally in 1332. Their surname, from the medieval word *pertriche*, originally described a hunter or snarer of partridges.

Pashley. See PATCHING.

Patcham. Originally the *hām* or settlement of a South Saxon named Pecca, it was recorded as Piceham by the Normans in 1086. Pecham (1291) became Pecheham (1377) before developing to Petcham (1794). The

village lies on the northern outskirts of Brighton, and is now much smaller than it was in the time of Edward the Confessor when it belonged to Harold Godwinson, who was to be Edward's successor as king of Saxon England. The Domesday Book gives its population as over 200, with 84 acres of meadowland, and woodland for 100 hogs.

Patching. The earliest record of this name dates from AD 960 when it was documented as Pæccingas, a Saxon tribal name meaning 'the people of Pæcci'. The Domesday Book lists it as Petchinges. Some 200 years later it's Passinges, shortened to Pacchyng in 1327 and spelled Poching in 1513. Pæcci himself, or possibly a member of his family group, is associated elsewhere in the county with a *lēah* or cleared area of woodland on the site of **Pashley** near Ticehurst. This appears as Pesselegh around the year 1230, Passeleye some 60 years after. In 1552 it's described as Great Pashele, to distinguish it from Pashley at Eastbourne, a place taking the name of the 13th century family of de Passelegh who had settled here from Ticehurst. **Pashley Farm** at Ninfield shares the same connection through another native of the Ticehurst area, Robert de Passeleye (1288).

Patchway. This name is of particular interest to scholars because it pinpoints the site of a pagan shrine or *wīg* built by a South Saxon called Pæccel – almost certainly the ritual building excavated here in 1957 within a group of trees known as Rocky Clump. A document dated about the year AD 765 refers to the place as Petteleswige, apparently mis-spelling the personal name, because subsequent records show it as Piceleswia (1121) and Paccheleswye (1263). By the start of the 17th century it was Patchwye.

Pattleton's. Pattleton's Farm near Westfield is all that remains to preserve the name of a Saxon tribal group called the Piertelingas, or Piertel's people, who had their farmstead on this site. Originally *Piertelinga tūn*, the place is found as Pertlingetun about 1215, Partlyngton in 1474. In 1625 it's described as Partlington *alias* Pattledens, a form from which the modern name has developed.

Paxhill Park. It has the alternative spelling of Packshill about 1780, having appeared as Backshells in 1636, and Bacshelve rather earlier in 1339. The first recorded mention of the name dates even further back, to a Saxon charter of AD 765, where it appears as bacanscylfes – 'Bacca's shelf' – describing land shelving here to the river Ouse.

Paythorne Barn. Somewhere here in Saxon days stood a thornbush that was used as a boundary mark or similar feature on land belonging to a settler called Paga. In time 'Paga's thorn' became the name of the place, Normanised in 1086 as Paveorne before returning to its older form as Pagethorne two centuries later. In 1633 it was Pawthorne, and in 1830 Peathorne.

Peacehaven. This is one of the county's more recent place names, chosen as the result of a national competition held in 1919. The resort developed on 6,000 acres of land purchased in 1914 by businessman Charles Neville, and for a time was known as **Anzac-on-Sea** because of the numbers of Australian and New Zealand troops stationed in the area at the beginning of the Great War.

Peakdean. Its name – 'the valley beneath the peak' – perfectly describes Peakdean's location below a hill on its western side. First mentioned as Pekedene in 1198, it appeared little changed as Peakedane in 1649. **Peckham Farm** at Framfield shares a similar origin: it lies on the hill-top site of a Saxon *pēac hām* or 'peak settlement' called Pecham in 1298.

Pease Pottage. A delightful name with an interesting history, it's more fully recorded as Peaspottage Gate in 1724, marking one of the old entrances into woodland nowadays known as **Peasepottage Forest**. Traditionally, prisoners under escort to Horsham Gaol were halted at this gate and fed a dish of cold pottage, a mash of boiled dried peas. Another version of the same story maintains it was guards preceding the Prince Regent on his way to Brighton who used the spot as a pull-up to partake of pottage – unlikely however, since the Prince Regent wasn't born until 1762 and the place name already existed some 40 years earlier.

Peasmarsh. This obviously describes an area of marshy ground where peas grew – not the cultivated kind but some wild plant of the pea family, probably marsh trefoil, which is also known as buck-bean. The place is called Pisemershe in 1247, a spelling that changes to Pesmarshe in 1420 and Peasmarshe in 1588. Lying three miles from Rye, this pretty village was the birthplace of William Pattison, a poet once fêted as 'the Chatterton of Sussex', who died in 1727 of smallpox and near-starvation, aged just twenty-one.

Pebsham. Now virtually a suburb of Bexhill, Pebsham occupies the site of 'Pyppel's *hām*', an early settlement taking its identity from its Saxon founder. Recorded as Papelesham, Paplesham and Pupplesham in the 12th and 13th centuries, it's described as Pepplesham *alias* Pepsham in 1738. **Pebsham Bridge**, a short distance away at Herstmonceux, appears as Pepsambridge in 1541, getting its name from a family who had settled here from Pebsham.

Peckham Farm. See PEAKDEAN.

Peelings. This is one of the 45 or so *ingas* names found in Sussex, and one of the few, like Hastings, that have hung on to their final *s*. Each identifies the territorial area of a South Saxon tribal group – in this case the Pydelingas, or Pydel's people. The Domesday Book records the name as Pellinges in 1086, but it's Pedlinga a century later, changing to Peeling in 1406. The same group seem to have had their *worð* or enclosure on land at **Piddingworth**, which is documented as Pydelingeworth and Pedelingeworth during the 13th century. Pydel himself – or some other Saxon sharing his name – is associated with a *hām* or settlement at **Pelsham**, Peasmarsh. This is listed as Pedelesham around the year 1200 before changing to the 14th century forms Petlesham and Pylsham, and becoming Pelsome in 1724. And it was a native of Peelings, Simon de Pellyng, who in the late 13th century moved to the Chailey area to make his home close to the river Ouse at what is now **Pellingbridge Farm**, mentioned as Pellyngesbregge in 1425.

Pegden. Peghedenn (1296) and Pegheden (1332) suggest to etymologists this little place near Lindfield was originally the *denn* or woodland pasture where a Saxon named Pecga kept his hogs.

Pell Green. Pell Green, Great and Little Pell, Pell Hill, Pellbottom and Pell Wood all lie in the same area on either side of a stream called Hook Water, which is spanned by Pell Bridge. Scholars think this stream must have been the original 'pell', a dialect variation of 'pool' still used in Sussex to describe the deepest part of a shallow stretch of water. **The Pells** at Lewes, and **Pells**, Buxshalls, likewise derive their name from this word.

Pellingbridge, Pelsham. See PEEL-INGS.

Pen Bridge. Called Penebrugge in 1295, it marks the site of an old bridge across the Adur identified by livestock pens in its vicinity.

Pen Hill. Pen Hill preserves the name of the old port of Pende here at the mouth of the river Adur (the river having been recorded as aquam de Pende in 1301). Mentioned as Ponde by Shoreham later that same century, Pende in turn took its name from *pund*, 'pound, enclosure', a description originally given to its harbour to denote an enclosed stretch of water.

Penhurst. Its spelling has hardly altered since 1086, when the Domesday Book listed this little hamlet as Penehest. It had originated in Saxon days as *Penan hyrst*, a hurst or wood owned by an early settler called Pena, whose property extended to a forest ridge at nearby **Pannelridge Wood**, which we find as Panegregg in 1296, Panyngrigge 70 years later, and Peninge Redge in 1405.

Pennybridge. The place name reminds us that tolls and taxes are nothing new, because it was mentioned as Penybrigge as far back as 1438 when one silver penny seems to have been the toll imposed on medieval travellers wishing to cross the bridge here at Wadhurst. And in case they took an avoiding route, there was a second bridge not far away near Mayfield at what's now **Pennybridge Farm**, recorded a century later in 1545.

Peppering. This was land originally settled by a South Saxon tribal group known as the Pipperingas, who took their identity from their leader, Pippera. Their territory was first documented about AD 725 as Piperinges, a name that resurfaced as Pipringues about 1160 before it changed to Piperinge and Peperyng in the following century. The same group apparently owned one or more streams in the area around **Peppering Eye Farm**, south of Battle, because the place owes its distinctive name to the Saxon description *Pipperinga ēa*, 'the river of Pippera's people', being recorded as Peperengee in 1189, Pipringey in 1383.

Pepperscoombe. The combe or downland valley here near Steyning gets its name from the family of John Pyper, living in the vicinity in 1354. It's noted as Piperescombe in 1425, changing its spelling to Peperscome in 1579. **Peppersgate** at Lower Beeding – Pepersgate in 1609 – is similarly associated with a family named Pepper who appear in the local parish register from 1569.

Peppersgate. See PEPPERSCOOMBE.

Perching. In the Domesday Book it's Berchinges, becoming Percinges in 1267. Sixty years later it's Perchinges, then in 1532, Parchyng. The name is clearly a Saxon *ingas* one, which etymologists believe originated as *Pearrocingas*, meaning 'the paddock dwellers', describing a group of families living on land that had been enclosed within a hedge or similar boundary. **Perching Sands Farm**, just to the north, is described as Saund by Poninges (Poynings) in 1267, but then changes parish to reappear as Perchynsonde in 1343. Its neighbours **Truleigh Sands** and **Tottington Sands** share the same reference to the distinctly sandy soil in this area.

Perryfield. We get our 'perry', the drink made from pears, from the Norman-French *peiré*, a word that became *pereye* in medieval English. So Perryfield was once 'the perry or pear land' where fruit-trees were growing, being described as Purifeud in 1230 and Piriefeld in 1320. **Perryfield Wood**, Brightling, likewise appears as Pirefeld in 1229; **Perryfields** near Tillington is called Peryfeilds rather later, in 1641; and **Perry Barn** at Poling was originally Perry fields in 1715.

Perryman's Cross. Described as Perymans Crosse in the time of Henry VIII, the land here appears to have been owned by an unrecorded individual named Peryman or Piryman – 'the pear-tree grower' – because there's also reference to a now lost Pirymans in the same area, together with Pirymannys gardyn – perhaps the original orchard. The surname is also associated with **Perryman's Grove**, Buxted (Perymans 1438), **Perryman's Farm**, Brightling (Perimans 1636), and **Perryman's Hill**, Danehill.

Petland Barn, Petley Wood, Petsalls Copses. See PETT.

Pett. It's found as Pette in 1195 and Pytte in 1443. The village actually lies on top of a hill, so the description of 'pit' originally must have referred to a distinctive hollow somewhere further down towards **Pett Level**, a flat expanse of watercourses and marshland stretching to the sea. Old pits or hollows are also responsible for the names of **Petland Barn** – 'the pit land' - noted as Pettlonde in 1544, and **The Petlands**, Haywards Heath – Petlandes in 1610. **Petley Wood** near Battle is in the hollow from which it gets its origin as *pytt lēah*, 'the clearing within the pit', referred to as boscus de Petlee in the mid 12th century before changing to Petleywode in 1496. And **Petsalls Copses** at Petworth mark the site of some early animal fold in a hollow, noted as Pittesfald and Pettesfold at the end of the 13th century. The modern name is a corruption of these forms.

Petworth. This handsome medieval town graced by fine old buildings along its many narrow, winding streets, entered history as a Saxon *worð* or enclosed farm belonging to a settler called Peota. Scholars have identified it with the Peartingwyrth mentioned in a charter of AD 785 in which Ealdwulf, last king of the South Saxons, granted land here to St Peter's church at Selsey. The Domesday Book lists Petworth as Peteorde in 1086, but its Saxon roots are more accurately mirrored as Petewurða in 1168, half a century or so before it was recorded as Petteworth. The town was a royal manor in the days of Edward the Confessor, later becoming the property of Roger de Montgomerie, who administered the combined Rapes (county divisions) of Arundel and Chichester for William I. One of its loveliest attractions is nearby **Petworth House**, dating from the 13th century but rebuilt completely by the sixth Duke of Somerset in the 1690s. Set within 2,000 acres of parkland, this great mansion is now National Trust property.

Pevensey. A little village full of picturesque old houses, Pevensey's quaint appearance rather belies its history as one of the most dramatic archaeological sites in the county. It owes its name to Pevensey Haven, one of the many streams draining the Levels or marshes in this area. In AD 947 it was described as Pefenesea – 'Pefen's river' – taking the identity of some early Saxon settler. The 1086 Domesday Book records the place as Pevenesel. By 1198 it's Pevenesee. And in 1639 it appears as Pevensey *alias* Pemsey, a pronunciation that persisted till quite recently. Its story begins in the third century AD, when the Romans enclosed ten acres of what had been an early British stronghold and built their great fortress of **Anderida** here as part of a chain of similar forts protecting 'the Saxon Shore' against barbarian invasion. After the departure of the Legions, Anderida was re-occupied by the British; but in AD 491 the South Saxon war-leader Ælla and his son Cissa attacked the fortress during their lengthy campaign to subjugate the region, massacring all within it. When, in their turn, the Saxons were conquered by the Normans, Pevensey was awarded by William I to his half-brother, Robert de Mortain, and in recognition of its strategic importance a new stronghold was built inside the old Roman walls. Since those days the sea has retreated, leaving the village and its ruined castle lying two miles inland from the pleasant coastal resort of **Pevensey Bay**.

Pickeridge. This originated as medieval *pigge rigge*, 'the pig ridge', describing a swine pasture on a ridge of the forest. It's noted as Pygherygg in 1332, becoming Pyckerage in 1565. **Pickforde**, on a tributary of the river Limden, appears as Pyggeuorde, Pegeford and Pikeford between 1296 and 1332, marking 'the pig ford' where these animals were herded across.

Pickforde. See PICKERIDGE.

Pickham. It's spelled Pekeham, Pykeham and Pykenham during the period 1220-1279, suggesting its derivation is probably *Pīcan hām* – 'Pīca's settlement'. This is a Saxon personal name we find in connection with **Picknill Green**, which is

first documented in AD 772 as on pican glinde, a reference to 'Pīca's fenced enclosure'. At the start of the 12th century it reappears as Pigglinde, a form from which the modern name has developed. The old bridge at Picknill, spanning one of the streams here in the Bexhill area, is mentioned as pontem de Piklyndebrugg and Piklingdebrigg in 1288. The same personal name is also associated with **Pickwell Farm**, south-west of Cuckfield, noted in 1296 as Pykehulle – 'Pīca's hill'. By the year 1400 its spelling had changed to Pekewell.

Pickhurst. Change of final -ers to -hurst is a fairly common feature of place names. This one actually started off as Piker's through its connection with the family of William Piker, whose name appears in the Lay Subsidy Roll of 1327. Interestingly, the place had earlier been the site of the very first English glassworks of which we have authentic record. A deed of 1226 granted 20 acres of land here to the Norman, Laurence Vitrarius, who by 1240 was known to be producing both clear and coloured glass for 'King Henry III's Abbey of Westminster'.

Picknill Green, Pickwell. See PICK-HAM.

Piddinghoe. Standing on a spur of the Downs above the river Ouse, Piddinghoe was first settled by a minor Saxon tribe called the Pyddingas, or Pyddi's people, from whom it took its name as *Pyddinga hōh* – 'the spur of the Pyddingas'. Its subsequent development shows little change from that original form, being Pydingeho in 1248, Pedynghoo in 1438, and Piddinhoo in 1675. The tribe's leader, Pyddi (or another Saxon of the same name) owned a *hām* or settlement on the site of **Pitsham Farm**, just south of Midhurst. This is listed in 1327 as Pidesham, before leaping five centuries to reappear as Pitsom on a county map of 1823.

Piddingworth. See PEELINGS.

Pigstrood. The first element has nothing whatever to do with pigs, but represents the personal name Bica – a name we find connected elsewhere with BIGNOR. The second element is a Saxon word denoting marshy land overgrown with brushwood. So here we have an origin of *Bican strōd*, variously recorded as Bygestrode, Bixstrode and Bycstrode between 1296 and 1327.

Pilstye. Pilstye Farm, beside the Ouse north of Cuckfield, marks the whereabouts of a path or track belonging to an early settler, hence its name, *Pīlan stīg* – 'Pīla's path' – noted as Pylestye in 1296, and then Pillstie in 1599.

Pilt Down. Famous for the 'Piltdown Skull' hoax that made it a household name, this little place was originally the *dūn* or hill of a Saxon called Pīleca. It's mentioned as Pylkedowne in 1455, before changing to Pyltedowne and Peltdowne in the time of Elizabeth I. The skull, discovered here by an amateur antiquarian in 1912, was acclaimed as the 'missing link' between ape and man, but subsequently proved to be a clever deception, probably perpetrated by the then curator of the Natural History Museum.

Pinkhurst. See PANGDEAN.

Piplye Wood. See PIPPINGFORD.

Pippingford. In 1352 it was called Pippingworth, reflecting its Saxon origin as the 'worth' or enclosure of someone with the rather modern-sounding name of Pippa. Later its ending was altered and in 1610 it reappears as Pyppenford, probably explained by its proximity to a tributary stream of the Ouse. Pippa seems to have been the same early settler who owned a *lēah* or cleared area of woodland not far away at **Piplye Wood**, Horsted Keynes, which is found as Pippele in 1437.

Pitsham. See PIDDINGHOE.

Pixton Hill. Recorded during the Tudor period as Pykestones and Pickstone, the place takes its name from the family of Richard Pikstan who were living here in the Forest Row area in 1296.

Plaistow. In earlier times there must have been all sorts of fun and games going on here at Plaistow, because its name – recorded as La Pleystowe in 1271 – literally meant 'the play place', describing a spot hereabouts where folk liked to gather for recreation. Perhaps their enjoyment included the old traditional Sussex game of stoolball (still played in villages around Midhurst), a sport that was popular for more than 300 years before being supplanted by cricket late in the 18th century. There was a similar recreation ground in the vicinity of **Plawhatch Hall** at Forest Row, although this one was simply described by the Saxon word *plega* as 'the play', appearing as Plege in

1139, Plaghe in 1285 and le Plawe in 1612. A hatch-gate into woodland here influenced the change of name to Playhatch by 1724.

Plashett Park. In 1397 we find the place mentioned in connection with LITTLE PARK, near Battle, apparently as the property of the abbot of Battle Abbey. Plashett Park itself (now a farm) is recorded as parc. de Plaseto just over a century earlier in 1288, and as Plasschette in 1323, taking its name from the old French *plaissiet*, meaning 'plaited', most likely a reference to some kind of woven fence originally enclosing the park.

Plawhatch Hall. See PLAISTOW.

Playden. A charming little village with an equally charming origin for its name, Playden lies near Rye on the site of a 'play pasture' where lambs or other young animals were to be seen frisking about. In Saxon times it was called *plega denn*, appearing in the 1086 Domesday Book as Pleidenā before developing to Pleydenne in 1332.

Plonk Barn. Plonke House, recorded here in 1618, sounds the ideal place for a glass of cheap vino; but its name actually refers to a building constructed of *planke* or planks – probably the weatherboarding so often seen in Sussex.

Plummerden. A medieval place name, it first appeared in the Lay Subsidy Roll of 1296 as Plumeresden and Plumereden, being the *denn* or woodland pasture of a Lindfield family called Plumer, whose name tells us they were plume-dealers originally.

Plumpton. The Domesday Book lists the place as Plumtone in 1086. Five years later it's Plumptune, which is a little closer to its Saxon origin of *plūme tūn* – 'the farmstead where plum-trees grow'. A mile or so north of this downland village with its fine 16th century moated manorhouse, lies the much later development of **Plumpton Green**, whose railway station serves **Plumpton race course**, venue of steeplechase events.

Pokerlee Farm. See POOKHILL.

Polegate. Like several other 'newish' communities in Sussex, Polegate owes its expansion to the railway system. Before the opening of the London-Eastbourne line in 1849 it had been a quiet rural backwater, mentioned in the days of Elizabeth I as Powlegate Corner and Poolgate, a name that obviously refers to an old gate by a pool hereabouts.

Poling. Poling preserves the identity of a South Saxon tribal group known as the Pālingas, or Pāl's people, who colonised this area just inland from the coast near Littlehampton. Its name has remained fairly constant over the centuries, appearing as Palinges in 1199, Palyng in 1580, and Powling in 1610. Scholars believe the group also held land about a dozen miles north near Petworth, because a Saxon document mentions a place there called Palinga schittas – 'the sheds of the Pālingas' – where they probably pastured their swine. This is now the site of **Limbo Farm**, whose older name of Palshuddes reflected its Saxon origin. Limbo itself – form *imp hæg* or 'sapling enclosure' – is first noted in 1327 as Imphaghe, before it became prefixed by *l'* to emerge as Lyme-howe and Lymhow in the Tudor period, and then Limboe in 1645.

Ponts Green. Originally it was associated with the family of James Ponte (1405) whose surname came from French *pont* to describe someone living by a bridge. This name is also connected with **Pontmills**, where the old mill seems to have been owned by William Ponte who's recorded here in 1531, the same year in which a now lost Pontyslond, or Pont's land, is mentioned nearby.

Pookhill. There are a number of places in Sussex, including Pookhill, that share a particularly unusual history, because they each owe their name to a supernatural spirit the Saxons called *pūca*. We know him better as the mischievous Puck in *A Midsummer Night's Dream*, and as the fairy who takes two children on a tour of English history in Rudyard Kipling's *Puck of Pook's Hill*. Perhaps Kipling was thinking of Pookhill itself while writing that story. Its name originated as *pūcan healh*, describing a corner of land haunted by a puck or fairy, and it was noted as Poukhale in 1350, Pokehale in 1457, and Powkehalle about 1520. 'Puck's glade' or *pūcan lēah* is now the site of **Pokerlee Farm** near Hen-field, recorded as Pokerlye in 1332; while **Puckscroft** was originally 'Puck's hill' until it changed its name – it's called Powkhill *alias* Powcrofts in 1614. An old hill-track at Hartfield was also thought to be haunted by this fairy, since **Puckstye Farm** here takes its name from *pūcan stīg* or 'Puck's path' – Pukestie in

1287. It shares its origin with **Puxty Wood**, Wadhurst, noted in the mid 15th century as Puxstye and Puk-stye. **Poppets** may look a thoroughly modern name but it actually dates to 1350, when it was spelled Poukeput, 'Puck's pit or hollow'. In 1405 we find a reference to two fields in the same vicinity described as my Lordespokeputt (belonging to the manor) and Townmannespokeputte (owned by the local townsfolk). A less mischievous fairy called a *puccel* or 'little Puck' was believed to inhabit a stubble-field on the site of **Purchase Wood** at Brightling. This name originated as *pucceles ersc* and was variously spelled Pokeleserse, Pocklesherse and Pochelesesse late in the 12th century.

Popmoor. See POPPINGHOLE.

Poppets. See POOKHILL.

Poppinghole. This was once 'Poppa's hothe', a patch of heath-land belonging to a Saxon called Poppa. It's first recorded about the year 1200 as Popenhodhe, reappearing as Popynhothe in 1529. The same personal name also seems to be associated with moor or wasteland at **Popmoor** near Fernhurst, together with a *healh* or corner of land at the now lost place of Pophall in the neighbouring parish of Linchmere.

Portfield. Noted as le Portefeld around the year 1150, the name at that time described an area of open land lying beyond the east 'port' or town gate of Chichester.

Portslade. The old village of Port-slade lies a little way inland from its more recent offspring **Portslade-by-**

Sea, deriving its name from Saxon *portes lād*, 'the harbour's watercourse'. For this derivation to be geographically correct, scholars suggest the mouth of the river Adur must have been as far east as neighbouring Aldrington when the name first came into use. In 1086 the Domesday Book listed the place as Porteslage, but in its modern form it's stayed virtually unchanged since 1179 when it was Porteslade.

Possingworth Park. Posingeworth in 1281, it began its history as the *worð* or enclosed farm of the Posingas, a group of South Saxons taking their identity from their leader, Posa. The place once shared its name with **Possingford Farm** at Hartfield, which is known to have belonged to the manor of Possingworth in 1327 and was recorded as Posyngworth as late as 1559 before its ending changed to -ford to avoid confusion between the two sites.

Potcommon. See POTWELL.

Potwell. Somewhere in this locality there once was a spring rising within a pit or hollow, giving the place its medieval description of *put welle* – 'the pit spring'. It's referred to as Puttewelle in 1369, and Potwelle four years after. A pit or hollow is also responsible for the name of **Potcommon**, which together with nearby **Pothill Farm** is mentioned as La Potte in 1392. A century before this the place had been the home of Margery atte Potte, whose name describes her dwelling 'by the pit'.

Poulter's Corner. Poulter is a development of Polletre, given for the place in 1518. This in turn had come

from le Pollet trew, recorded exactly 100 years earlier. It's clear the name originated as 'the polled or pollarded tree', referring to one that had been cut back to produce a round, knobby head of young shoots.

Poundfield Corner. Pondefoldefelde in 1563, Poundsfould in 1650, the place lies on what was once a patch of unenclosed land where there was a pinfold, or pound for stray cattle. That old word *pund* – 'pound, enclosure' – has likewise given us **Pound Corner**, called Poundland in 1361, and **Pound Hill** at Crawley.

Poundsford. This is actually a migrant name from the south Midlands, because it originated with Richard de Polesworth, a native of Polesworth in Warwickshire, who settled here late in the 13th century. In 1574 the place is referred to as Pollysford *alias* Pollysworth.

Pounsley. One of many little places once associated with Sussex's iron industry, appearing as Pounsley Furnace in 1586. Just over 100 years earlier it had been recorded as Pounteslegh and Ponteslegh, suggesting a Saxon derivation, *Puntes lēah* – 'Punt's woodland clearing'.

Poynings. Once the South Saxons had successfully subdued and colonised the area we know as Sussex, their warrior-chiefs became the leaders of early tribal groups of families called *ingas* who settled down to farm the land here. Old ways died hard though, and the nicknames they'd earned themselves as fighters stuck with them as farmers, including Billa 'the dagger', Glott 'the sneerer', Heafoc 'the hawk' – and Pūna 'the hammer', whose tribal name, Pūningas, survives as Poynings. It's first documented in its Saxon form in AD 960. The Domesday Book lists it as Poninges. And in 1369 it's spelled Poinynges.

Preston. The place now has been virtually absorbed by the growth of Brighton and Hove, bequeathing its name to **Preston Park**, but at one time this was Bishop's Preston, or Preston Episcopi, reflecting its early status as a Church-owned manor. Its name originated as *prēosta tūn* – literally 'the farmstead of the priests' – and at the time of the Norman Domesday Book, in which it appeared as Prestetone, it belonged to the Bishop of Chichester. By 1319 it was called Bisshopes Preston to distinguish it from EAST PRESTON further along the coast.

Preston, East and **West.** Both places share the same history as the preceeding entry, marking the sites of farmsteads or manors owned by the Church. East Preston is Prestetune in 1086, Prestona in 1180, becoming Est Preston in 1327; while West Preston is first mentioned as 'West' around the year 1230.

Prestwood. 'The priests' wood', recorded as Prestewode in 1312, it must have been part of Church-owned land at some time in the past.

Prickett's Hatch. The name refers to some old hatch-gate associated with the 'yeoman prickers' or huntsmen attached to royal hunting parties. It dates back to Tudor times, when the oakwoods of Sussex provided excellent sport for the nobility, being recorded between 1546 and 1579 as Prikers hatch, Prikkett hatche, and Priggers hatch. Incidentally, 'pricket' was the old term for a fallow deer buck in its second year, before its antlers had started to branch.

Prinkle Wood. Its name comes from the family of Ada Prynkel (1296) who are also registered as owners of **Prinkle Farm** in the neighbouring parish of Dallington. The derivation of their surname isn't certain, but it's most likely a diminutive of medieval *prink*, used to describe somebody pert or forward.

Prinsted. There was probably an old orchard here originally, since the name stems from *peren stede* – 'the place of pears' – appearing as Pernestede in 1253 before it changed to Prynsted late in the reign of Elizabeth I.

Puckscroft, Puckstye. See POOKHILL.

Pulborough. The older part of the village stands with its parish church of St Mary's along the top of a hill above the young river Arun. Both hill and river feature in its name, because it was once *pōle beorg*, 'the mound near the pools', described as Puleberge in the Domesday Book (1086). By the first half of the 13th century its spelling had altered to Pollebergh and Pulbergh. The 'pools' – probably bends in the river – nowadays offer excellent fishing and boating.

Punnett's Town. The village has developed on land shown as Pannets Farm on a county map of 1823. It originally acquired its name during the period of the English Civil

War from an Anthony Pannet of Herstmonceux, recorded in 1645.

Purchase Wood. See POOKHILL.

Purster. This has a rather sinister history as a place once associated with an outbreak of plague or other contagion, because its name began as *Puddan steorfa*, meaning 'Pudda's pestilence'. We don't know who Pudda was or what became of him, but Purster Farm here at Brede marks the site of his misfortune, being noted as Podesterf in 1296, Potesterf *alias* Pusterves in 1374, and Poster in 1428.

Pyecombe. Pyecombe is a derivation of *pēac cumb* – 'the peak valley' – owing its description to the southern edge of Wolstonbury Hill which juts out into the valley here. It's mentioned around the year 1100 as Piccumbe, changing its spelling to Pykcumbe two centuries later.

Pythingdean. The only early recorded form of this place name dates from 1279, when it's given as Pytingedene, suggesting to etymologists that it probably originated as *Pyttinga dene*, 'the valley of Pytta's people', a minor Saxon tribal group.

Quabrook. The exact definition of Quabrook is a mystery. Its first element is medieval *quabbe*, meaning a boggy place, while its second certainly looks like 'brook' or marshy

ground. But in 1285 we find the name documented as Quabbalke, a form that apparently contains the word *balke* – a timber beam – suggesting a balk of timber at one time could have been laid over the bog, enabling people to get across. The name reappears as Quabback in 1546, but significantly it doesn't change to Quabrooke until 1625.

Quedley. In 1605 it was spelled Quodleigh. Etymologists think it comes from the same source as our old word 'quoth' and originally referred to a *lēah* or clearing in a wood where discussions took place. Perhaps like MADEHURST and MOTCOMBE, Quedley was once the meeting-place of a local moot.

Quickbourne. From medieval *quik bourne*, 'the lively bourne', the name obviously describes a fast-flowing stream. In 1498 a place in this vicinity is mentioned as Quykbonecrouche – 'the cross by the Quickbourne'.

Quiddlewell Mount. There's no mention of the name earlier than 1630, when it's spelled Quiddleswell, but scholars believe it may well contain a diminutive form of the Saxon personal name Cwīda, giving us a derivation of *Cwideles wielle*, or 'Cwidel's spring'. The affix 'Mount' simply describes an area of higher ground here in the marshes of Hooe Level.

··R··

Rackham. There must have been hayfields here at one time, because Rackham was first known as *hrēac hām*, 'the rick settlement' – it's recorded as Recham in 1166, Rakham in 1295. Similarly, **Racklands** – Rakelond in 1492 – was originally land on which hayricks were built.

Racton. Lying in the narrow valley of a stream known locally as the Racon, the place almost certainly derives its name – *hraca tūn* or 'gullet farmstead' – from its location. It's listed in the Domesday Book of 1086 as Rachetone, becoming Raketon 200 years later. We find the same use of *hraca*, 'throat/gullet', used in connection with **The Rake**, where there's a gulley on the eastern side of the long ridge on which neighbouring **Rake Hanger** and **Rake Common** lie. In 1296 the place was the home of John ate Rake.

Raffling Wood. See RATFORD.

Ranscombe. Rammescombe (1291) describes a downland combe or valley where rams used to be kept. The name stayed unaltered for centuries, appearing as late as 1823 as Ramscombe.

Ratford. In the 13th century this was La Rudeford, Redeford and Rotford – 'the reed ford'. It must have been a larger place than now, because its land included nearby **Raffling Wood**, once known as 'the wood attached to (*ing*) Ratford', and first mentioned in 1314 as Rotforthyngwode. By 1533 its name had altered to Rattesfarthingwood, and at the end of that century is found as Ratfalling Wood.

Ratham. The name's shown as Rotham on Greenwood's map of Sussex (1823), changing very little over the centuries since 1279 when it had been Roteham – 'the settlement of Rōta' – a Saxon personal name we also find connected with ROTTINGDEAN.

Ratton. Once the *tūn* or farmstead of an early settler called Ræda, this was Radintone in the Domesday Book (1086) and Rattone in 1247. The Ratton estates formerly included the HAMPDEN PARK district of Eastbourne.

Raughmere. Raughmere Farm lies beside the river Lavant at a spot once known as 'the heron pool' or *hrāgra mere*. It's recorded as Raghmere in 1323 and Rawmere in 1411, acquiring its present spelling early in the reign of Henry VIII.

Reddyke. See REDFORD.

Redford. This name looks as though it might share the same origin as RATFORD'S 'reed ford', but it first appears in 1296 as Rydeforde, suggesting it started as *rīed ford* – 'the ford at the rid place' – where encroaching saplings and undergrowth had been cleared away. The Saxon word *rīed* likewise forms part of **Reddyke** – 'the cleared ditch' – recorded as la Rede-diche about 1180; and also **Redgrove Wood** – 'grove by the clearing' – Redegrove in 1375; while **Redlands** was 'cleared land' mentioned as Redelande in 1363. But **Redland**, near Salehurst, began its history as *hrȳðer land* or 'cattle land', being listed as Retherlonde in 1305.

Redgrove Wood, Redland(s). See REDFORD.

Renhurst. See ROUNDHURST.

Rewell Hill. Scholars believe this hill just outside Arundel derived its name from an old French word *roelle*, meaning 'little wheel', originally given to a circular track that skirted the foot of the hill at FAIRMILE BOTTOM. It's mentioned as La Ruele in 1275, just four years after neighbouring **Rewell Wood** had been noted as 'forest of Roell'.

Rickney. In early times Rickney formed one of a number of 'islands' of firm ground standing above the surrounding marshes of the Pevensey Levels. Recorded as Rykeneye in 1291, this particular *ēg* or island took its name from a Saxon called Rīca who'd made his home on it. In 1371 we find **Little Rickney Bridge** here referred to as Rykenyesbregge.

Ridge Hill. A place name that explains itself, it's Rydghyll and Redgehill at the start of the 17th cen-

tury, sharing its old spelling with **Redgeland Wood** near Hollington, which had appeared rather earlier (1399) as Ruggelond. **The Ridge** is the name of the prehistoric track running from Ore to Baldslow.

Ridlington. See WARTLING.

Ringden Wood. It covers the site of an old woodland pasture probably lying in a circular depression, hence the name 'ring pasture' or *hring denn*, recorded as Ringedenn in 1271.

Ringles Cross. In 1489 we find the place mentioned both as Ryngylcros and Rynglescrosse. Etymologists think the first element is almost certainly the dialect word 'ringle', meaning 'little circle', here describing a wayside or boundary cross in the Celtic style, with arms banded by a decorated circle.

Ringmer. There's no trace of any natural pool in the village now; but this was once an area of river marshland, so Ringmer's derivation – *hring mere*, 'the ring mere' – must have originally applied to some large, circular marsh-pool in its vicinity. The name first appeared in its modern form during the Tudor period, having developed from Ringemere (1276) and Ryngmere (1290). The older spelling is preserved still by nearby **Ryngmer Park**.

Ripe. In Saxon times this was *rip* – 'the edge' – because of the settlement's location on a ridge of land. Incredibly, the name hasn't altered at all since the Normans recorded it in their Domesday Book of 1086; although in 1573 it was noted as

Rype *alias* Eckyngton, from the proximity of Eckington Corner.

Riseden. Rysdenne (1332) and Ryseden (1438) suggest this began as *hrīs denn*, 'brushwood pasture', denoting a woodland pasture where brushwood was lying about, ready to be gathered for fuel.

River. Although River lies within a mile or so of the western Rother, the name has no connection as such with the river. It's the Saxon word *yfre*, meaning 'hill brow', a reference to the steep slope on which this pretty hamlet and neighbouring **River Common** are situated. During the Middle Ages the place was described as *atter evre* – 'at the brow' – abbreviated to *'ter evre* to produce the forms Treva (c.1145), Treue (1262) and Trewerre (1352). In 1396 the name first appeared as Rivere. In 1542 it was Ryver *alias* Tryve. The same process of abbreviation has been at work with **Riverhill**. Like River it lies on a steep slope, and was recorded in 1380 as atte Euere before changing to Ryvers in 1487, Riverhill in 1602. Similarly, **Riverhall** near Mountfield is noted as Eures around the year 1200. Here the affix -hall seems to be a corruption of -hill, since the ground rises steeply from the river Line. But the name of **Riverhall**, Wadhurst, obviously does refer to its local stream because it's mentioned as Watergates *alias* Ryverhall in 1600.

Riverhall, Riverhill. See RIVER.

Robertsbridge. This popular little town, associated with the manufacture of cricket bats since 1876, takes its name from Robert de St Martin, a nobleman of Norman descent who founded a Cistercian abbey by the eastern Rother towards the end of the 12th century. The ruins are now incorporated in farm buildings at the end of Fair Lane, a mile east of the town. The bridge spanning the Rother at the neighbouring hamlet of **Northbridge Street** dates back to the founding of the abbey, hence 'Robert's Bridge', first recorded in Latin in 1199 as Pons Roberti, and anglicised to Pount Robert in 1310, before appearing as Robartesbregge in 1445.

Rock. Despite its appearance, this is actually 'the oak-tree'. It's one of those names, like RIVER and RYE, that have suffered a medieval misplacement of letters, turning *atter ook* – 'at the oak' – into *atte rook*. We can follow the process in the name of a family once living at Rock, listed in 1296 as atte Rock, but in 1327 as atter Oke. **Rocklands Farm** near Wartling has an entirely different origin, though – it was 'the rook land', recorded between 1226 and 1328 as Rokeland, Rokelonde and Rokland.

Rodmell. Lying at the foot of the Downs by the river Ouse, Rodmell gained its Saxon name *rēada mylde*, meaning 'red soil', from the distinctive colour of the earth in this area. In the Domesday Book of 1086 it's given as Redmelle. During the period 1199-1296 it appears as Redemelde, Radmelde and Rademylde. And by 1638 it's Radmell. The village is associated with the writers Leonard and Virginia Woolf, who lived at **Monks House**. Tragically, Virginia was to drown herself here in the Ouse while suffering a mental breakdown in 1941.

Rodmill. Rodmill derives its name from RODMELL through a native of that village, William de Rademylde (1296) who owned the manor of a now lost place nearby called Beverington, of which Rodmill was formerly part.

Roedean. It appears as Rowdean Gap in 1724, a reference to the gap or break in the cliffs here. The name probably originated as *rūh denu* – 'the rough dean or valley'. Roedean is famous for its girls' public school, founded in 1885 in Brighton before being moved to its present site in 1898-9.

Roffey. This began as *rūh hæg*, 'the rough hay', describing a hay or hedged enclosure on uncultivated land. It's recorded as La Rogheye in 1281, Roughey in 1446, and Ropheye in 1574. **Roffey Place** has close links with the Jesuit poet Robert Southwell (1561-1595), author of *The Burning Babe*, who was executed at Tyburn for his faith.

Rogate. 'The roe-deer gate', it marks one of the old forest entrances in this area, appearing as la Ragate in 1229 before acquiring its modern spelling in 1275.

Rose Green. Research associates this name with the family of John Rose, living in Pagham early in the 15th century. The same surname – either from old French Rohese, Roese, or else an inn-name, 'at the sign of the Rose' – is possibly also connected with **Rose Lands**, Eastbourne (Rowesland 1587) and **Roseland Shaw**, Alciston (Roseland 1337) – although the latter could equally have originated as *horsa land*, 'horses' land'.

Roser's Common. It gets its name from a native of Hadlow Down whom we find listed in 1288 as Sayer de Roseye, and in 1296 as Saer de Roseg. His surname probably began as a place name, *hors ēg* or 'horse island'.

Rother, River (eastern). The Rother's older name is recorded as Lymme in 1474, a development of Lymmene or Lymene (1279) and Liminel (c.1180), which in turn had derived from a British word *lem*, meaning 'elm-tree'. The river is first mentioned as the Rother in 1575, from ROTHERFIELD where it rises.

Rother, River (western). Like the eastern Rother, this river once had an older name. It's first mentioned in the 10th century as Scir and Scyre – 'bright, clear' – a description of its water, and appears thereafter as Schire about 1160, Shyre in 1413. The present name is a fairly modern back-formation from ROTHERBRIDGE.

Rotherbridge. Once the meeting place of the Rotherbridge Hundred, it's given its name to the western Rother on which it lies, marking the site of a Saxon river-crossing called *hrȳðer brycg*, 'the cattle bridge', recorded about 1280 as Rutherbrig. By the mid Tudor period this had developed to Rother bridge.

Rotherfield. A prosperous Wealden village, Rotherfield developed on an area of unenclosed land where cattle were put to graze in Saxon days. A document dated about AD 880 described it as æt Hryðeranfelda – 'at the land of the cattle' – a name repeated as Hryðerafeld some 30 years before the Norman Conquest of 1066. Towards the end of the same century it's variously recorded as Retheresfeld, Rederesfeld and Retherfeld. Land for the parish church of St Denys was given to the village some time during the 8th century by Bertwald, Duke of the South Saxons, who owned a considerable amount of territory in this area. He intended the church to be an expression of his gratitude to the monks of the Abbey of St Denys near Paris, who had successfully cured him of a serious illness. The building was enlarged at the beginning of the 13th century, when it was decorated with wall frescoes which were rediscovered in 1893.

Rottingdean. Its Saxon name was *Rōtinga dene*, 'the valley of the Rōtingas', denoting the territory of a tribal group who took their identity from their leader, Rōta. The Domesday Book lists the place as Rotingeden in 1086. Six centuries later in the time of Charles II its pronunciation is shown as Rottendeane. The Rōtingas also appear to have had land at **Ruttingham**, near Fletching to the north, where they gave their name to a *hamm* or watermeadow recorded as Rotingehamme in 1200. The author Rudyard Kipling lived at **The Elms** in Rottingdean for five years, until sightseers forced him to move away in 1902 to BURWASH. Kipling's neighbour in the village was the artist Sir Edward Burne-Jones, who spent the final 20 years of his life here, dying in 1898.

Rounden Wood. It's Rawindenne about 1197, Ruindanne in 1225, and Rowenden in 1539. Etymologists think these forms probably go back to Saxon times as *æt þæm rūgan*

denne, meaning 'at the rough woodland pasture'.

Roundhurst Common. In local parish records the name appeared as Rundhurst until about 1866. At the start of the 17th century it had been noted as Rendhurst and Randhurst, and earlier still (1296) as Ryndhurst. Its derivation seems to be *rȳmde hyrst*, 'the cleared wood', an origin also shared by **Renhurst** near Mayfield, which is listed as Rendherst in 1439.

Roundstreet Common. See ROWNER.

Rowfant. Etymologists connect this name with the same Saxon word associated with FRANT, giving Rowfant a derivation of *rūh fyrnþe*, 'rough fern-covered land'. It first occurs in the Lay Subsidy Roll of 1327 as the family name of Adam de Ronferth, and then appears as Rowfraunte in 1574 and Rowvant in 1610.

Rowhook. A name that hasn't altered at all since the early 14th century, it originally meant 'the rough hook or spur', a reference to the projecting hill-spur here.

Rowley. This began as *Rūnan lēah*, a cleared area of woodland owned by a Saxon called Rūna. In fact a document of 1018 details the perimeter of this property as runanleagesmearc – 'the boundary of Rūna's clearing'. Between 1296 and 1332 it appears as Runle, Rumlegh and Rondlegh, forms from which a later unrecorded Rowdley would have developed to give us the modern place name.

Rowner. Rowner lies beside the river Arun marking a spot identified in earlier times as *æt þæm rūgan ōran* – 'at the rough bank'. By the 13th century the name had evolved to Rugenor and Ruwenore, and the following century it's found as Roughenore and Rughenor. The place has given its name to **Roundstreet Common**, two miles away across the river, which is recorded in 1738 as Rowner Street.

Rudgwick. There was a little Saxon farm here originally, standing on a ridge of land above the surrounding oakwoods of the Weald. In time 'the ridge farm' or *hrycg wīc* became Regwic (1210) and Reggewik (1225), changing its name to Rudgweeke in the 17th century. Interestingly, its pronunciation still preserves something of its origin as 'Ridgick'.

Rumboldswhyke. Listed in the 1086 Domesday Book simply as Wiche, Rumboldswhyke began its history as a Saxon *wīc* or farm. But then some time during the 12th century the chapel of its church was dedicated to St Rumbold, and as a consequence we find the place mentioned in 1225 both as Wikes and Rumbaldeswic. In 1262 it's described as town of St Rumbold, appearing rather less grandly in 1623 as Rumballsweek. The original Saxon name now survives as **Whyke** on the outskirts of Chichester. St Rumbold himself was the son of an 8th century king of Northumbria and his wife, a Mercian princess. Legend relates that the saint died when only three days old, having declared himself a Christian, demanding baptism, and delivering a lengthy sermon to his parents. His birthplace is believed to have been at King's Sutton, Northamptonshire, where St Rumbold's Well still exists.

Runcton. In 1540 the name was recorded in some detail as Rongeton *alias* Rounton commonly called Romton. During the 12th century it had appeared as Rongenton and Rogentona. And in the Domesday Book (1086) we find it listed as Rochintone. Etymologists believe it possibly goes back to a Saxon tribal group called the Rūningas – Rūn's people – who had their *tūn* or farmstead on this site.

Runtington. Originally *Hrunting tūn*, Runtington Farm at Heathfield marks the site of an earlier farmstead owned by a Saxon named Hrunta, whose property also included a hill at the now lost place of Runtingdown just to the south near Hailsham. Runtington was first recorded about the year 1100 as Runctintuna, developing to Runtyngton in the 13th century.

Rushlake Green. 'The rush-fringed watercourse' or *rische lac* must have been the medieval name given to one of the streams in this vicinity before it was eventually transferred to the village. It's first noted in 1537 as Rysshelake, changing just 30 years afterwards to Ruslake grene.

Rusper. Rusper began as *rūh spær*, 'the rough enclosure', a name scholars describe as being characteristic of this old forest area. Its 13th century spellings included Rugespere, Rughesparre and Rusparre. In 1529 it appeared as Roosper.

Russell's Green. Described in 1367

as Russelleslond, the hamlet stands on land once owned by the family of a William Russell, recorded in the Ninfield area around 1300. Their surname originally began as a nickname meaning 'red-haired/faced'.

Rustington. We can hazard a guess that the Saxon who built his *tūn* or farmstead on this site had red hair, because his nickname, Rusta, came from the same word as our 'rust'. The place name hasn't altered its spelling since 1255. In the time of Elizabeth I (1589) it's mentioned in an abbreviated form as Ruston *alias* Rustington.

Ruston Wood. The wood lies between the Ouse and a tributary stream on land once occupied by a farmstead known as 'the rush farm' or *rysc tūn*, noted as Ryghston, Riston late in the 13th century, and The Ryshton in 1546.

Ruttingham. See ROTTINGDEAN.

Rye. Something of a tourist showplace with its pretty little cobbled streets and medieval houses, Rye epitomises everything that's most attractive about Sussex. It was built on a rocky promontory above sea-flooded marshes that in earlier times separated it from the mainland, thus its Saxon name *æt þ̆ǣre īege* – 'at the island'. In the English of the Middle

Ages this became *at ther ye*, the *r* later getting carried over to give *at the rye*, a form recorded as Ria and Rya in the mid 12th century. By 1222 it had become La Rye. A thriving seaport during the 15th and 16th centuries, Rye's prosperity as one of the Cinque Ports gradually diminished once the sea began to recede, leaving the town eventually standing high and dry above the Romney marshes. It has long been a favourite haven for artists and writers, including Henry James who lived at **Lamb House** from 1897 until his death in 1916. The house (which is open to the public) subsequently became the home of the novelist E.F.Benson, who used Rye as the setting for his 'Miss Mapp' stories.

Ryecroft. See RYEFIELD.

Ryefield. Recorded as la Riefeld in 1263, it signifies land on which rye was once grown. Greenwood's map of Sussex (1823) shows the place as Rivall Fm, giving the dialect pronunciation of the day (preserved in the name of **Rival Lodge** nearby). **Ryecroft** shares the same origin as Ryefield, being mentioned as Ryland in Nuthurst in 1560.

Rye Foreign. This is the name given to the area around Rye, 'Foreign' coming from Latin *forinseca*, meaning 'outside the bounds'.

· · S · ·

Saddlescombe. The clue lies in the hamlet's location on a ridge of land rising saddle-like at either end to the summits of Newtimber Hill and Devil's Dyke. Its situation gave it the original descripton of *sadoles cumb*, 'the valley of the saddle', recorded as Salescombe in 1086, Sadelescumbe a few decades later, and Sadlescomb in 1327. Interestingly, the 1086 Domesday Book form is closest to the name's modern pronunciation.

St Anthony's Hill. The name here is not Anthony, saint or otherwise, but Anta, identifying an early settler whose land included this hill, rising like an island above the coastal levels near Eastbourne. *Antan ēg* – 'Anta's island' – had become Antenye by 1249, a form corrupted to Anthony Hill in the time of Elizabeth I. In 1624 we find it fancified as St Anthonies Hill. But then a map of Sussex published in 1823 shows it nearer its medieval form as Anthon Hill.

Saint Hill Green. The earliest record we have of this name dates only as far back as 1568, when it appears as Saynt Hill. Scholars think it could be a derivation of *sænget*, meaning 'singed/scorched', suggesting the hill at some time had been burnt by fire. This is almost certainly the origin of **St Ives Farm**, Hartfield, once *sænget tēag* – 'the scorched tye or enclosure' – found during the Tudor period as Sentye, Seynt Tye and Saynt Tye, before developing to Saint Tyes by 1792.

St Ives Farm. See SAINT HILL GREEN.

St Leonards. Quieter and more sedate than its neighbour Hastings, St Leonards developed as a seaside resort early in the 19th century when a London builder James Burton (father of the noted architect Decimus Burton) bought an estate here on which to create a watering-place similar to Brighton. The town is named for its church, mentioned as ecclesia Leonardi de Hastynges in 1279, and Seynt Leonards in 1557. Further north near Horsham, **St Leonard's Forest** – foresta S.Leonardi in 1213 – in all probability took its identity from some medieval chapel likewise dedicated to St Leonard – a saint revered as the patron of prisoners, whose cult had been introduced by returning Crusaders.

St Roche's Hill. St Roch or St Rock, still a popular saint on the Continent, is invoked to give protection against physical disease. Until the dissolution of the monasteries, there had been a chapel dedicated to him here – it's described as the 'late chappell of St Rooks' in 1570. Soon afterwards, we find the site referred to as St Rokeshill, becoming St Rock's Hill in 1625 and Rook's Hill a century later. The whole hill is nowadays known as **The Trundle**, after the Iron Age earthwork – *tryndel*, 'the circle' – that crowns its summit. Occupied from the 5th to the 1st centuries BC, this had been the stronghold of a British tribe whose territory lay between the rivers Lavant and Arun.

Saffrons, The. See EASTBOURNE.

Sakeham. It lies beside the Adur on the site of a *hām* or settlement belonging to a Saxon named Saca, appearing in the Domesday Book (1086) as Sacheham before acquiring its modern spelling in 1279. Close to Sakeham Farm is **Sake Ride**, which gets its affix from *rīed* – 'ridded' or cleared land.

Salehurst. This began as *sealh hyrst*, 'the sallow hurst' or willow wood, an appropriate name for a place lying in an area long associated with the manufacture of cricket bats. In 1086 the Domesday Book listed it as Salhert. And in the 13th century it was Salherst and Salhurst.

Saltcote, Saltdean. See SALTHAM.

Saltham. A name that hasn't changed since 1272, it originally described a settlement where seasalt was worked – in fact the place is only a few miles from **Saltmill**, called Lityl saltmyll in 1460. **Saltcote** marks the site of a medieval cot where salt was probably stored. It's first recorded in 1307, and its name was once used as an alternative for Playden, the parish in which it lies, the two being mentioned together as Salcott *alias* Pleyden in 1629, and

Playden *alias* Salcote in 1675. **Saltdean**, on the coast east of Brighton, was simply 'the salt dean or valley' forming a break in the cliffs, shown as Saltdean Gap on a map of 1740.

Salvington. Lying just a couple of miles from the coast, Salvington began as the *tūn* or farmstead of a South Saxon who was called either Sæwulf – 'the sea wolf' – or less romantically, Sælāf, which translates literally as 'sea leavings', suggesting a nickname something like 'flotsam'. In the 13th century Salvington was recorded as Saluinton and Saluynton, forms easier to understand when we remember that medieval *v* was written as *u*.

Sapperton. The spelling of this place name shows very little variation over the centuries. It's Sabertona in 1210, Saperton in 1450, and Saperton *alias* Saberton in 1590. Etymologists think it goes back to *Sǣbeorhting tūn*, denoting the farmstead of a Saxon attractively named Sǣbeorht or 'seabright'.

Saxby. This looks an older name that it actually is, dating only from the mid 17th century when the land here was owned by a Stuart gentleman, Robert Saxby of Eastergate. Research suggests he may have been descended from a family called Saxepe or Saxpe, recorded in the parish of Ashurst early in the 1300s.

Saxonbury Hill. As with neighbouring DANEGATE, romantic fancy has been at work here, turning Socksbury Hill (1809) and Soxenbury (1842) into something a little more imaginative. In fact the name's first element is Saxon only insofar as it's the old word *soca*, 'the soaking or sucking place', describing a quagmire. There must have been some kind of defensive site on the hill at one time, because the name actually means 'the stronghold above the quagmire' or *soca burh*, recorded late in the Tudor period as Sockburie.

Sayers Common. Called Sayer's Common in 1665, but Sawyers in 1823, it lies close to a Sawyersbridge noted in 1611, both deriving their name from the family of Walter le Saghier of Poynings (1327) whose surname tells us he worked as a timber sawyer.

Scaynes Hill. The name – most likely that of an early owner – appears as Skerns Hill in 1586, Skaines Hill in 1849. The district includes an area formerly known as Henfield Common (**Henfield Wood** lies just to the north) which has a much older provenance, dating all the way back to AD 765 when it appeared in a Saxon charter as heanfelde, 'at the high land'. It was subsequently noted as Henefeld in 1327, and Hendfeild in 1636.

Seabeach. Despite its seaside description, Seabeach is actually some way inland. First recorded around the year 1187 as Seuebech, in 1521 it was noted as Sebeche *alias* Sewenbeche. Etymologists offer us two possible origins for the name. Either it began as *seofon bēcan*, 'the seven beeches', describing some prominent landmark in the vicinity; or it was *Seofan bece*, 'Seofa's stream' which once flowed through the valley here. Interestingly, we also find *bece* – 'beck, stream' – as an element in **Waterbeach**, close by.

Seaford. Early in its history this was 'the ford by the sea', a crossing-place over the river Ouse, documented in 1180 as Seford. Until the time of the Tudors the place was a thriving harbour, but in 1579 a terrific storm altered the course of the river, causing it to enter the Channel instead at NEWHAVEN, and Seaford's importance as a commercial port never recovered. It was described as being already 'decayed' in 1592, although still referred to as the 'old' haven well into the 19th century.

Sedgewick Park. It's recorded as Segwike in 1222, Seghwyk just over a century later, marking the site of a Saxon *wīc* or farm that took its name from the sedge growing at the margin of some nearby pool – probably the large pond that still exists here. To the north of the park lies **Sedgwick Castle**, built in the time of the Normans but now completely in ruins.

Sedlescombe. Although the name looks very similar to SADDLESCOMBE, etymologists think this pretty East Sussex village originated as the property of some unidentified Saxon who chose to make the valley here his seat or residence – hence *setles cumb*, 'the combe of the seat'. The Norman Domesday Book recorded the place as Salescome and Selescome, but its Saxon roots show more clearly in the forms Seteles-cumbe (c.1180) and Sedelescombe (1342). In 1584 we find it spelled Selscome, which is how it's still pronounced. Just to the south lies the **Pestalozzi Children's Village**, where deprived children from overseas are provided with care and education. It can be visited only by appointment.

Sele Priory. The name means 'hall' from the Saxon word *sele*. It's mentioned as Sela about 1075, the year in which the Benedictine priory was founded here by William de Braose, administrator of the Rape (county division) of Bramber, so the description probably referred to the monastic buildings. In 1600 the place is mentioned as Seale *alias* Beedinge, from its proximity to Upper Beeding.

Selham. This began as *syla hām*, 'the settlement of the wallowing-places', conjuring up a rustic picture of livestock cooling themselves in the river mud at the edge of the Rother. The Domesday Book (1086) lists the place as Seleham, a spelling that changes to Suleham, Sulleham and Selham in the course of the 13th century. Aptly enough, there's now a **Noah's Farm Yard Nature Trail** just across the river.

Selhurst. Selhersh, Selherse (1275) and Selersh (1356) are medieval forms suggesting the name goes back to *sele ersc*, 'the hall earsh', identifying a stubble-field bordering some early hall or building. Corruption of final -erse to -hurst is a common development of this type of place name. There was also once a hall of some kind standing on the edge of open land at **Selsfield**, which is recorded both as Selefeld and Selesfeld in 1279.

Selmeston. A South Saxon bearing the typical warrior nickname Sigehelm – 'victory helm' – chose this ancient downland location on which to build his *tūn* or farmstead. Recorded as Sielmestone in 1086, the place name has been Selmeston since 1242, although its pronuncia-

ton is better shown as Symston in 1578, Simson in 1765. Long before the Saxons came, this had been an important centre during the Mesolithic period, pits excavated here in 1933 yielding over 6,000 worked flint implements. It was later re-occupied by Neolithic tribes, who left behind potsherds and traces of their hearths.

Selsey. The Selsey peninsula, south of Chichester, is steeped in the history of the South Saxons, with many of its farms and villages dating at least to the 7th and 8th centuries AD. Despite a belief that its name orginated as *selig ēg* or 'holy island' because of its links with St Wilfred, proof that it was actually *seoles ēg* or 'seal's island' is furnished by no less an authority than the Venerable Bede, whose writings describe Selsey as *insula vituli marini* – 'the island of the marine calf'. In its Saxon form the name is recorded as Seolesige in AD 683, Selesie in AD 957. St Wilfred, the evangelist of the South Saxons, sought refuge here from Northumbrian persecution in AD 681, founding a monastery that was later to become the seat of the diocese of Selsey, and later still, of Chichester. The site of his monastery is now covered by the sea, lying several miles out beneath the coastal waters off Church Norton. Selsey village, at the tip of the peninsula, occupies the site of a Suthton or Sutton, 'south farmstead', corresponding to neighbouring NORTON's 'north farmstead'.

Selsfield. See SELHURST.

Sessingham. It marks the *hām* or settlement of an early tribal group known either as the Seassingas, 'Seassa's people', or the Seaxingas, 'the people of the axe', taking their identity from the nickname of their leader. The Domesday Book (1086) records the place as Sesingeham and Sasingham. In the 13th century its spelling varies as Sessingeham and Cessingham.

Seven Sisters. Referred to as 'the Seven Cliffes or hills' in the *Mariners Mirrour* of 1588, these are the series of chalk cliff heights which are such a noted feature of the Sussex coastline. From Birling Gap, they undulate westward to Cuckmere Haven, beginning with the smallest height, Went Hill Brow (over which runs the Went Way, a prehistoric track), then Baily's Brow, Flagstaff Point, Brass Point, Rough Brow (the highest), Short Brow and Haven Brow.

Sharnden. See SHARNFOLD.

Sharnfold. This name contains the dialect word 'sharn' or cow-dung, derived from Saxon *scearn* – hence 'the dung fold', noted as Scherneuolde in the 13th century, Shernfold in 1527. **Shernfold Park** at Frant is similarly found as Scharnefold in 1327; while **Sharnden Old Manor** near Mayfield stands on a medieval 'dung pasture', appearing as Sarden, Scharden and Sharndenne between 1296 and 1307 – an origin also shared by **Shornden Wood**, Hastings, which is spelled Sarndenne in 1296.

Sharpenhurst. 'The sharp hurst' or wooded hill, describing the fairly steep slope on which lies Sharpenhurst Farm, just south of Itchingfield, it's recorded early in the 13th century as Scearpherst, and first became Sharpenhurst in 1312 before briefly reverting to its older form as Sharpherst a century later.

Sharpthorne. This could be 'the sharp/steep place where thorns grow', but it's more likely to be simply a reference to a prickly thorn-bush once used as a boundary mark. The name is spelled Sharpethorne in the time of Elizabeth I (1597).

Sheep Combe, Sheeplands, Sheepwash. See SHEPHAM.

Sheffield Park. Once upon a time, sheep used to graze on open land here where nowadays cascades of water link the lakes which are among the beauties of these National Trust gardens. The Saxons knew the place as *scēap feld*, 'the sheep land', a name recorded by the Norman Domesday Book as Sifelle before it became Sypfeld, Shepfeud and then Sheffeld (1303). Created for John Baker Holroyd, 1st Earl of Sheffield, around 1775, the park has given its name to the nearby southern terminus of the **Bluebell Line**, the last remaining steam railway in the county, opened in 1960 to operate vintage rolling stock through five miles of unspoilt woodland between here and Horsted Keynes.

Shelley Plain, Shelley's Wood. See SHELLIES GREEN.

Shellies Green. It appears as Shillersgrene, Shellers grene and Shelleis greene during the period 1543-1603, taking the name of an early landowner. **Shelley Plain**, on the outskirts of Crawley, is spelled Shulley in 1428, but its origin can be traced back via Shelflegh (1317) and Sulfleg (1279) to *scylf lēah*, 'the shelf clearing', denoting a cleared area of woodland on the narrow strip of land here, falling away on either side to valleys. **Shelley Wood** at Peasmarsh is mentioned as Seligh *alias* Sedleys in 1610, perhaps a derivation of *sealh lēah*, 'willow clearing'; but **Shelley's Wood**, Itchingfield, gets its name from the family of Richard Shelley, recorded locally in 1625.

Shepham. This little place on the edge of the Pevensey marshes marks the site of a *hamm* or watermeadow once grazed by sheep. It's found as Sheppham in 1591. **Sheep Combe**, on the Downs near Findon, has a much older provenance, being first recorded in 1073 when it was Sicumba – 'the sheep valley' – later apearing as Schypcumbe (1261) and Shipcombland (1477). **Sheeplands** explains itself – it's Sheepeland in 1641; and **Sheepwash Farm** at Nuthurst was a place where sheep were dipped in medieval days, being the home of Philip atte Shepewassh, a native of West Grinstead, in 1332.

Shermanbury. This place name is of particular interest because it began as *scīrmannes burh* – 'the stronghold of the shire-man'. The Domesday Book of 1086 records it as Salmonesberie, but it's closer to its pre-Norman form as Shyremanesburi (1280) and Shirremannebury (1366). A shire-man or shire-reeve (the forerunner of our modern county sheriff) was the chief official of his district, with judicial and executive powers to act on behalf of the king. We don't know the identity of whoever fortified Shermanbury, but it

was obviously an important site in Saxon days and still retains traces of later defensive works in its vicinity, including a moat.

Shernfold Park. See SHARNFOLD.

Sherrington. The Domesday Book (1086) gives the name three different spellings – Sirintone, Serintone and Esserintone. A century later it's Sirinton. And in 1296 we find it as Sherynton. It originated as *Scīring tūn*, denoting the farmstead of a South Saxon called Scīra.

Shillinglee Park. The location is fairly high, with the land shelving away all round, leading etymologists to suggest the name may go back to *Scylfinga lēah* – 'the woodland clearing of the Scylfingas or dwellers at the shelf (of land)'. In 1279 it was recorded as Sullingelegh, developing to Shullynglegh in 1350, and Shellingley in 1570.

Shipbourne. See SHOPWYKE.

Shipley. This pretty village, noted for its associations with the poet and historian Hilaire Belloc, stands at what early settlers in the area referred to as *scēapa lēage*, '(at the) sheep clearing', a cleared patch of woodland where sheep were kept. It appeared in the Domesday Book as Sepelei, having been recorded as Scapeleia 13 years earlier in 1073, subsequently developing to Shepeleye by the beginning of the Tudor period. Hilaire Belloc came to live here in 1906 and remained until his death in 1953, reflecting his love of Sussex in many of his best-known poems. Next to his house stands the fine old wooden smock-mill he preserved, now restored as his memorial.

Shipreed, Shiprods Farm, Shipton Green. See SHOPWYKE.

Shoesmith's Wood. Called Old Shosmiths in the year 1600, it gets its name from the family of William Sosmyth, a 'shoeing smith' who made horseshoes, whom we find recorded in the Lay Subsidy Roll of 1296.

Shopham Bridge. There has been a bridge here since at least the 13th century, spanning the western Rother at a place once known as *Sceobban hamm*, 'Sceobba's watermeadow', recorded as Schobeham in 1288, Scopham in 1437. The bridge itself is mentioned as pontem de Shobeham in 1279.

Shopwyke. A hamlet just to the east of Chichester, Shopwyke began its history as a Saxon sheep farm or *scēap wīc*, supplying mutton to the townsfolk. It's named as Sepewica around the year 1150, and Shapewyke in 1212, changing its spelling to Shopwick and Shopweek early in the 18th century. The importance of sheep as a source of food and wool shows in a number of other place names, including SHEPHAM and SHIPLEY. **Shipbourne Farm**, Wisborough Green, lies on a stretch of the Arun that must be the original 'sheep bourne' where the animals were watered – it was called Shipburne in 1313. **Shipreed** was 'rid' or cleared land where flocks grazed, described as Sheprede in 1543, sharing its derivation with **Shiprods Farm**, Henfield – Schiprede in 1279, Sheeprods in 1830. And **Shipton Green** on the Selsey peninsula must take its name from some unrecorded *tūn* or farmstead where sheep were once reared.

Shoreham-by-Sea. One of the largest privately owned commercial ports in the country, with an airport on its western side, it owes its name to **Old Shoreham**, lying just a little way inland from the mouth of the river Adur. The Saxons knew this older site as *scora hām*, 'the settlement at the steep place', a reference to the downland slopes above the river. First mentioned as Sorham in 1073, it was recorded by the Normans in their Domesday Book as Soreham, altering to Shorham in 1167. Early in its history Old Shoreham had been used as a Roman ferry terminal. A little later (according to traditional accounts) Ælla of the South Saxons landed here with an army of warriors during his eight-year campaign to subjugate the British tribes. For a time after the Norman Conquest the place served as a main harbour and was the port of the Rape of Bramber, but once the river Adur started silting up Old Shoreham's importance gradually waned, and we find it already being described as Eldesorham in 1279. 'New' Shoreham-by-Sea – Nywe Shorham in 1288 – had first been documented in 1151 when its church of St Mary de Portu was given to Sele Priory. Interestingly, it's also recorded in 1457 as Porte of Hulkesmouth *alias* Shorham, suggesting to scholars that some hulk or wreck once lay for many years in the estuary – the port's seal bears a hulk on its reverse.

Shornden Wood. See SHARNFOLD.

Shortbridge. A name that needs no explaining, it's Schirtebreg' in 1287, describing a bridge once spanning a tributary stream of the Ouse. **Shortridge** is similarly self-descriptive – Shorteredge in 1606. And **Shortwood** is first recorded back in AD 772 when it was sceorta wida, developing to Shortewod in 1288.

Shortridge, Shortwood. See SHORT-BRIDGE.

Shovelstrode. The clerks who recorded Saxon place names for the Domesday Book tended to be somewhat hit-or-miss in their Normanised interpretations. Thus we find the origin of this particular name – *scylf strōd*, meaning 'overgrown marshy ground by the shelf (of land)' – listed as Calvrestot and Celrestius in 1086. It was more accurately rendered as Soluestrode and Sheluestrod during the 13th century (when *v* was written as *u*), becoming Sholstrode in the mid Tudor period, then Sholvestrode *alias* Showlestrode in 1619. The site, near East Grinstead, is now a farm.

Shover's Green. This develops as le Sholuere (1402), Sholfere (1418), Shover (1562) and finally Shover Green (1724). Etymologists find it a difficult name to interpret. It possibly derives from *scylf ōra*, 'the shelf or shelving bank'; but more probably from *scylfre*, a Saxon word loosely meaning 'see-saw' – though in what sense this would have been used isn't clear.

Shoyswell. Somewhere hereabouts once welled a spring belonging to an early settler called Sceoh, a rather endearing nickname meaning 'the timid or shy one'. Sceoh's spring – *Sceohes wielle* – eventually gave its name to the Shoyswell Hundred, listed in the Domesday Book (1086) as Esseswelle. The original site, now occupied by **Old Shoyswell Manor**, is named around the year 1100 as Scouueswelle, changing to Schoweswelle and Shoswelle by the early 14th century.

Shripney. In its earliest form, the name is documented in a Saxon charter of AD 680 as Scrippan eg. The second element is 'island', denoting some higher ground in this flat, well-watered area just inland from Bognor Regis. Scholars suggest the first element may have had the original meaning of 'sharp, steep', with reference to some local feature probably altered considerably over the centuries. In 1229 we find the name recorded as Scrippeneye. By 1288 it was Shripeneye.

Shulbrede Priory. Shulbrede can be literally interpreted as 'shelf breadth' to describe the topography of its site, a valley widening out between two hills, with a steep shelf of land to the east of the priory. In its original Saxon form the name was *scylf brǣdu*, evolving to Shelebrede, Shelbrede and Schulbrede by the 13th century. The Augustinian priory was founded about the year 1200 by Sir Ralph de Arderne. Dissolved at the time of the Reformation, it subsequently became part of a house which was a farm until 1902.

Sidlesham. Like so many of its neighbours on the Selsey peninsula, Sidlesham's history begins with the arrival of the South Saxons – in this case, a warrior-farmer named Sīdel.

We find Sīdel's *hām* or settlement documented as Sidelesham as early as AD 683, and as Sideleshamstede, or homestead, 30 years afterwards. In their Domesday Book of 1086 the Normans inaccurately recorded the name as Filleicham. Over five centuries later, in 1606, its pronunciation was shown to be Sidlesame.

Sidley. This was Sidley greene in the time of Charles I (1636). During the late 13th century it had been noted as Sidelegh and Sedeleghe, deriving from *sīd lēah* – 'the wide clearing'.

Singleton. Singleton lies at the edge of an area of ancient forest on a site identified by early settlers as *sængel tūn*, 'the farmstead by the brushwood thicket'. The Domesday Book (1086) gives the name as Silletone, but a century later we can see its Saxon roots reappearing as Sengelton and Singelton. The village is home to the **Weald and Downland Open Air Museum**, in a lovely countryside setting containing many fine examples of old timber-framed buildings brought here from their original locations and exactly reassembled.

Slathurst. This was *slīete hyrst*, 'the sleet wood', a name with a bleak and wintry feel, recorded as Sluthurst in 1296. Etymologists think *slīete* was used here in the sense 'slush, mud', a meaning shared by **Sluts Wood**, Peasmarsh, **Sluts Lane**, Lindfield, and **Sluts Cottage**, Horsham, which stands on land called Slutlond in 1474, Slutt in 1515. Interestingly, 'slut's farthings' is the local dialect term for the hard little bits found in loaves when the dough hasn't been kneaded properly.

Slaugham. Long before the village appeared, there was a water-meadow here beside the river Ouse where sloe or blackthorn grew. In Saxon times it was known as *slāh hamm*, 'sloe meadow', a name recorded as Slacham early in the Norman period. During the 13th century it developed to Slagham and Slaweham, acquiring its modern spelling (pronounced 'Slaffham') in 1324. West of the village, Slaugham Common overlooks the lake on the old estate of **Slaugham Place**, an Elizabethan mansion now in ruins – its staircase is in Lewes Town Hall.

Slaughter Bridge, Slaughterford Farm. See SLOUGH GREEN.

Sleeches Cross. Spelled Sleaches in 1639, the place acquired its name from a William Slech of nearby Rotherfield, recorded in the Lay Subsidy Roll in 1327.

Slifehurst. This has the curious derivation of 'sleeve wood' or *slīef hyrst*, being mentioned as Slefhurst in 1199, Slifhurst in 1296. Either the name originally described the hollow in which Slifehurst lies or – as scholars suggest – it meant 'slippery', in the way that a sleeve is something 'slipped' on. However, there's also a **Sleeves Wood** just south of Hadlow Down, and it's interesting to compare these two place names with the French term for the Channel, La Manche – 'the sleeve' – so called from its shape.

Slindon. An important centre during the Palæolithic (Old Stone Age) period, Slindon stands on the edge of what was once a raised beach, about 200 ft above present sea level.

Its name reflects its site, meaning 'the hill by the slope' – *slinu dūn* – recorded in the Domesday Book as Eslindone, and found as Slindon a century later in 1188. Much of the village and surrounding beech-woods are now part of the large **Slindon Park Estate**, managed by the National Trust.

Slinfold. Slindefold and Slyndefold, forms of this name frequently found between 1225 and 1409, suggest it originated as *slind falod*, 'the enclo-sure on the side or slope', which fits in well with Slinfold's location. The place used to be noted for its Hor-sham Stone quarries, once widely used in Sussex as a roofing material, giving rise to the local term 'slabcas-tle' used derisively of a small house roofed with these slates.

Slonk Hill. Situated just inland from Shoreham, this is believed by scholars to be the *mearc rædesburn* on whose slopes Ælla and his South Saxons crushed the native British forces in AD 485, during their cam-paign to subjugate their new terri-tory. Slonk Hill probably derived its name from the Saxon word *slōg*, part of their verb *slēan*, 'to slay or strike'.

Slough Green. The parish register of 1607 spells it Slowe Greene. A little earlier, in 1543, it had been described as the manor of Slowes. And earlier still, in 1332, the place had been the home of John atte Slo, whose sur-name tells us he lived 'at the slough or mud-filled hollow' – *slōh*. This old word in its alternative form *slōhtre* is probably also an element in the names of **Slaughter Bridge**, Slin-fold, over which ran a way men-tioned in 1279 as via de Slouhtre;

Slaughterbridge Farm, Shipley – Sloghtrebrugge in 1399; and **Slaugh-terford Farm**, Itchingfield, recorded as Sloghtreford in 1276, Sloghterford in 1482, and Slawghterford in 1547. Alternatively, etymologists suggest these three names are a derivation of medieval *sloghtre* (from Saxon *slāh-trēo*) meaning 'sloe-tree or black-thorn'.

Sluts Lane, Sluts Wood. See SLATHURST.

Snailham, Upper and **Lower.** This is unique in the county's place names because it's the only one that men-tions the humble snail. Here beside the river Brede once lay a *hamm* or watermeadow known as 'snail meadow' mentioned as Sneilhamme and Sneylham in the 13th century (the latter spelling preserved by **Snaylham Farm** here). It's been sug-gested Upper Snailham was origi-nally called Grafhurst or 'grove wood', appearing as such in records of 1296 and 1332. In fact there's still a Grove Wood close by.

Snape. The dialect word 'snape' or 'snapey', used of boggy land useless for cultivation, comes directly from Saxon *snæp*, which had the same meaning. Snape itself – la Snape in 1279 – shares the derivation with **Snap Hill**, Lullington, and **Snap Bottom**, South Heighton, as well as **Snapelands Copse**, Selham – described as Le Snapelond in Sule-ham in 1317.

Socknersh Manor. It lies close to the river Dudwell on what was once a 'soaked earsh' or saturated stubble-field – *socen ersc*. Around 1195 the name was spelled Swokenerse, developing to Sokenershe by 1428. In the 18th century it was noted as Socknershe *alias* Sockness. We also come across the word *socen* in connection with **Sokenholes Farm** at Tillington, which gets its name from 'the soaked hollow' in which it lies. The place is first noted in the time of Henry VIII as Sowkenowlles and Soak Knowles.

Sokenholes. See SOCKNERSH.

Somerley. This little village on the Selsey peninsula stands on the site of a Saxon *lēah* or cleared patch of woodland that was only used during the dry months of summer. Listed in the Domesday Book as Summerlege, it's mentioned two centuries later in 1298 as Sumerlegh.

Sompting. Although this is obviously an -ingas name, signifying Saxon tribal territory, etymologists are stumped for an explanation of its first element, *sunt*, which they take to be a topographical word. All they can say with certainty is that the tribe originally owning the land were called the Suntingas, because in AD 956 a charter refers to Suntinga gemære, 'the boundary of the Suntingas' in this area. The Norman Domesday Book records the place as Sultinges. A century later it's Suntinges, becoming Sumptinges in 1242 and Somptyng in 1380. The older name was never completely abandoned though, since we find it noted as Sompting *alias* Sounting as late as 1641. The village's showpiece is its parish church of St Mary's – one of Sussex's three 'Saxon treasures' – crowned by the famous Rhenish helm tower. It was rebuilt and enlarged by the Knights Tem-

plars after Sompting had been granted to them in 1154.

South Binns. See BINEHAM.

Southbrook. See NORTHBROOK.

Southease. A little downland village lying above the valley of the Ouse, Southease was known to early settlers in this area as *sūð hēse*, 'the south brushwood (land)', from its position a mile or two below 'the north brushwood' now occupied by **Northease Farm** at Rodmell. First recorded in AD 966 as Sueise, Southease appears in the Domesday Book as Suesse, developing to Suthese in 1268, Sowthees in 1590. Northease is found as Northesia and Northeise early in the Norman period, before becoming Northhese in 1347, Northees in 1635.

South Eaton. See EATONS.

Southerham. Southerham Farm, on the Ouse just south of Lewes, is all that now remains of a Saxon site called *sūþerran hām*, 'the more southerly settlement', from its position in relation to MIDDLEHAM and NORLINGTON. It was recorded as Suthram in 1262, Southram in 1403.

South Heighton. In Saxon times this was 'the high farmstead' or *hēah tūn*, standing at the edge of the Downs above the Ouse estuary. The Domesday Book gives its name as Hectone in 1086. By the mid 14th century it was already being distinguished as South Eghton to avoid confusion with **Heighton Street**, just to the north at West Firle. This is first recorded around 1150 as Hiectona, becoming Heghton in 1262, and at one time had the alternative name St Cleres (1422) after John de Sancto Claro who had held the manor here in 1347.

South Malling. The area was originally settled by a branch of the Meallingas, or Mealla's people, who had their main tribal base in Kent at East and West Malling. We find South Malling first mentioned in AD 838 as (æt) Mallingum. In the 1086 Domesday Book it appeared as Mellinges, and by the early 13th century was already being distinguished as Suthmelling. Norden's map of 1610 gives the name as Mawling, which is how it's still pronounced.

Southover. Now part of Lewes, Southover was the original 'south bank' or *ōfer* from its location on the Winterbourne stream. Appearing as Suthovere in 1121, Southenover *juxta* Lewes in 1342, it was the site of **St Pancras' Priory**, the first Cluniac house in the country, founded in 1077 by William de Warenne and his wife Gundrada, daughter of William the Conqueror. The priory was dissolved in 1538 and is now in ruins – some of its stonework was used in the gardens of **Southover Grange**, a large Elizabethan house in Keere Street. **Anne of Cleves' House**, one of several properties given by Henry VIII to his fourth wife on their divorce (another is at DITCHLING) is now a folk museum with a fine display of Sussex ironwork.

Southwater. It's difficult to know which 'water' this originally referred to, unless it was one of the several streams in the area. The village lies south of Horsham, sharing its name with **Southwater Street** about a mile away, and appears as Suthwatre in 1346, Southewater in 1570. The poet Wilfred Scawen Blunt, who lived at CRABETT PARK, Worth, from 1872, died here in 1922 and was buried in **Newbuildings Wood** without religious rites, as he had requested.

Southwick. We know the place began its Saxon history as *sūð wīc*, 'the south farm' – but south of what? Scholars aren't sure. Either the description applied to its position on the coast or – as has been suggested – because it was the southern 'wick' of the manor of neighbouring Kingston (by Sea). Whichever is right, Southwick was first mentioned in 1073 as Sudewic, and its location noted 200 years later as Suthewick *juxta* Shorham. Interestingly, it was simply called Week in 1675. From around 1700 BC, long before the Saxons came here, the place had been the site of a succession of settlements, including a Roman villa excavated during the 1930s.

Sparrow's Green. Recorded as such in the year 1600, this East Sussex village originally acquired its name from a John Sparwe (1333) 'the sparrow', indicating a rather chirpy little character. He was also identified with a now lost Sparwyscrosse listed close by in 1452.

Sparrwood. From *spær wudu*, 'the enclosure wood', the name's given as Sparwode in 1314. **Spar Wood** at Billingshurst similarly appears as Sparrewood in 1618 having earlier been the home of John atte Sparre (1296) who dwelt 'by the enclosure' that stood on land at neighbouring **Spurland** – called Sperlond in 1375. Another enclosure, this one in a 'hale' or corner of land, identifies **Sparhall Spinney** at Cowfold, which is Sparro Halle in 1598 and Spurhale a decade later.

Spithurst. Splytherst (1296) and Splidhurst (1327) suggest the site was originally occupied by a hurst or wood that was 'split' in some way. Perhaps it was divided by a path running through it, though it's hard to know what exact interpretation can be put on this name.

Spitlye. The first element here is our word 'speed' used in its old sense of 'good fortune, prosperity', as in the expression 'God speed'. The second element is medieval *legh*, denoting a woodland clearing. So this was a place regarded as being in some way fortunate by its early owners. Recorded as Spedelegh in 1333, it was variously noted as Spedlywud and Spydlycrosse during the Tudor period, becoming Spitleigh in 1622.

Splayne's Green. This is found as Splanes green in 1607, and must take its name from some unrecorded family living locally in the parish of Fletching.

Spray's Wood. Lying west of Battle, it seems to have been part of the property of an Elizabethan landowner, John Spraye of Mountfield, whose name we also find associated with **Sprays Wood** at Ninfield, and **Spray's Farm**, Penhurst, places all fairly close to each other.

Spurland. See SPARRWOOD.

Stammerham. See STANMER.

Standard Hill. Recorded as le Standard in 1470, this is believed by many to be the hill on which William the Conqueror raised his standard before engaging the English Saxon army at BATTLE, four miles away, on 14th October 1066.

Standean, Standgrove Wood. See STANSTED.

Stane Street. Called Stanestret in 1270, this is the famous Roman road running from London Bridge to the east gate of Chichester, a distance of almost 60 miles. The Saxon origin of its name, *stān strǣt* – 'the stone street' refers to the stone-slab surface of the old *via strata* or highway constructed about AD 70. Much of the labour for the Sussex section was provided by the Regni, whose tribal capital was Regnum, later to become CHICHESTER. Their work seems to have been entirely voluntary since no military posts were built; moreover their king Cogidubnus is known to have been on excellent terms with the Romans – in fact the splendid palace at OLD FISHBOURNE was probably built as a residence for him. Stretches of Stane Street have now become busy modern roads. Others survive as quieter byways to be enjoyed by walkers and horse riders.

Stanmer. Stanmer Park, formerly owned by the Earls of Chichester, is the site of the **University of Sussex**, built in the late 1950s, within whose grounds can still be seen the 'stony mere' that gave the old village its Saxon name *stān mere*. It's found recorded in this form in AD 765, and appears in the Domesday Book as both Stanmere and Stamere before becoming Stonmere in 1291. Stammer (1690) shows the local pronunciation of the name – a spelling shared by **Stammerham Farm** at Rusper, which stands on the site of an old stone quarry near a lake, hence *stān mere hām*, 'the settlement by the stony mere', recorded as Stamerham in 1255.

Stansted. Stanesteda in 1179, it's a name that has changed very little since its first appearance as *stān stede*, 'the stony place'. The village is bordered by Stansted Forest, called boscus (wood) de Stansted in 1271, one of the seven 'forests' of Sussex that once were part of the vast *Andredesweald* of Saxon times. Stony sites have also produced several other place names in the county, including **Standean** at the edge of the Downs, whose dean or valley was once noted for its large stones. In 1086 the Domesday Book listed it as Standene. **Standgrove Wood** at Ardingly used to be known as 'the stony grove' – it's Stonegrove in 1613; while **Stoneham Farm**, Glynde, marks a stony *hamm* or watermeadow mentioned as Stonhamme in 1328. The county's two **Stonelinks**, one at Fairlight, the other at Brede, both lie on a *hlinc* or 'link' of rising ground, the former appearing as Stanling around 1210, Stonlinke 60 years later, and the latter as Stonling in 1261, Stonlynk in 1327.

Staplecross. We can follow the development of this name from Stapele, recorded around 1180, via Cruche de Staple (1296) to Staple Cross (1768). The original *stapol* or post that preceded the later medieval *crouche* or cross was probably a marker of some kind for the meeting-place here of the Staple Hundred (a district division). Similar posts have given us the names of **Staplefield** near Slaugham, 'open land by the staple' (Stapelfeld 1315), and **Staplefields**, Steyning (Staplefeild 1612); while **Stapleash Farm**, West Dean, is on the site of 'the *ersc* or stubble-field by the staple', being recorded as Stapelers in 1296.

Stapleash, Staplefield. See STAPLE-CROSS.

Starnash. This little place is on low-lying land beside the river Cuckmere, leading etymologists to suggest its name may go back to *stearn ersc*, describing a stubble-field hereabouts where tern or sea-swallows were often seen. During the 13th century it's found as Sternerse and Sternesse, developing to Sternersh by 1535.

Stedham. Steddanham, recorded in a document of AD 960, leaves no doubt that this village on the western Rother began much earlier as the *hām* or settlement of a Saxon bearing the nickname Stedda, 'the steed or stud-horse', a not untypical name for the period. The Domesday Book listed it as Stedeham in 1086, and its modern spelling first appeared in 1308.

Steyning. We don't know anything more about the original settlers of Steyning other than that they were probably known as the Stæningas, who had their communal village at the *stæne* or 'stony place'. It's first recorded about AD 880 as æt Stæningum, and listed in the Domesday

197

Book two centuries later as Stan-inges, becoming Steyninge in 1316. The village – a port in Saxon days when the estuary of the river Adur stretched further inland – has close links with the 9th century St Cuth-man, who founded the first church here. In fact it's recorded as portus Cuthmanni (St Cuthman's port) in 1103. Legend tells how the shep-herd-saint left Devon at his father's death, trundling his aged mother in a handcart as far as Steyning, where the cart collapsed. His little church was succeeded by a second, larger one in which were interred the remains of King Æthelwulf (d.858) father of Alfred the Great, who him-self had a royal residence here.

Stockbridge. The old meeting-place of the Stockbridge Hundred, it gets its name from an early bridge con-structed of stocks or logs – *stoccen brycg* – spanning a stream that's since become part of Chichester Canal. In 1217 the place was recorded as Stok-kenebrugg, becoming Stokbrugge by the end of the same century.

Stoke, North, South and **West.** North and South Stoke lie opposite one another on either side of a wide loop of the river Arun, while West Stoke is further away close to Chich-ester. All three villages derive their name from a single source, the Saxon word *stoc*, meaning 'place', and interestingly, they each appear in plural form in early records. **North Stoke** is Stoches in the Nor-man Domesday Book (1086), North-stoke in 1271. Its partner opposite likewise appears as Stoches in the Domesday Book, becoming Suth Stok in 1281 – both sites probably originating as strongholds guarding

a strategic fording-place across the river. **West Stoke** is Stokes in 1205, and Stoke *juxta* Cycestre (Chich-ester) in 1288, not being identified as 'West' until the time of Elizabeth I.

Stoneham, Stonelink. See STANSTED.

Stopham. Recorded in the Domes-day Book as Stopeham, the village owes its name to a South Saxon called Stoppa, who chose to build his *hām* or settlement opposite the ruins of a Roman station here where the rivers Rother and Arun con-verge. **Stopham House**, overlooking the little medieval bridge, is the fam-ily seat of the de Stopham Barttelots, whose ancestor, a Norman knight, adopted the name of the manor on being awarded it by William the Conqueror in recognition of his ser-vice at the Battle of Hastings.

Storrington. Etymologists admit this is a difficult name to interpret with any accuracy, but they believe its most likely derivation is *storca tūn*, 'storks' farmstead', indicating a place where storks were occasion-ally sighted. Just to the north of the village there are river marshes, and the pools at nearby Parham have long been noted for their heron colonies, so the presence of storks in the area, say the scholars, isn't improbable. The Domesday Book listed the place as both Storgetune and Estorchetone in 1086. During the 13th and 14th centuries its spelling varied from Storgeton to Storketon and Storweton, and not until 1583 do we find it mentioned as Storghton *alias* Storrington. The name of the **river Stor**, which rises here, is simply a back-formation.

Stoughton. This West Sussex village has a significant place in local Saxon history. Its origin as *stoc tūn*, 'the farmstead by the place', almost certainly refers to the site just northeast of here of the Battle of Stoughton Down (AD 685), in which the South Saxon king Æthelwald was defeated and slain by Ceadwalla, exiled prince of the West Saxons. Traditionally (though erroneously) Æthelwald is believed to lie buried in one of the long barrows on the down. Stoughton itself (pronounced Storton) was recorded in the Domesday Book as Estone, and appeared in the 12th century as Stoctona and Stohton before becoming Stoghton in 1327.

Streat. The village lies at the northern end of an old Roman road or *via strata* that once ran across Plumpton Plain to the foot of the Downs. The Saxons adopted their word *strǣt* (our modern 'street') directly from the Latin one, hence Streat, recorded as Estrat in 1086 and Strete in 1271. Another Roman road, leading to a fording-place across the Adur, gave its name to **Streatham** – 'the *hām* or settlement on the street' – listed at the end of the 12th century as Stretham. And **Streetfield Wood**, Ewhurst lies beside the main Robertsbridge-Rye road which follows the line of a Roman one. At one time there must have been an area of unenclosed land or *feld* here, producing the forms Stratfeld (c.1230) and Stretfeld (1279).

Streatham. See STREAT.

Streele. First noted in 1677, it's a name going back to the Saxon word *strǣl* or 'arrow', signifying a narrow, straight piece of land. We find the same meaning attached to **Streele Farm**, Pulborough – Strele in 1528 – and **Streel Farm**, Mayfield, where Strelewode and Strelane were noted in 1333.

Streetfield Wood. See STREAT.

Strettington. The little Saxon community that built its farmstead here beside Stane Street knew the place simply as *strǣt tūn*, 'the farmstead by the (Roman) street', while outsiders identified it as *strǣt hǣma tūn*, 'the farmstead of the street-dwellers'. The Domesday Book recorded the name in its earlier form as Stratone in 1086, but two centuries afterwards it appeared as Strethamton, developing to Strittington by 1696.

Strood Green, Stroodland Barn, Stroud Lane, Strudgate Farm. See STRUDGWICK WOOD.

Strudgwick Wood. In a list of Saxon swine pastures dating from the mid 10th century, this name appears as Strodwic, 'the farm in the marshy place'. Roughly 300 years later, around 1330, it's described as boscus (wood) de Strodwike, and shortly afterwards identified more fully as Strodewykeswood in Kyrdeford (Kirdford). During the period of the English Civil War we find it recorded as Stroodwiches Wood. Also in the Kirdford area is **Strood Green** – le Strode in 1405 – which probably takes its name from the same *strōd* or 'marshy place' as the wood. It shares its derivation with a dozen other places throughout the county, including **Stroud Lane**, Ambersham, **Strudgate Farm**, Ardingly, and **Stroodland Barn**, Little Horsted; while a second **Strood Green** – this one near Slinfold – is listed as the home of William de la Strode, 'of the marsh', in 1279.

Stumbleholm, Stumblett Wood, Stumlets Wood. See STUMBLEWOOD COMMON.

Stumblewood Common. A Parliamentary survey of 1658 gives this name as both Stumblett Common and Stamblett Common. The word *stumblet* seems to be connected with several old areas of woodland in East Sussex, leading etymologists to suggest it probably applied to places where there were tree-stumps. We find **Stumlets Wood** at Frant called Stomblets grene in 1559, le Stumblet in 1600; and the word is clearly also the origin of **Stumlet Wood**, Waldron, **Stumblett Wood**, Ticehurst, **Stumblott's Wood**, Ewhurst, and **Stumletts Gill**, Rotherfield. **Stumbleholm Farm** at Ifield falls in much the same category, taking its name from medieval *stumbel holwe* or 'stump hollow', recorded as Stombelhole in 1327, Stumblehole in 1565.

Stunts Green. A hamlet close to Herstmonceux, it was originally connected with the family of a John Stonte whose name appears in court records of 1520.

Sullington. Opinion is divided as to the interpretation of this particular name. Its second element is obviously *tūn*, denoting a Saxon farmstead. The first may be *syling*, a derivation of *syle* or 'wallowing-place' (found at SELHAM). Alternatively it could be *sielling* or 'gift'. So Sullington originated either as a

farmstead by a miry place where livestock wallowed, or as one possessing land given as a gift. Around the year 1050 the place was recorded as Sillingtune, appearing just under 40 years later in the Domesday Book as Sillintone. In 1641 it was Sullington *alias* Sillington.

Summersdale. Spelled Sumeresdale in 1233, it was originally *Sumores dæl*, the dale or valley of an early settler called Sumor – a name meaning 'summer' which had its opposite in Wintra or 'winter', also used as a personal name, albeit a less agreeable one.

Summertree. A charming name with an equally charming origin, it dates back to the old May Day festivities once heralding the fruitful months of summer. A centrepiece of the celebrations was the 'summertree', either a real one or more often a pole decorated with flowers, ribbons and greenery. Summertree Farm, on the site of a little medieval hamlet north of Herstmonceux, preserves the memory of this ancient custom, being recorded in 1520 as Somertre, Somertregate and Somertre crosse.

Sunninglye. Sonnyngelegh early in the 14th century, it stems from *Sunninga lēah*, denoting a cleared area of woodland belonging to a minor Saxon tribe called the Sunningas, or Sunna's people, who had their home in this part of the ancient Wealden forest.

Sutton. The West Sussex village of Sutton has its roots in a Saxon settlement known as 'the south farmstead' or *sūð tūn*. It's recorded as such around the year AD 880, probably so called because of its position in relation to Barlavington, half a mile to the north-west. In the Domesday Book of 1086 it's Sudtone, and in 1331 Sutton by Bygenyure (Bignor). A similar farmstead on the site of the county's other Sutton, now virtually part of Seaford, was originally 'south' in relation to Bishopstone, as NORTON was to its north. It's recorded as Suthtona in the first half of the 12th century, and Sutton without (outside) Seford in 1259.

Swaile's Green. Noted simply as Swale in 1523, the name originated either as Saxon *swylle* or 'swill', denoting some now-vanished watercourse, or - equally possible – it's the old word 'swale, swayl' (from *swælan*, 'to burn') signifying a place where heather or gorse had been burned off. **Swale Bank**, the name given to the lower slopes of Mount Caburn, is found as Swylle in 1332, the Swyll in 1581, clearly so called because of the number of streams that 'swilled' down it to join Glynde Reach. Until Elizabethan times, when the land was drained, there was a large area of water just here known as the Brodewater.

Swanborough. Standing at the end of the Downs just below Kingston near Lewes, Swanborough Manor marks the meeting-place of the old Swanborough Hundred at *swāna beorg*, 'the hill of the swains or peasants'. During the reign of William the Conqueror its name appeared as Swanberga. By 1724 this had developed to Swanborow. The manor, part of which dates to the 12th century, was once a grange or farm estate of the Priory of St Pancras in Lewes, so perhaps it's not too far-fetched to suggest the 'swains' – peasant farmers – may have worked the same land at an earlier date.

Swandean. Scholars think this is probably the same place as a swanu dionu mentioned in a Saxon charter as one of the swine pastures of neighbouring Durrington. If so, it fits well with the name's origin as *swāna dene*, 'the valley of the swains or peasants', recorded rather later in 1326 as Swaneden.

• • T • •

Tablehurst. The name isn't found in its modern form until the Tudor period, appearing as Tabilherst about 1530, Tablehurst *alias* Tavelherst in 1569. Records of the 13th and 14th centuries show it uniformly as Tavelhurst, suggesting to etymologists that its first element is the medieval word *tavel*, 'to quarrel, argue, contend'. If so, then the name must refer to a hurst or wood whose ownership had once been in dispute.

Tanbridge. Called Tanbruggelond in 1427, it lay close to an old tanyard mentioned as le Tannehouse just over a century later in 1548. Such yards held curing sheds next to a series of pits containing vegetable solutions, including tannin from tree-bark, where hides were processed into leather. One who followed this occupation, Adam le Tannere (1346), gave his name to **Tanner's Hill**, East Grinstead, recorded as Tannershyll in 1580; while another Adam Tanner, a native of Framfield (1332), is remembered by **Tanner's Wood** at Buxted. A Tanners bridge is noted in the same vicinity in 1622.

Tangmere. First documented as Tangmere around the year AD 680, this is probably the oldest un-changed Saxon name in Sussex. But what do we make of its meaning – 'the tongs mere'? Opinions differ. Either some pool here was shaped like a pair of curved tongs, or it was skirted by two ancient tracks con-verging at one end. The pool itself has long disappeared, but interest-ingly there was also a Tangstede – 'tongs place' – somewhere in the neighbourhood. Just south-east of the village lies a disused airfield that played an historic role as a frontline station during the Battle of Britain, when it was operated jointly by the RAF and Canadian Air Force. It finally closed in 1970.

Tanner's Hill and **Wood.** See TAN-BRIDGE.

Tarring Neville. Here on the down-land slopes above the estuary of the Ouse lay the territory of a tribe of South Saxons identified as the Teor-ringas – Teorra's people. The site was recorded in the 1086 Domesday Book as Toringes, and in the 13th century appeared as both Torringes and Tarringes. Early that same cen-tury its manor came into the posses-sion of the Nevile family, and we find the place subsequently noted as Thoryng Nevell (1339) and Tarringe Nevell (1588) to avoid confusion with **West Tarring** at Worthing, where the Teorringas had held another area of territory. During the 10th century this site is found docu-mented as Terringges and Teor-ringas, while the Domesday Book spells it Terringes. In order to distin-guish it from Tarring Neville it was given a slightly different spelling in the medieval period (Tering 1210, Terrynges 1313), first appearing as Westtarringe in 1613.

Tedfold. Tuddefolde (1296) and Tudefold (1338) are early forms sug-gesting Tedfold originated as *Tuddan falod*, marking the fold or enclosure of an early settler called Tudda.

Tegdown Hill. This area of the Downs at Patcham gets its name from the Sussex word 'teg' for a yearling sheep; while **Tegleaze**, near Graffham, preserves another old dialect word 'teglease' or 'taglease', denoting the right to graze flocks on the Downs.

Tegleaze. See TEGDOWN HILL.

Teise, River. Spelled Theise in 1577, the name is a back-formation from TICEHURST, which is found as Theise Hirst at the same date.

Telegraph Hill. This is the site of one of a series of signalling stations built to convey semaphore messages between Portsmouth dockyard and the Admiralty in London during the Napoleonic Wars. It's marked as Semiphore on a map of 1823. At its northern end lies the Neolithic long barrow known as BEVIS'S THUMB.

Telham. Telham Hill, Telham Place and Telham Court (now a school) are all situated close to Telham itself, just south-east of Battle. Telham Court seems to be the oldest site, from which the others took their name. It's recorded in the 12th century as Telleham, identifying the *hām* or settlement of a South Saxon, Tella (or possibly Tylla) who had his farmstead or *tūn* a couple of miles away at **Tilton**. This place appears as Telletone and Telton early in the medieval period, changing to Tylton by 1555. We come across the same personal name attached to another Saxon farmstead on the site of **Tilton Farm** near Alciston, listed in 1086 in the Domesday Book as Telitone and Telentone. Late in the 12th century it's Telletun, then reappears as Telton *alias* Tilton in 1688.

Telscombe. A village on the breezy Downs above Peacehaven, Telscombe is first mentioned in AD 966 as Titelescumb, the combe or valley of a Saxon whose name was either Tytel or Tittel. The place isn't listed in the Norman Domesday Book, but resurfaces in 1248 as Tittelescumbe. Its modern form is a corruption of Titlescomb, noted at the beginning of the reign of Henry VIII (1509).

Terrible Down. In fact Terrible Down is rather a terrible comedown, because its name actually originated as *tord hyll*, 'the turd-hill or midden'. It's recorded as Tordehelle in 1296. Only later towards the mid 15th century was it altered to conceal its unpleasing beginnings, with -down attached for good measure. Thus we find it reappearing during that period in its new disguise as Turbyldoune and Torbildoune, and then Terbill Downe (1563) and Tyrryble doune (1573). Local imagination seized upon this more dramatic form and wove about it the legend of some fearful battle once fought on the site, the slaughter being so dreadful, says the story, that warriors had waded up to their knees in the gore of their foes.

Terwick. Like the previous entry, Terwick is a place name containing one of those everyday Saxon words now considered inappropriate in polite society. Poor sanitary hygiene may have accounted for it being known originally as *tord wīc*, 'the turd farm'. In 1291 it was recorded as Turdewyk, a name that lasted surprisingly long given its associations, because as late as 1560 it's found as Turwick *alias* Turdwyke, and Turwike *alias* Tourdwike. By 1714 it had changed completely however, appearing as Terwick *alias* Terrick, which is how it's still pronounced.

Thakeham. Scholars find this a difficult name to interpret accurately, but they take it to be a derivation of *þæc hām*, 'thatch settlement', apparently identifying a homestead whose main buildings were thatched instead of roofed with tiles or wood shingles. In its earliest forms the name's recorded as Tacaham (1073),

Taceham (1086) and Takeham (c.1200). From the 13th century onwards its development is towards Thackham – the local pronunciation – with variations of spelling such as Thacombe in 1549, and Fakeham, a form in which it appears between 1610 and 1789.

Thorney Island. A true island, separated from the mainland by the Great Deep channel, it juts out into Chichester Harbour and marks the southernmost point of the Hampshire-Sussex border. The Saxons knew it as þorneg, 'the thorn-tree island', recording it as such in 1052. Just over 30 years later it was listed as Tornei in the Norman Domesday Book. The village of **West Thorney**, the island's only settlement, is mentioned as Westthorneye in 1291 – 'West' to distinguish it from **Thorney Farm**, across the harbour at East Wittering, which is all that now remains of a Saxon site recorded as Torneia in AD 945, Thorny in 1340.

Three Bridges. A place that developed with the opening of the London-Brighton railway in 1841, Three Bridges has been amalgamated with IFIELD and the old village of CRAWLEY to form Crawley New Town. It owes its name to a number of streams that had been bridged in earlier times to allow the road from Charlwood to pass over them. In 1598 the Elizabethan writer John Rowe mentioned 'three bridges between Worth and Crawley', and in 1613 we find 'the bridge called Le three bridges' also recorded.

Three Leg Cross. Noted as Thre-legged Crosse in 1556, the name possibly describes an old boundary mark or signpost with three arms indicating the separate directions of neighbouring Wadhurst, Ticehurst and Hawkhurst.

Three Oaks. Obviously a reference to some prominent group of trees, it appeared as le three Ok' in 1543, Three Oakes a century afterwards.

Thunder's Hill. It gets its name from a Tudor gentleman, Thomas Thunder, who was registered here in the parish of Chiddingly during the reign of Edward VI (1547-53). His family must have been already living in the area for several generations because 60 years earlier we find the surname also associated with a place called Thunderyscrosse, and a field or croft, le Thonderscrofth.

Ticehurst. This pretty Wealden village stands close to the Kentish border on what was once a wooded hill where young goats were kept. Its Saxon description, *ticcenes hyrst*, 'the kid's wood', appeared as Tichesherst and Tyceshurst early in the 14th century, acquiring its modern spelling by 1590. Young goats also grazed a forest ridge at **Tickerage Wood**, Framfield, recorded as Tykeregge in 1395, Tyckeredges in 1617. And they were penned on land at **Tickfold Farm**, Warnham, which is found as both Tickefeld and Tyckfolde in 1551.

Tickerage Wood, Tickfold. See TICE-HURST.

Tidebrook. In 1439 the spelling was Tydebroke, which scholars take to be a derivation of *Tidan brōc*, identifying an area of marshy ground owned by an early settler called Tida.

Tile Hurst. This little place just outside Hailsham is on the site of an old lime-oast or kiln where roofing tiles were produced during the Tudor period. Between 1557 and 1598 it's mentioned as Tylehost land, le Tylehouse, and Tylehoste.

Tilgate. The clue to its origin is probably provided by the surnames of William Yllegate (1296) and John de Illegate (1340) who had their homes in the vicinity. Etymologists think these names derived from an earlier source, *Illan geat*, 'Illa's gate', identifying one of the entrances into what's now Tilgate Forest. In medieval times the site would have been referred to as atte Illegate – 'at, by' – abbreviated to 't Illegate to give the place name its modern form, recorded as Tylegate in 1567.

Tilkhurst. The Sussex dialect word 'tellow', used of a young oak-tree, comes directly from Saxon *telga* – 'branch, bough' – giving Tilkhurst the meaning of 'young oakwood'. It's first found in 1285 as Telghurst, developing via Telkeherst (1302) to Tilkerst (1574).

Tillingham. Tillingham Farm, which shares its name with the river Tillingham on which it lies, is all that now remains of the settlement of a group of South Saxons known as the Tillingas, the people of Tilli. Originating as *Tillinga hām*, the place was recorded in 1296 as Tyllyngeham, and has been spelled in its moden form since 1428.

Tillinghurst. Until the 17th century this was Tittinghurst (it's noted as Tettinghurst in 1665), so the change from *t* to *l* is a late one and can't really be explained. It began as a Saxon name, *Tittinga hyrst*, identifying a wooded hill belonging to the tribe of the Tittingas, or Titta's people, appearing as Tytyngehurst in 1296. Scholars believe the original site was actually some miles south at **Tillinghurst Wood**, Plumpton, the name being transferred when early settlers migrated to live here just outside Ardingly.

Tillington. The village lies on the banks of the western Rother, a location that recommended itself to a South Saxon called Tulla as a site for his *tūn* or farmstead. Its name is first found as Tullingtun in a charter of AD 960, and changes very little until the Tudor period when it appears as Telyngton and Tyllington.

Tilton. See TELHAM.

Tiltwood. Its first element – Tylthe in 1476, Tilt in 1567 – is the dialect word 'tilth' describing arable land that's kept tilled or cultivated.

Timberley. Originally 'the timber *lēah* or clearing' where a patch of woodland had been cut down, the place is recorded as Tymberle in 1415.

Tinsley Green. Greenwood's map of Sussex (1823) shows this name as Tensley. Earlier, in the days of Elizabeth I, it had been Tynsley, and earlier still (1353) Tyntesle. Its source seems to be *Tintes lēah*, signifying the woodland clearing of some early settler called Tinte or Tinti.

Tisman's Common. The only record we have of this name dates from 1651, the time of Oliver Cromwell, and gives it as Tishmorth Comon. Without anything else to go on, it's impossible to speculate how it might have originated.

Toat Hill. See TOTE HILL.

Toddington. Totintune in the Domesday Book of 1086, Totyngton two centuries later, the place originated as the *tūn* or farmstead of a South Saxon called Totta. As late as 1688 it was still spelled Tottington, probably taking its modern form to avoid confusion with **Tottington** near Upper Beeding, where another Totta had his farmstead at what's now Tottington Manor Farm. This too appears in the Domesday Book as Totintune, becoming Totington in 1291. The same personal name is connected with two more places in the county. **Totease**, near Buxted, began as *Tottanhēse*, 'Totta's brushwood', developing from Totenhesse (1200) and Tottehese (1327) to Totease Oak (1724). And **Tottingworth** at Heathfield marks the site of Totta's 'worth' or enclosure, Old Tottingworth Farm being recorded as Tottingwerthe, Totingworth and Todyngworth in the late 13th and early 14th centuries.

Todham. Generally spelled Tadeham and Tadham between 1086 and 1500, the name goes back to Saxon times as *Tadan hām* – 'Tada's settlement'. Scholars have found one isolated instance of it being noted as Todham in 1279.

Topleigh. The early forms of this particular name – Topely (1249) and Topley (1501) – suggest it's a straightforward derivation of *Toppan lēah*, describing a cleared patch of woodland belonging to an early settler called Toppa.

Torberry Hill. This would have been *torr burh* originally – 'the stronghold at the tor' – identifying the ancient hillfort here. Around the year 1250 its name was recorded as Torburi, and a century afterwards it appeared as Torrebury.

Tortington. Situated below Tortington Common on the lower reaches of the river Arun, the place owes its existence to a South Saxon named Torhta who built his farmstead or *tūn* at this spot. In 1086 the Domesday Book listed it as Tortinton, a spelling that changes only slightly to Tortyngton in 1397. Interestingly, it appeared in 1304 as Torton, which is still the local pronunciation.

Totease, Tottington, Tottingworth. See TODDINGTON.

Tote Hill. The name is actually the old dialect word 'toot-hill' or 'watch-hill', which has its roots in the Saxon verb *tōtian*, 'to peep out'. In 1627 it was noted as Tothill. **Tote Copse**, Aldingbourne, and **Toat Hill**, Slinfold, identify similar vantage points. In 1357 the latter was the home of Peter atte Tote, 'dweller by the look-out'; and **Toat Farm**, Pulborough, was once similarly connected with the family of Ida atte Tote (1332) who took their name from the prominent hill close by.

Town Littleworth. In 1571 this hamlet north of Barcombe was described by the writer John Rowe as 'land late

John a Towne', identifying some former owner. Its affix may either denote a small 'worth' or enclosure (perhaps the original medieval *toun* or farmstead), or else refer to the land being of 'little worth'.

Treyford. The village lies below the steep slope of Treyford Hill where a stream rises, flowing north to join the western Rother. In Saxon times this stream was forded by means of a tree trunk – either one that had fallen down across it, or been deliberately dragged there to make a primitive bridge. We actually know this from Treyford's name. It originated as *trēow fyrde*, 'the tree-forded place'. In the Norman Domesday Book it was listed as Treverde, developing via Trefferde and Trefurde in the Middle Ages to Treaford in 1585.

Trotton. Unlike its neighbour TREYFORD (above) where the stream was 'tree-forded', here at Trotton, on the Rother, the crossing was apparently achieved by means of 'treading' or stepping stones, because etymologists believe this name started as *trædding tūn*, 'the farmstead at the treading-place'. The Domesday Book (1086) abbreviated it to Traitone, but slightly later records give it more fully as Tratinton and Tradington. Noted as Tratton *alias* Tradyngton in 1421, it acquired its modern spelling the following century.

Truleigh. The name is shared by Truleigh Manor Farm and Truleigh Sands, lying just below Truleigh Hill. The farm is the earliest site. It occupies what was originally a cleared area of woodland where one or several trees had been left standing, hence *trēow lēah*, 'the tree clearing'. The Domesday Book recorded the name as Trailgi in 1086. In 1261 it was Treweli, becoming Truly in 1610.

Trundle, The. See ST ROCHE'S HILL.

Turners Hill. Its recent development has been stimulated by the growth of neighbouring Crawley, but in previous days Turners Hill was an insignificant little place, probably hardly changed since 1427 when it was recorded as Turnoureshill. It had acquired its name some time earlier from the family of Galfridus le Turnur, registered in the Lay Subsidy Roll of 1296. Their surname – it denoted a wood-turner, or maybe a jouster (one who tourneys) – is also associated with **Turner's Green** at Wadhurst and at Warbleton, and **Turner's Wood**, Beckley.

Turzes. Occupying what was once a stubblefield or 'earsh' belonging to an early settler named Tīrheard, Turzes is first recorded right at the start of the 13th century as Tiridesherse, Tyerdesherse and Tyresherse. Its modern form is obviously a contraction.

Tweazle Wood. This rather charming name is the Saxon word *twisla*, meaning 'fork', here applied to the fork of two streams that join in the wood. They must have been crossed by a bridge at one time, because we find pons de Twysle mentioned in 1288, while a little earlier the place had been described as terr. (land) de Twisell. In 1840 it's found as Twizzle Farm. It shares its origin with **Twissell's Mill** at Heathfield, where two streams also join, giving their name to Magota atte Twisele who was living here in 1379.

Twelve Oaks. Noted simply as 12 Oaks in 1740, this name falls into the same category as FIVE ASHES, THREE OAKS etc., identifying a spot noted for its prominent group of trees.

Twineham. Its location between two streams converging into the river Adur is what originally gave Twineham its Saxon description of *æt tweoxnēam*, '(the place) at two waters'. Although not recorded in the Domesday Book of 1086, the name appeared before the end of that century as Twienen, Tuineam and Twyenem. In 1280 it was Twynham, but as late as 1509 its Saxon form remained evident as Twyneam.

Twisly. It's recorded as Twystley in 1520, Twyste lee in 1544. Scholars think the name contains an obsolete medieval word *twist*, meaning a twig or branch, which makes its derivation 'the twig clearing'. The same word is shared by **Twist Wood** at Brede, noted as Twiste in 1410.

Twissell's Mill. See TWEAZLE WOOD.

Twist Wood. See TWISLY.

Tyes Cross. Tyes Cros in 1600, this is the frequently-found dialect word 'tye' denoting an area of outlying commonland or any large open field. It stems directly from Saxon *tēag*, 'enclosure', and as a place name is found elsewhere in the county at **The Tye**, Berwick, **Tye Lane**, Warbleton, and **Tye Oak**, Harting.

Tyler's Green. In 1578, the time of Elizabeth I, the name is given as Tylehouse. Like TILE HURST, once it must have been the site of a lime-oast producing house tiles.

·· UV ··

Uckfield. Now the terminal of the old London-Lewes railway line and one of the largest villages in East Sussex, Uckfield owes its existence to a Saxon named Ucca, who owned an area of open land or *feld* here between two tributary rivers of the Ouse. The settlement that later developed on the site is recorded as Ukkefeld in 1220, and Uckefeld in 1428.

Udiam. There was once a *hamm* or watermeadow here on the banks of the western river Rother, belonging to a settler called Hūda – a personal name we also meet at HEADFOLDSWOOD. About the year 1180 the place was recorded as Hudeham, and half a century or so later, Hodihame. A map of 1823 shows it as Udgeham, which is still its local pronunciation.

Udimore. In the Domesday Book it appeared as Dodimere, but later records prove the origin of this name to have been *Udan mere*, 'Uda's mere or pool' – 13th century spellings include Hudimere, Odimere and Odemore. Local legend however tells a different story, one that involves the village's Norman church of St Mary's. Originally its intended site was to be down by the river Brede, but each morning the builders arrived to find its stones pulled down, and a supernatural voice urging them to build instead 'o'er the mere'. The church now stands firmly on high ground.

Uppark. In a lovely location high on the Downs where it enjoys magnificent views towards the Solent and Isle of Wight, Uppark takes its name from a deer park created here late in the 13th century to serve the family seat of the Husseys, lords of the manor of Harting. A valuation of Henry Hussey's estate in 1370 mentioned 'the Park on the Down' and 'a certain park called Le Upparke...' Twenty years earlier it had been referred to as le Overpark (together with le Netherpark, recorded as Down Parke in 1440, and now the site of **Down Park Farm**). The house at Uppark, built about 1690 on slightly older foundations, has interesting connections with Lord Nelson's beloved Emma, Lady Hamilton; and also with the author H.G.Wells, whose mother worked here as housekeeper. It appears as

'Bladesover' in his novel *Tono Bungay* (1909). Since 1954 Uppark has been in the care of the National Trust and is open to the public.

Upperton. There are three Uppertons in Sussex, each originating as an upper or higher farmstead. The one near Eastbourne was recorded as Uppeton in 1176; that at Harting shared the same spelling four years later; while Upperton near Tillington had already acquired its modern form in 1191.

Upwaltham. Like COLDWALTHAM to the north-east, Upwaltham lies in an area of ancient forest where some natural clearing offered early settlers a suitable site for their homestead. *Weald hām*, 'the forest settlement', was listed in the 1086 Domesday Book simply as Waltham. Later on, when it became necessary to distinguish the two villages, this one appeared first as West Waltham (1288), then Up Waltham (1371) – 'up' in the sense of 'higher'. In 1641 the name's found as Uppwaltome, which is how it's still pronounced.

Valdoe, The. Scholars think The Valdoe originally could have been woodland called Waldey, recorded in 1492, part of Goodwood Park that had been fenced off or otherwise enclosed for hunting. This fits in well with Waldey's derivation as *weald (ge)hæg*, 'the forest enclosure'. It's still a well-defined area of woodland.

Varncombe Barn. This was once 'the ferny combe or valley', noted as Farncombe in 1279. The influence of dialect pronunciation has been at work since then to change the initial letter to its modern form.

Verdley Wood. An interesting name, it appears to owe its origin to some long forgotten military presence here in the Fernhurst area. Maybe a cleared area of woodland had formerly been used as a camp, or a mustering point – no one knows. All we can say for sure is that Verdley began as *fierd lēah*, 'the army clearing', and was recorded as Verdelay in 1318.

Vert Wood. See FATLAND.

Vinehall. Called Vynawes in 1566, it had appeared during the 14th century as Fynhage, Fynhagh, and Fynhawe. Etymologists take the first element of the name to be *fin*, meaning 'heap' – possibly a reference to the hill on which Vinehall lies (as with FINDON). The second element is *haga*, 'enclosure'. So this was either 'the enclosure on the hill', or 'the enclosure by the wood-heap'.

Vines Cross. It acquired its name from an Elizabethan landowner, John Vyne, a native of neighbouring Hellingly whom we find registered in 1595.

Vining Rough, Vinings. See FYNING.

Vinnetrow. Vinnetrow Farm borders the modern leisure centre just south of Chichester, but its site dates back to the days of the South Saxons. The flat marshlands hereabouts were the territory of a small tribal group called the Fenningas, or 'fen-dwellers', whose boundary was marked by an isolated tree that identified the place as *Fenninga trēow*, 'the tree of the fen-dwellers'. Some time in the 1100s its name was recorded as Feningetrowe. At the close of the following century it was Fengetrewe. And by 1531 it had been smoothed down to Venytrowe.

Waddle's Wish. See WHATLINGTON.

Wadhurst. A popular village set in lovely countryside close to the Kentish border, Wadhurst owes its existence to an early settler called Wada, whose land included a wooded hill or hurst hereabouts. Its name has changed scarcely at all since it was first recorded as Wadehurst in 1253, although Wodhurst, noted early in

the 15th century, is closer to the modern pronunciation.

Wakeham. Lying beside the western river Rother, it marks the site of Waca's *hamm* or watermeadow, and has been Wakeham since 1279. The same personal name is also found in connection with **Wakehurst Place**, the National Trust property at Ardingly, which occupies the site of

Waca's *hyrst* or wood, first mentioned as Wakehurst in 1206. The Elizabethan mansion here is surrounded by more than 100 acres of gardens, lakes and woodland managed by the Royal Botanic Gardens, Kew.

Wakehurst Place. See WAKEHAM.

Walberton. Walberton began its history as a *tūn* or farmstead owned by one of the handful of Saxon women whose identities have been preserved down the centuries by the place names they left behind. This particular lady was called Wealdburh (a somewhat masculine name meaning 'forest stronghold'), and her property was listed in 1086 in the Domesday Book as Walburgetone. It first appeared as Walberton in 1203, but less than 30 years afterwards we find its older Saxon form resurfacing as Walburgheton. In 1672 the name is spelled Warburton – which is how it's still pronounced.

Walderton. Although the modern form of this name actually dates from 1167, we also find it as Waldryngton in 1331, and Waltertoune in 1570. Most likely it identifies the farmstead or *tūn* of a South Saxon called Wealdhere, meaning 'forest army'.

Waldron. Many centuries ago when this part of Sussex was covered in the dense oakwood forests of the Weald, some enterprising Saxon built his *ærn* or house just here. In time a little settlement developed, and itself became identified as *weald ærn* – 'the forest house' – appearing in the Norman Domesday Book as Waldere and Waldrene. During the 12th and 13th centuries it was Waldrena and then Waldern, acquiring its modern spelling in 1336. Kynges Waldron, noted in 1585, suggests that surrounding remnants of the old forest had become a royal hunting ground by Tudor times. Northwest of the village lies **Waldron Down**, recorded as Walderon downe in 1543.

Wallhurst. See WALTON.

Walstead. Walstead Place Farm and its neighbour **Great Walstead**, just outside Haywards Heath, take their name from an early settler called Walca, who had his *stede* or place in the vicinity. It was documented as Walcanstede as long ago as AD 765, before appearing as Walkstede in 1295, Walsted in 1475.

Walton. The Saxons referred to the defeated British Celts as *wēalas*, a term that indicated both 'foreigner' and 'serf'. (Incidentally, the same word is the source of 'Wales' and 'Welsh', from the Britons who sought refuge beyond the border country of the Marches in what was to become known as the land of the Wēalas.) Walton itself was once a British farmstead or *wēala tūn*, probably attached to the royal manor at Bosham. It's mentioned as Waleton *juxta* Boseham in 1295. And the site of **Wallhurst Manor**, at Cowfold, seems to have been a wood in some way connected with the native British, because its name originated as *wēala hyrst*, recorded as Waleherst in 1279, Walhurst in 1332.

Wannock. Etymologists suggest this began as a Saxon stream-name, *wannoc*, 'the little dark one', describing the stream that rises on the Downs just here. The Domesday Book recorded it as Walnoch. During the 13th century it was Wannoc or Wannok. And in the time of Elizabeth I the stream was called the Ryver of Wannocke, and the site itself Wannockebridge.

Wantley. During the period 1296-1340 this is found as a manorial name spelled Wantelya, Wantelye or Wantelee. It probably originated with someone who moved to live here in the Sullington area from Wantley at Henfield (now a farm), which had itself originated as *Wantan lēah* – 'Wanta's woodland clearing' – appearing in the Domesday Book of 1086 as Wantelei before being recorded as Wantely in the 14th century.

Wapelgate Corner. See WAPSBOURNE.

Wappingthorn. See WEPHAM.

Wapsbourne. The bourne is Longford Stream, a tributary of the Ouse, beside which lies historic Wapsbourne Farm, a designated site known locally as 'Wapses Boorn'. Its name actually originated in Saxon times as *werpels burna*, 'the wapple stream' – 'wapple' being the dialect word for a bridle-way. The earliest records give it as Weplesburn and Werplesburn. In 1439 it's found as Waplesbourne, and in 1551, Wappysborne. We come across the same dialect word in the name of **Wapelgate Corner** at Houghton, marking the location of an old gate leading on to a wapple-way for riders.

Warbleton. Medieval records for this particular name are confusingly

similar to those for WALBERTON. The two villages even share a common origin, as the *tūn* or farmstead of a Saxon lady of property. In the case of Warbleton, the lady was called Wǣrburh, and in 1086 the Domesday Book documented her farmstead as Warborgetone. Eighty years later the name had developed to Warberton, then Walberton (1340) and Warbelton (1351).

Wardley. Wardelegh, noted in 1279, and Wardely, 1332, suggest this stems from *Weardan lēah*, signifying a cleared area of woodland owned by a settler called Wearda – a personal name meaning 'the warder or sentinel'.

Warminghurst. Its original Saxon form was *Wyrming hyrst*, 'the hurst or wood of Wyrma', a rather unflattering nickname derived from *wyrm*, which meant 'worm or serpent'. In the 12th century the place was recorded as Wurmincgehurste, changing to Wermingherst in 1291, and Wourmynghurst in 1341.

Warnham. Found as Werneham in 1166, the village lies between Horsham and the Surrey border on the site of a *hām* or settlement owned by a Saxon, Werna. One of its main claims to fame is its connection with the poet Percy Bysshe Shelley, son of a country squire, who was born here at **Field Place** in 1792.

Warningcamp. Local legend attributes the name to some early look-out point from which warning of attack could be sent over the river to Arundel Castle. In fact this is a bit of romantic nonsense, because Warningcamp owes its name to a settler called Wærna, whose *camp* was actually the Saxon word for 'field'. The Domesday Book noted the place as Warnechamp in 1086. In 1263 it was Warnecampe, and in 1316, Wornecamp. Not until the Tudor period do we find it changing to Warmyngcamp (1593), and then later to Warninge Campe (1641).

Warninglid. The first little settlement here developed on sloping ground within the tribal territory of a minor group of Saxons called the Weardelingas – Weardel's people – hence *Weardelinga hliþ*, 'the slope of the Weardelingas'. It's recorded in 1279 as Wardingelithe and Wardlinglithe, then develops via Warnynglyth (1456) to Warninglead (1629). The village was for a time the home of Alfred Lord Tennyson, Poet Laureate, before he moved to live near BLACK DOWN in 1869.

Warningore. The Norman Domesday Book listed the place as Waningore and Venningore. And in 1302 it was Wannyngore. Etymologists trace its name back to *Wænninga ōra*, 'the bank of Wænna's people' – now the site of Warningore Farm at Chailey. A Saxon sharing this tribal leader's name is also associated with **Wenbons Farm** near Wadhurst, which takes its identity from Wænna's bourne or stream, recorded as Waneburn in 1296, and Wenbourne in 1823.

Wartling. Wartling lies just above the marshlands of the Pevensey Levels, in what was once the territory of a group of Saxons called the Wyrtelingas, the people of Wyrtel. The 1086 Domesday Book lists the name as Werlinges, but records of the following century show it more accurately as Wertlinges. By 1199 it's Wortling. Wyrtel himself was the owner of a *hām* or settlement on the site of **Worsham Farm**, just east of Bexhill, documented in AD 772 as Wyrtlesham. By 1385 the name had changed only slightly to Wortlysham, becoming Wersham by the time of Elizabeth I. The same personal name, though probably not the same individual, appears elsewhere in connection with **Ridlington Farm** at Burton, once *Wyrteling tūn*, 'Wyrtel's farmstead'. Although we have no late records for its modern form, the place was mentioned as Writelington and Wrytelingeton in the 13th century. And **Wortleford**, near Chailey, identifies the site of 'Wyrtel's ford', being noted as Wyrtleford in 1291.

Washingham. This little area between the rivers Arun and Stor is networked with streams, so it's not surprising that the people who once had their *hamm* or watermeadow here were known as the Wæssingas, 'the dwellers in the *wæsse* or wet place'. The name was Wassingham in 1296, and hardly altered at all over the next five centuries, appearing as Wasingham in 1823.

Washington. It shares its name with America's capital city – but there the similarity ends. This Washington is a pleasant village lying below the swell of the South Downs, marking what was once the farmstead or *tūn* of the Wassingas, a tribal group of Saxons led by one named Wassa. Documents of the 10th century record the site as Wessingatun, æt Wassingatune, and Wassengatun in Sudsexon (Sussex). In 1086 the

Domesday Book lists it as Wasinge-tune. And in 1261 it's Wassington, acquiring its modern spelling towards the close of the following century. The poet Hilaire Belloc, who lived just up the A24 at SHIPLEY, knew the village well, ending his *West Sussex Drinking Song* – 'the swipes they take in at Washington Inn is the very best beer I know.'

Watcombe. Records of the 13th century spell this name variously as Wescumbe, Wetescumbe, Weat-cumbe and Watecombe. Etymologists think it possibly started as *Hwætes cumb*, denoting the combe or valley of a settler called Hwæt.

Waterbeach. See SEABEACH.

Watersfield. A hamlet on a stream flowing into the river Arun, it appeared as Watresfeld in 1226 and Wateresfeld 30 years later, its name describing an area of open land 'of or by the water'.

Weald, The. To the South Saxons, the vast oakwood forest once covering the hinterland of the Downs was *Andredesweald*, 'the forest of Andred', named for the Roman fort of Anderida at PEVENSEY. In AD 893 se micla wudu – 'the great wood' – was described as being some 30 miles wide and over 120 miles long, stretching from the marshes of Kent to the New Forest in Hampshire. The name 'weald' by itself came into use quite early, appearing as þe welde in 1290, le Walde in 1330.

Wellhead Wood. See WELLINGHAM.

Wellingham. Upper Wellingham and neighbouring Wellingham House occupy the site of a Saxon *hamm* or watermeadow here beside the river Ouse. It belonged to a minor tribal group who appear to have taken their identity from a spring-fed stream in the vicinity, since they were known as the Wiellingas – 'the dwellers by the welling-place or spring'. From its original form, *Wiellinga hamm*, the place name has altered very little since the closing years of the 11th century, when it was recorded as Wellingeham. We find a separate group of 'spring dwellers' also owning land near Ewhurst, at what's now **Wellhead Wood**. In 1086 the Domesday Book listed this place as Waliland, and about 1230 it was Welilonde, becoming Wellond Felds in 1535.

Wenbons. See WARNINGORE.

Wenham. So spelled in 1195, Wenham Manor Farm began its existence as the property of a Saxon named Wēna, who chose to build his settlement or *hām* just here on the western Rother near Rogate.

Wepham. Recorded in the Norman Domesday Book as Wepeham, this had earlier been *Wæppan hām*, the settlement of a South Saxon called Wæppa – a personal name we also find connected with **Wephurst**, once Wæppa's *hyrst* or wood, noted as Webbehurst, Weppehurst and la Wephurst during the 13th century. A different Wæppa was leader of his own tribal group, whose land lay in the Steyning area at **Wappingthorn**. This had originated as *Wæppinga þorn*, 'the thorn-bush of the Wæppingas', identifying a prominent boundary mark on their territory. In

1086 its site was listed as Wapinge-torne. In the 1260s it appeared as Wepingethorn and Wappingethorn. Although no one knows for certain, it's possible this particular little tribe could have been a branch of the Wæppingas who bequeathed their name to Wapping in London.

Wephurst. See WEPHAM.

Westbourne. The 'bourne' of this place name is the river Ems which flows past the village, marking the county boundary between Sussex and Hampshire. The Domesday Book noted it simply as Borne and Burne, but by the beginning of the 14th century it started being called West-bourne to avoid confusion with the county's other Bourne, now EAST-BOURNE. However the original name lingered on in official documents as late as 1646, and the village is still known locally simply as Bourne.

West Burton. This was the *tūn* or farmstead to the west of Bury, appearing in the 13th century as Westburgton, Westburgheton and Bury Westburton. In 1740 the bones of a number of elephants were dis-covered buried here some nine feet below ground level. Since the village was once part of the large Roman estate centred on nearby BIGNOR, it's thought the animals possibly could have originated there, a theory endorsed by the fact that Vespasian is known to have brought elephants with him to use against the native British when he landed at Chich-ester Harbour in AD 44.

West Dean. See DEAN, EAST and WEST.

Westdean. It stands in a lovely set-ting above the river Cuckmere, with the woods of Friston Forest as a backdrop and the **Seven Sisters Country Park** just a stone's throw away. The first little village here got its name from the dean or valley in which it developed, appearing as Dene in the Domesday Book. It's first noted as Wesden in 1189 – 'West' to distinguish it from nearby EASTDEAN. It's also occasionally found as West Dean *orientalis* (or 'eastern') to avoid confusion with WEST DEAN, near Chichester.

Westergate. Recorded in the 13th century as Westgate and Westregate, this was originally 'the western gate' that led on to an area of common land closed off on its opposite side by neighbouring EASTERGATE. In early Saxon documents the site is also mentioned as Geinstedisgate, Genstedegate, signifying 'the gate opposite the place'.

Westerton. The spelling hasn't altered since the 12th century, when this was 'the more westerly *tūn* or farmstead', identifying its position in relation to Strettington, half a mile away.

Westfield. Spelled Westewelle in the Domesday Book of 1086, Westfield developed on unenclosed land or *feld* to the west of Guestling. During the 12th century its name was West-efelde.

West Firle. See FIRLE.

West Grinstead. In contrast with the busy market-town bustle of EAST GRINSTEAD, West Grinstead is still a quiet country village with a school, a couple of pubs, and a Norman church. Like its counterpart however, it was a spot once noted for the particular verdant lushness of its vegetation, hence the shared description 'green *stede* or place'. In 1261 this 'green place' was recorded both as Grenstede and West Grenstede, and its position further clarified in 1288 as Grenestede *juxta* Knappe (by Knepp). **West Grinstead Park** is well known in the equestrian world as one of the homes of the National Stud for breeding racehorses.

Westham. A marshland village popular with holidaymakers, Westham occupies the site of a *hamm* or watermeadow lying to the west of Pevensey. It's spelled Westhamme in 1252, and is Westham *juxta* Pevenese (by Pevensey) in 1312.

Westhampnett. Like its near-neighbour EAST HAMPNETT, this village on the edge of Chichester originated as a little Saxon settlement known as (*æt þæm) hēan tūne*, '(at the) high farmstead', from its location. The Domesday Book recorded it as Hentone, but not long afterwards the diminutive ending -et was added and we find the name reappearing around 1187 as Hamptoneta. In 1279 it was Westhamptonette. St Peter's church here was founded at the start of the 8th century AD, replacing an earlier one that had been built of material from the ruined Romano-British fort of Noviomagus (modern Chichester).

West Itchenor. See ITCHENOR.

Westmeston. It lies at the foot of the Downs west of Plumpton, and in Saxon times was 'the westmost farmstead' or *westmæst tūn* from

Lewes, being recorded as such in a charter dated about AD 765. The Norman Domesday Book listed the name as Westmestun, a spelling that altered to its modern form in 1291.

West Tarring. See TARRING NEVILLE.

West Thorney. See THORNEY ISLAND.

Whalesbeech. The Domesday Book gives this as Waslebie, but a later spelling – Walesbech in 1265 – is more closely linked to the original Saxon *Hwæles bece*, describing 'Hwæl's beck', a stream flowing through the valley near what's now Whalesbeech Farm at Forest Row. The personal name is somewhat less than flattering because it meant 'the whale'.

Whatlington. Whatlington lies on the little river Line, marking what was once the *tūn* or farmstead of a tribal group called the Hwætelingas, or Hwætel's people. In the 1086 Domesday Book its name appeared as Watlingetone. In 1320 it was Hwatlington. And in 1724 we find it spelled Whartlington, reflecting the local pronunciation of the day. Hwætel himself owned a *wisc* or bog meadow on the site of **Waddle's Wish** nearby at Battle, recorded as Wattleiswysshe in the year 1500.

Whiligh. Although the South Saxons were converted to Christianity towards the end of the 7th century AD, their pagan practices took a long time to die out, lingering on at places like Whiligh near Ticehurst, and **Whyly** at East Hoathly. Both these sites were once a *wīg lēah*, a clearing among woodland that was used for pagan rites or else contained a pagan sanctuary. In 1018 Whiligh was recorded as (to) wiglege – '(to) the clearing of the pagan temple'. Later on, between 1279 and 1366, the name was spelled Wyleghe and Willegh. We find Whyly as Willee in 1246, Wylegh 50 years later, and Wylee in 1451.

Whitehawk. In the time of Elizabeth I it was White Hawke Hill, 'white' describing the chalk of the Down, not the bird. At its summit lie the remains of a Neolithic causewayed camp, overlooking Brighton Racecourse and a modern television station.

Whitemans Green. Recorded in 1520 as Swetemannegrene, this hamlet near Cuckfield originally seems to have been connected with a family named Sweatman or Sweatman (it meant 'sweet creature'). The initial S had been lost by 1604, when the name reappears as Whitman's Greene.

White's Green. A little place on a tributary of the western Rother, it gets its name from a Georgian gentleman, John White, recorded in 1716. **White's Bridge**, noted as Whyte Bridge lands in 1650, is similarly associated with a Richard White of Horsham, who was alive at the outbreak of the English Civil War in 1642.

Whitesmith. A whitesmith is one who works with tin, and this was the site of a tin smithy as far back as the 15th century, when the name appeared as Wythesmyth. The hamlet lies only a few miles from UPPER and LOWER DICKER, where there were ironworks.

Whydown. Scholars believe this place, just outside Bexhill, marks the site of a swine pasture referred to as swinhamme in a Saxon charter of AD 772. It was recorded as Swinham in 1189, and as Swynhamme in 1307. By 1706 the name had disappeared, and instead we find White Down, which may well be a corrupt form. Interestingly, **Whydown Bridge** close by is mentioned as Swyneshambrigge in 1455.

Whyke. See RUMBOLDSWHYKE.

Whyly. See WHILIGH.

Wick, Wicklands, Wick Street. See WICKHAM.

Wickham. Wykeham in 1279, this is the Saxon word wīchām, signifying a small settlement with a farm. It's also the origin of **Wickham Farm**, Icklesham (Wicham 1200) and **Wyckham Farm**, Steyning (Wicam 1073, Wycham juxta Stenygge 1307). Used by itself wīc denoted a dependent farm with a specific function, usually dairy production. In this form it's responsible for the names of **Wick** near Lyminster (Wyke 1261), **The Wick** at Hove (Wyk 1327, the Weeke 1656), and **Wick Wood**, Chithurst (boscus de la Wyk c.1286, Weekwood 1642). **Wicklands** at Little Horsted began as farmland, recorded as Wyklonde at the end of the 13th century, sharing its origin with **Wickstreet**, Arlington, which appears as le Wyklonde in 1372 before becoming Wykestret in 1501. Similarly, **Wick Street** near West Firle was Wyk in 1296, and Weeke Strete in 1576.

Wiggonholt. This is spelled Wickenholt in 1675. During the time of the Tudors it had appeared as Wiging-holt and Wyginholt. And earlier still, in the 13th century, it was Wygeholt, Wykenolt and Wyghenholt. Etymologists think the name goes back to *Wicgan holt*, identifying the holt or thicket of an early settler, Wicga. In recent times excavations have revealed the remains of a Roman villa dating from the 2nd century AD, and apparently destroyed by fire towards the middle of the 4th century.

Wigsell. There are two Wigsells here near Bodiam. Great Wigsell lies low down near the Kent Ditch stream, while High Wigsell stands more prominently to the south. The latter is probably the original site of *Wicges hyll* or 'Wicg's hill', recorded as Wiggesell about the year 1200, Wiggesulle in 1339. A native of the place may have taken the name with him to **Wigsell** at Rotherfield, which is first noted in 1646 as Wigsells.

Willingdon. Willingdon and Lower Willingdon, just north of Eastbourne, get their name from the downland height of Willingdon Hill, once the property of a Saxon called Willa. His *dūn* or down appeared in the 1086 Domesday Book as Willendone (which incidentally is how the name's still pronounced). By 1229 it had become Wylindon, and by 1295 Wyllingdon.

Willingford. In its modern form, the name is a corruption of Wynham-ford, recorded in 1315. The place lies on the river Dudwell – which was obviously fordable at this point – and marks the site of a *hamm* or watermeadow belonging to an early settler called Wina. In 1241 we find

mention of the mill of Winham, and later, in 1535, Wynchamford mill. There's no mill marked on the map here now, only a farm.

Wilmington. Several round barrows near 'The Long Man' (see WINDOVER HILL) and long barrows and flint mines just south-east of the village, show this was an important centre for Neolithic tribes long before a South Saxon called Wilma chose the downland site for his *tūn* or farmstead. The Norman Domesday Book of 1086 listed its name as Wineltone and Wilminte, but it was more accurately recorded as Wilminton 100 years later, when the priory (now ruins) was built here.

Wilting, Upper and **Lower.** Just west of Hastings, these two places have been farms for many years, but their name stretches back beyond the Domesday Book to Saxon times, when the land here belonged to a tribe called the Wiltingas – the people of Wilta. We know they probably had a *hām* or settlement on the site because its name is given as both Wiltingham and Witinges in 1086. The following century it reappeared as Wiltinges, and by 1442 had lost its ending and acquired its modern form.

Winchelsea. A picture postcard village whose grid-pattern streets belie its medieval origins, 'New' Winchelsea was planned and built by King Edward I as a successor to 'Old' Winchelsea, which had been destroyed by the sea during the great storms of 1287. The earlier site, situated at shore level about a mile from Camber Castle, took its name from *Winceles ēa*, 'Wincel's river', whose little estuary had provided the town with its harbour and boat-building yards. It was recorded as Winceleseia in 1130, and Old Wynchchelse in 1321, by which time King Edward's 'New' Winchelsea was already taking shape on a promontory called Higham (its name now preserved by HIGHAM STREET) rising above a wide inlet of the Channel. The new town prospered and became one of the Cinque Ports, but as the coastline gradually silted up so Winchelsea's fortunes declined, and by the 15th century – when the name was spelled Winchelsey – its port had ceased to function.

Windfallwood Common. It was Windfold Wood in 1780, and before that in 1547, simply Winfold. The earliest record of the name dates from 1296, when it appeared as Wyndefeld and Wingefold. Etymologists think it probably originated as *Windan falod*, 'Winda's fold or enclosure'. We meet the same Saxon personal name in connection with **Wyndham Farm**, Shermanbury, which lies on what was once Winda's *hamm* or watermeadow beside the river Adur. It's recorded in the 13th century as Windeham and Wyndehamme.

Windover Hill. In 1779 this was called Windore hill, a name stemming from *wind ōra*, or 'windy bank'. The hill, just south of the Hastings-Lewes road, is famous for the chalk figure known as the **Long Man of Wilmington** carved into its turf – at 240 ft long believed to be the highest of its kind in the world. It was first mentioned in an 18th century manuscript, but is clearly far older, lying

surrounded by Neolithic, Bronze and Iron Age remains and ancient trackways, including one that leads eventually to the great Neolithic capital of Avebury in Wiltshire. Debate still rages whether the Long Man represents some prehistoric war god, King Harold's emblem of 'The Fighting Man', or a pilgrim directing travellers to shelter at Wilmington Priory.

Winkenhurst. This isn't an easy name to interpret, although its second element is clearly *hyrst* or wood. It's noted as Wytonesherst in 1296, and Wiltonesherst, Wyltonhurst in the 1330s. In 1729 it's Winkinghurst. This last form resembles a word found in the name of woodland at East Dean called **Open and Closed Winkins**, recorded as Winkingas around 1220. Scholars suggest its derivation is from Saxon *wince*, 'a nook or corner', and that *wincing* was a term for woodland of an irregular shape. **Winkins Wood** at Kirdford probably shares the same obscure description.

Winton. The Domesday Book lists the name as Wigentone. In 1203 it was Wingeton. And in 1548 the spelling was Wynton. The hamlet began as a farmstead belonging to a Saxon called Wīga – hence *Wīgan tūn*.

Wisborough Green. The village stands on a little hill above a tributary stream of the Arun, at a spot known to its earliest settlers as *wisc beorg*, 'the mound by the wish or bog meadow'. Thirteenth century spellings of the name include Wyseberg, Wysberwe and Wyseberuwe. We first find the affix 'Green' appearing in 1517, when the place was called Wysebarughgrene. Three years later it was simply referred to as Grene. And in 1604 it alternated as Wysebrough *alias* Grene.

Wish. This is the Saxon word *wisc*, signifying a bog meadow, generally one lying in the bend of a stream. Its most notable example in Sussex is the martello tower on Eastbourne's sea front, the **Wish Tower**, which gets its name from an old 'wish' or meadow nearby. Others include **The Wish**, Eastdean – Wysse in 1327 – and **Wishdown** at Ticehurst, preserving the name of Wysshlondstrete recorded in 1418.

Wiston. Lying below one of the county's most striking landscape features, Chanctonbury Ring, this attractive village began its history as the *tūn* or farmstead of a Saxon called either Wīgstan or Winestan – etymologists can't decide which. The Domesday Book recorded its name as Wistanestun in 1086. At the turn of the 13th century it appeared as both Winestanestone and Wicstaneston. And in 1628 it was Wiston *alias* Wisteneston. The Elizabethan mansion in **Wiston Park** to the north of the village was the home of Charles Goring, who as a schoolboy in 1760 planted the grove of beech-trees that crowns Chanctonbury.

Withdean. It's now been absorbed into the northward spread of Brighton, but in earlier days Withdean was a quiet little village that had developed in one of the deans or valleys of the Downs. Its original owner was Wihta, a Saxon settler, and the place was first recorded in the 1090s as Wictedene. The follow-

ing century its spelling was Wighteden, a form that continued in use well into the Tudor period, when we find the name mentioned as Wighdean *alias* Withdean (1574).

Witherenden Hill. A hamlet just north-west of Burwash, it marks the site of *Wiðering denn*, 'Wiðera's swine pasture', that once sloped towards the western river Rother. By 1180 its name had virtually acquired its modern form as Wytherenden, although Greenwood's map of Sussex (1823) shows it as Witherden.

Withyham. This was originally *wiðig hamm*, 'the withy watermeadow', a pretty name for a pretty place, describing its location between two willow-shaded streams. First recorded around 1095 as Wideham, its Saxon roots show more clearly as Wythyhamme in 1266. The village and neighbouring Hartfield are on the **Buckhurst Park** estate of Earl de la Warr, whose family, the Sackvilles, owned Withyham manor from 1200 until they removed to Knole in Kent in the 16th century. All that remains of their manor house at **Old Buckhurst**, (a name meaning 'beechwood') south of the village, is the early Tudor gatehouse.

Wittering, East and West. This pair of seaside villages on the Selsey peninsula occupy one of the most historic areas in the county. It was through the narrow inlet between West Wittering and Hayling Island that Vespasian's fleet sailed into Chichester Harbour in AD 44 to take the British tribal capital of Regnum, thus spearheading the Roman occupation of Sussex. When the Romans finally departed four centuries later, their Saxon successors included a group called the Wihtheringas – the people of Wihthere – whose territory, now covered by the two villages, is documented in a charter of AD 683 as Wihttringes. The Normans recorded its name as Westringes in their Domesday Book of 1086, and it was called Witteringes and Wyteringe in the first half of the 13th century. The western settlement was identified as Westwyghtryngge in 1292, and the eastern one as Estwightryng in 1320.

Wivelsden. See WIVELSFIELD.

Wivelsfield. Sharing its name with neighbouring Wivelsfield Green, Hall and Station (at Burgess Hill), the village occupies an area of *feld* or unenclosed land belonging to an early settler called Wifel. In a document dated about AD 765, it's mentioned as Wifelesfeld, altering its spelling to Wyvelesfeld in 1408, and the rather odd Weevelsfield in 1637. The same Saxon settler very likely had his *denn* or swine pasture just two miles away on land now occupied by **Wivelsden Farm**.

Woldringfold. Spelled Wolfringfold in 1327, and Wolveringfold in 1700, this little place just north of Cowfold owes its name to a Saxon called Wulfhere, who had a fold for his livestock on the site. The same personal name may also be connected with **Wolverstone** near Cocking, which possibly began as Wulfhere's *tūn* or farmstead. It's recorded as Olvestone in 1296. Interestingly, Wulfhere (it meant 'wolf army') was the name of one of the followers of Ælla, the South Saxon war-leader.

Wolstonbury Hill. A map of 1740 shows this as Wolsonbury hill. There are no earlier records for the name, but scholars think it could go back to *Wulfstānes burh*, 'Wulfstān's stronghold', describing the ancient hill-fort here.

Wolverstone. See WOLDRINGFOLD.

Woodcote. A hamlet just outside Chichester, it was once nothing more than a few simple peasant cots on the edge of woodland, mentioned as la Wudecota about the year 1200. Towards the close of the same century the place is identified as Wodecote *juxta* Westhamptonet (Westhampnett). It shares its origin with **Woodcote Farm** at Chailey, similarly noted as Wodecote in 1331.

Woodgate. The medieval greenwood that once was a major feature of the Sussex landscape has not surprisingly left a number of place names dotted about the county map. Woodgate plainly marks an old gate leading into enclosed woodland, and is Wodegate in 1327. **Woodhorn** at Birdham was 'the wood near the horn-shaped piece of land' – Wudehorn in 1232; as was **Woodhorn Farm**, Oving, sharing the same spelling some 30 years earlier. **Woodhouse, Woodhurst** and **Woodlands** are self-explanatory medieval names, while **Woodsell** at Dallington comes from *wudu sele*, 'the hall by the wood', appearing as Wodeselle in 1288, Wodsell Asshe in 1520. **Woodstock** near Slinfold identifies an old tree stump – maybe one used as a boundary mark – and is spelled Wodestoke in 1288. However **Woodknowle** at Burwash has got nothing at all to do with wood. Its first element is the Saxon word *wōh*, meaning 'crooked', making the derivation of this particular name 'the crooked knoll or hillock'. It's Wocnolle about 1230, Wokenoll in 1369, and doesn't emerge as Woodknoll for another three centuries.

Woodhorn, Woodhouse, Woodhurst, Woodknowle, Woodlands. See WOODGATE.

Woodmancote. There are two places of this name in Sussex, both once upon a time the site of woodmen's cots – simple dwellings of wattle and daub and thatch where forest workers raised their families. The village south-east of Henfield appeared as Odemanscote in the Domesday Book, but was more correctly spelled Wodemanescote and Wodemancote in the 13th century. The other Woodmancote, at Westbourne, is found as Wodemancot in 1332.

Woodmansgreen. Noted as Woodmansgrene in the time of Elizabeth I (1583), the hamlet gets its name from the family of William Wodeman, living in the Linch area in 1332.

Woodsell, Woodstock. See WOODGATE.

Woolavington. See EAST LAVINGTON.

Woolbeding. A quiet hamlet on the banks of the western Rother, Woolbeding marks the territory of the Wulfbǣdingas, a group of Saxons identified from the name of their leader, Wulfbǣd. The Normans recorded the place as Welbedlinge in their Domesday Book. In the 13th century its spelling changed from Wulfbeding to Wolbeddyng. And in 1633 it appeared rather quaintly as Woolbedding – which is actually how it's pronounced.

Woolborough. This particular place name is a wolf disguised in sheep's clothing, because in its original form it was *wulf beorg*, 'the wolf mound', describing a barrow or hillock haunted by these animals. In 1296 it was recorded as Wolbergh, developing to Wolborough in 1485, Woolbarrowe in 1606. **Woolfly Farm** at Henfield shares much the same origin, taking its name from 'the wolves' *lēah* or clearing', a woodland glade where they were known to gather. The Domesday Book listed the place as Ovelei in 1086, while medieval spellings include Wlfely, Wlvely and Woluelie. In 1685 it was Woolvely. A 'wolf pit' where the animals were trapped and killed lay somewhere in the vicinity of **Woolpack Farm**, north of Fletching, which may well be identical with a *wulfpytt* recorded hereabouts in Saxon times. In 1203 it was noted as Wlfpot, and in 1327 as Wolputte, forms of which the modern name is clearly a corruption. **Woolbridge**, on a tributary of the Rother just west of Mayfield, was actually once what its name suggests – a bridge over which bales of wool were carted. It was called Wolbridge in 1562.

Woolbridge, Woolfly, Woolpack. See WOOLBOROUGH.

Worsham. See WARTLING.

Worth. This attractive north Sussex village gets its name directly from Saxon *worð*, signifying an enclosure of some sort – probably an enclosed farm or settlement. In the 1086 Domesday Book (which gives the place as a manor of Reigate in Surrey) it's listed as Orde, reappearing as Wurða in 1175. Although the modern spelling has been in use since the 13th century, it's interesting to find the original name as late as 1716, when the village is called Woord *alias* Worth. Its parish church of St Nicholas has been described as one of the three Saxon treasures of Sussex (the others are the churches of Bosham and Sompting). From the churchyard there's a splendid view of **Worth Forest**, once denuded to feed the forges of the Wealden iron industry but now restored to much of its former beauty.

Worthing. Popular with both holidaymakers and London commuters, many of whom have bought homes here, Worthing began its history as a small settlement in the territory of the Weorðingas, a South Saxon tribal group of warrior-farmers led by one called Weorð. The Domesday Book records the name as Ordinges and Mordinges, while 13th century spellings include Wordinge, Worthinges and Wurthing. The place was a quiet little fishing village in 1798 when Princess Amelia, a daughter of George III, was sent here by her father to 'recuperate' from a love affair with one of his equerries. In the following years it grew rapidly in popularity, and by 1820 had firmly established itself as a rival to Regency Brighton.

Wortleford. See WARTLING.

Wych Cross. Etymologists say this is a rare example of Saxon *wicg* – originally meaning 'steed', but later

'mare, beast of burden' – being found as a place name. It suggests this East Sussex hamlet stands on land once used to corral horses for some purpose, perhaps a relay station for travellers. It's first recorded in 1274 as la Wigge. By 1407 the site had become associated with a 'crouche' or cross and appears as Wygecrouche, changing to Wiggecrosse in 1564, and 15 years later, Witchcrosse. Local tradition attributes the place name to Richard de la Wych (c.1197-1253), Bishop of Chichester, claiming that his body rested here overnight on its journey from Kent to Chichester for burial. The story in part may be true, insofar as the bishop's name appears to have influenced the modern spelling.

Wyckham. See WICKHAM.

Wyndham. See WINDFALLWOOD COMMON.

Yapton. Records of the 12th century give the name of this West Sussex village as Abyngton and Abbitona. In 1288 it was Yabynton, and seven years later, Yapeton. It was originally the *tūn* or farmstead of a Saxon either called Eabba or Eappa – maybe the same Eappa who was one of the four disciples of St Wilfred of Northumbria, responsible for converting Sussex to Christianity towards the end of the 7th century AD. His companions were Burghelm, Eddi (associated with EDGERLEY) and Padda (associated with PADGHAM).

Yokehurst. This began as *geoc hyrst*, 'the yoke wood', a name scholars think either described a yoke of land joining two strips of woodland, or else referred to a wood from whose trees ox-yokes were made. It was recorded as Yocherst in 1307, Yoke-hirst in 1358.

Yorkhurst Wood. It means 'the gowk hurst' or cuckoo wood, spelled Yeakehurst in 1640 and Yawkhurst in 1850. In common with many other Sussex dialect words derived from the language of the South Saxons, 'gowk' comes from their word *gēac* for the cuckoo.

Yotham. The name now only survives as that of Yotham Stream, one of the many watercourses draining Pevensey Levels, mentioned as Yottum stream in 1653. Earlier it seems to have referred to a medieval *hamm* or watermeadow marked by a *yord*, a yard or enclosure of some sort, being recorded as Yortham in 1396.

Selected Bibliography

J. R ARMSTRONG, *A History of Sussex*, Darwen Finlayson, 1961.
DONALD ATTWATER, *The Penguin Dictionary of Saints*, Penguin, 1965.
ALEC BARR-HAMILTON, *In Saxon Sussex*, Arundel Press.
KENNETH CAMERON, *English Place-Names*, Batsford, 1961.
W. V. COOK, *The Story of Sussex*, Moore & Wingham, 1920.
G. J. COPLEY, *English Place Names and their Origins*, David & Charles, 1968.
BASIL COTTLE, *The Penguin Dictionary of Surnames*, Penguin, 1978.
E. EKWALL, *The Concise Oxford Dictionary of English Place Names*, 4th Edition, Oxford University Press, 1960.
S. C. KENDALL (ed.), *Sussex County Book*, Lindsay Drummond, 1938.
A. MAWER and F. M. STENTON with the assistance of J. E. B. GOVER, *The Place-Names of Sussex*, 2 vols., Cambridge University Press, 1929-30.
A. MAWER and F M. STENTON (ed.), *Introduction to the Survey of English Place-Names*, Cambridge University Press, 1924.
ALLEN MAWER (ed.), *The Chief Elements used in English Place-Names*, Cambridge University Press, 1924.
ARTHUR MEE, *Sussex (The King's England* series), Hodder & Stoughton, 1937.
BRUCE MITCHELL, *A Guide to Old English*, Basil Blackwell, 1965.
JOHN MORRIS, *The Age of Arthur*, Weidenfeld & Nicholson, 1973.
IAN NAIRN and NIKOLAUS PEVSNER, *Sussex (The Buildings of England* series), Penguin, 1965.
REVD W. D. PARISH, *A Dictionary of the Sussex Dialect* (expanded and augmented by HELENA HALL), Gardner's of Bexhill, 1957.
JACQUELINE SIMPSON, *The Folklore of Sussex*, Batsford, 1973.
KEITH SPENCE, *The Companion Guide to Kent and Sussex*, Collins, 1973.
MARTYN F. WAKELIN, *English Dialects: an Introduction*, Athlone Press, 1972.
BARBARA WILLARD, *Sussex*, Batsford, 1965.
Sussex Life magazine.